Praise for *Trampled by Unicorns*

"Gavet has delivered a very important piece of work, which highlights the issues around technology, information, democracy, and the human condition. Everyone will benefit from reading her analysis and will come away questioning not only the ethos of tomorrow's companies, but also the foundations upon which we train leaders for the future—from financial incentives to education to culture. This is a must-read book for anyone who cares about business, government, and progress."

—**Rob Siegel**, Stanford lecturer, VC

"Maëlle Gavet gives an insider's view of how tech companies and their investors become addicted to financial growth in the same way that they addict their users to attention, 'influence,' or other unsustainable pleasures. In the end, everyone wants more and no one is satisfied. The narrative arc of life becomes an endless loop in search of unsustainable growth. It reflects our short-term culture. But enough complaining! In the second half, Gavet proposes a number of remedies—not quick fixes, but fundamental shifts into more equitable, long-term thinking that will actually make everyone much happier without the addictive highs of 100x returns and CEO worship."

—**Esther Dyson**, Founding Chair, ICAN, Executive Founder, Wellville

"Despite being a tech insider, Maëlle Gavet successfully applies outside-in thinking to the tech backlash. She answers how these companies that endeavored to 'change the world' got so off course and how employees, boards, and other stakeholders need to demand a new brand of leadership. What if every company had a Chief Empathy Officer, or better yet, what if every employee was empowered to bring their humanity to the products and services that have so radically changed our lives? The future of tech depends on it."

—**Christa Quarles**, Former OpenTable CEO, Board Member Kimberly Clark and Affirm

"Maëlle Gavet takes the reader on a tour of the tech industry that only a tech insider with decades of experience could provide. She understands the business, the culture, and the personalities. More importantly, she helps the reader understand the industry and how and why it has moved from golden child

to problem child in just a few short years. Gavet doesn't just discuss the current and emerging problems confronting the tech industry and those of us who use their products; she recommends thoughtful and implementable solutions. This is a book for anyone who cares about the future of technology and the technology industry."

—**Larry Irving,** Former U.S. Assistant Secretary of Commerce, Member, Internet Hall of Fame

"Peter Drucker was adamant that leaders of organizations and institutions have a fundamental responsibility to create a functioning society. Maëlle Gavet shows impressively how the tech giants shape our future by optimizing society their way, thereby distancing us from the human core of our existence. It is all happening around us while we sit there like the frog in the fable, not realizing that the water in the saucepan is getting hotter by the day. Maëlle Gavet has written a book that should be an alert to us all—not by pointing a finger, but through sound diagnosis leading to a credible course of action. A great contribution to inform a public debate that needs to happen now."

—**Richard Straub,** Founder and President, Global Peter Drucker Forum

"Trampled by Unicorns is essential reading for anyone who leads or aspires to lead people and companies. The questions and stories held within are uncomfortable and go against many of the well-worn tracks pursuing growth at all costs. But as Gavet argues, we are all worse off today thanks to the fake news and false information that is so quickly propagated through the biggest tech powerhouses and must change ourselves as an industry before it's too late."

—**Shan-Lyn Ma,** CEO, Zola

TRAMPLED BY UNICORNS

MAËLLE GAVET

TRAMPLED BY UNICORNS

BIG TECH'S **EMPATHY PROBLEM**

AND HOW TO FIX IT

WILEY

Published by John Wiley & Sons, Inc., Hoboken, New Jersey.

Published simultaneously in Canada.

For general information on our other products and services or for technical support, please contact our Customer Care Department within the United States at (800) 762-2974, outside the United States at (317) 572-3993 or fax (317) 572-4002.

Wiley publishes in a variety of print and electronic formats and by print-on-demand. Some material included with standard print versions of this book may not be included in e-books or in print-on-demand. If this book refers to media such as a CD or DVD that is not included in the version you purchased, you may download this material at http://booksupport.wiley.com. For more information about Wiley products, visit www.wiley.com.

Library of Congress Cataloging-in-Publication Data is Available:

ISBN 978-1-119-73064-4 (Hardcover)
ISBN 978-1-119-73065-1 (ePDF)
ISBN 978-1-119-73062-0 (ePub)

Cover design: C. Wallace
Cover image: Unicorn Horn © Chereliss/Getty Images
Author photo courtesy of Maélle Gavet

Printed in the United States of America

SKY10020442_081320

To M

Contents

Introduction   **1**

PART ONE

Monsters of Scale

CHAPTER 1

Making the World a Better Place   **7**

Tech as Driver of Economic and Social Progress   7
Hidden Effects   10

CHAPTER 2

Culture Bubble   **13**

"What Do Engineers Know About the World!"   16
"Steve Jobs Didn't Build Apple by Being Humble
   and Caring About People"   19

CHAPTER 3

Emerald Cities   **23**

"Landlords Pounding on the Door"   25
"We Know Our Responsibility to Help Starts at Home"   28
"Shockingly Poor Value for Taxpayers"   29

CHAPTER 4

The New Feudalism   **35**

The Human Impact of Tech Disruption   35
"They Do a Lot More Revenue with a Lot Fewer People"   39
$1.42 per Hour   41

CHAPTER 5
Anti-Social Networks   **43**

Undermining Facts and Science   44
Democracy Under Attack   47
Unrelenting Hate   50
"When She Showed Me the Messages, I Just Felt Sick"   53
"#NewZealandmosqueattack"   54
"The Ugly"   57
YouTube Recommended Alex Jones 15 Billion Times   58
Section 230   60
"You're Arguing About Whether the Baby's Dead"   61
"I'm Going to Show You More Car Crashes"   65

CHAPTER 6
Venture Capital and the Holy Grail of Scale   **67**

The Good, the Bad, and the Ugly   69
"It's All About Scale"   70
"You Don't Scale Fast If You Try to Get Everything Perfect"   72
FOMO   73
Harvard or Stanford?   74
A New Investor Class?   76

CHAPTER 7
Psychos of the Valley   **79**

A Grandiose Sense of Self-Worth and Poor Behavioral Controls   81
Shallow Affect (Superficial Emotional Responses)   83
Pathological Lying   85
A Lack of Remorse or Guilt and a Failure to Accept Responsibility for
    One's Own Actions   86
Callousness and Lack of Empathy   87
Juvenile Delinquency   88

CHAPTER 8
**Between Scylla and Charybdis: What Happens
If We Do Nothing**   **91**

The Orwell Scenario   92
The Huxley Scenario   96

PART TWO
Fixing the Chaos Factory

CHAPTER 9
We Should All Be Chief Empathy Officer | **105**

What Does an Empathetic Company Look Like? | 107
1. People | 108
2. Decision-Making Processes | 114
3. Business Model and Economics | 119

CHAPTER 10
A Multiplayer Game: Corporate Governance in Tech | **121**

1. Investors | 121
2. Boards and Shareholders | 122
3. Stock Exchanges | 125
4. Investment Bankers and Proxy Advisors | 126
5. Industry Bodies | 127

CHAPTER 11
Breaking Up Big Tech? | **129**

Big Tech's Anticompetitive Behavior | 130
The Anti-Antitrust Cocktail | 132
Reinvigorating Antitrust | 133
Zuckerberg's Pushback (And Where He's Wrong) | 139
Antitrust Is Not a Universal Tool | 143

CHAPTER 12
Tax, Privacy, and Other Running Sores | **145**

Implementing Fair and Equitable Taxation | 146
Modernizing Employment and Labor Protections | 151
Protecting Privacy and Rethinking Data Ownership | 153
Fighting for the Preservation of Facts and Civil Discourse | 158
Setting Standards for Algorithms, Artificial Intelligence,
and Facial Recognition | 166

CHAPTER 13
Big Tech Broke the News Media: What's Next? | **173**

"Sign a Big Check, Then Get Out of the Way" | 174

Facebook and Google *Are* New Versions of Media Companies   177
News Organizations Need More Than Ever to Keep Big Tech
   Accountable   178

CHAPTER 14
People Power   **181**

Epilogue: A Manifesto for Change   **185**

Acknowledgments   **191**

About the Author   **193**

Index   **195**

Epigraph

"People will try to convince you that you should keep your empathy out of your career. Don't accept this false premise."

Tim Cook, 2017 MIT commencement address

Introduction

I came to tech accidentally. Almost two decades ago, not long after completing a bachelor's degree in Russian language and literature at the Sorbonne in Paris, I enrolled at the ENS Fontenay-St-Cloud, a school whose graduates go on to pursue careers in academia or rise through the ranks of government. It wasn't for me. So after a few weeks, I switched to a very different school: the IEP Paris, better known as Sciences Po. My new course turned out to be a gateway to a new world. In addition to an immersion in the humanities, it exposed me to sociology, political science, macro- and microeconomics, history, and so many other things. It was in many ways a map of the world.

Where did that map lead me? In an unexpected direction toward technology startups, building the "Amazon of Russia" with Ozon.ru, then to an online travel agency and restaurant reservation system with Booking.com, Priceline, and OpenTable, and from there to Compass, a pioneering real estate technology platform. Over the years, some skeptics in the tech world—and elsewhere—have argued that the only "practical" use for my humanities background was as preparation for a lifetime of late night existential conversations in Parisian cafés, and I would have been far better off, given the field I ended up in, attending engineering school instead. I emphatically disagree. If 15 years in tech has taught me anything, it's this: The more a company relies on tech, the more it needs people who are curious about the world around them. People who have studied the past to try not to repeat it. People who understand how others will feel and react to a set of circumstances and changes.

Over the years I've come to the conclusion that we tech leaders all too often over-value analytical, technical, and IQ-based skills rather than the social, EQ variety. We tend to ignore what history has taught us, look down on "soft skills" and subjects like philosophy, sociology, and literature because of their lack of a solution-oriented approach (in our eyes, at least), and yes, sometimes chase money over humanity's advancement. We often accept the idea that damage to human lives caused by our innovations is a price to pay for progress, rather than think long and hard about how to steer clear of these negative effects in the first place. That unwavering faith in technology, that blindness toward human cost in the name of a "vision," and that greed has led many of our companies to build technology that exploits humanity's

1

weaknesses and makes it subservient to tech, which is the opposite of what most of us intended.

At this point, let me say that I remain, for the most part, an eternal optimist. Technological advances have incrementally improved almost every aspect of the way we live, work, and enjoy ourselves. Thanks to machine intelligence we're on the threshold of a new era of medical breakthroughs, automated vehicles will make our roads safer (even if they also conjure other harms), pollution will be slashed, cities will become more efficient, space travel will no longer be science fiction, and, gradually, humans will cease performing repetitive, demeaning, and backbreaking tasks.

But technology has smashed open a Pandora's box of devastating side effects, too: disinformation, hate and harassment, catastrophic privacy breaches, disruptions unleashed by the gig economy, monopolistic bullying, and more. Technology giants like Facebook, Apple, Google, Amazon, Alibaba, Uber, YouTube, Twitter, Airbnb, and a handful of other unicorns stand at a crossroads as users are increasingly concerned about these issues: Do they continue to sow chaos and eschew moral responsibility in the remorseless pursuit of scale? Or do they reboot to put ethics and empathy—defined by one UK company as "the emotional impact a company has on its people—staff and customers—and society"[1]—at the very heart of what they do?

As I write, with COVID-19 plunging much of the planet into lockdown, and America named one of the world's coronavirus epicenters, the best and worst of tech is on display. On the one hand life would be far harder now without Amazon to bring essentials to our doorsteps, Zoom and Skype to talk to our colleagues and families, and Netflix for streaming TV and movies. On the other, tech has also enabled a flow of misinformation and sometimes dangerous lies about the virus, disseminated in minutes across the globe on Twitter, Facebook, YouTube, and others. It has also exposed, once again, the perils for delivery drivers and warehouse workers without proper social protections, and so obliged to risk their lives by continuing to work just to put food on the table.

I wrote *Trampled by Unicorns* to lift the lid on all of this and show how, in my view, many of the industry's household names sidelined morality as a price for technological leaps forward, and abandoned their original ideals. Instead, they have built products that pay little attention to their effect on users, and still less attention to their social impact. No one expects these innovators to be perfect. When you're doing something new, mistakes, even major ones, are inevitable. But too often these companies have concealed their errors and stopped asking questions that were too difficult or uncomfortable to answer.

---

[1]The Empathy Business, http://theempathybusiness.co.uk/

Drawing on my journey in high-growth tech companies across Europe, Russia, Asia, and the United States, this book is my personal take on where Big Tech—that exclusive club of tech unicorns, decacorns, hectocorns, and now trillion-dollar companies (a name remains to be found for these new animals) with increasingly dominant positions in their respective industries—went wrong. And why many of the world's 471[2] (at the time of writing) unicorns—tech companies with a valuation of over $1 billion—are now confronting a whirlwind of their own making. I'll trace the origins and effects of what I've come to call the tech industry's "empathy deficit," and argue that many of the most celebrated founders and companies share some of the key personality traits of psychopaths.[3]

The first part of this book takes stock of the situation and drills down into how we got here. Some of it will be all too familiar, particularly if you have spent many years working in tech. But while researching these chapters, I was taken aback by the extent and depth of the problems generated by my industry when I put them all together. The number of unspoken trade-offs that have been made and continue to be. The long-term impacts that we don't really talk about because we're too busy fire-fighting the immediate problems.

And then, when you add it all up, you're faced with a question I have been asked hundreds of times, after criticizing the industry's humanity problem in a speech, an article, or a private conversation:[4] "Yeah, it's bad, but how is that different from the damage caused by Wall Street/the auto giants/Big Oil/Big Food/pick your villain?" The answer to that is clear: it is different. No other industry has so rapidly, profoundly, and extensively changed every aspect of our lives. No other industry has made us all both victim and villain at such scale. No other industry has built new tools, such as AI, which just a few years after their creation we do not know how to control and which may one day replace us rather than complement us.

As a champion of the beneficial side of tech, I couldn't write about these problems without trying to offer solutions that, while benefiting the world, should also make businesses more sustainable. At a high level, the framework for the much-needed transformation is pretty simple:

1. Tech giants must accept their extraordinary power and the responsibility that comes with it. It is rather hypocritical for technologists to tout the massive changes they can bring to the world, but then downplay or hide from their influence when some of those changes go awry. Tech executives and lobbyists

---

[2]CB Insights, "The Global Unicorn Club," https://www.cbinsights.com/research-unicorn-companies

[3]As per Wikipedia, psychopathy is a "personality disorder characterized by persistent antisocial behavior, impaired empathy and remorse, and bold, disinhibited, and egotistical traits." Psychopaths are not necessarily clinically insane, nor violent.

[4]Note that any unsourced quotations throughout this book are taken from interviews conducted by the author or conversations with the speaker in question.

are quick to decry the so-called unintended consequences of potential regulation or laws. That same concern should be applied to their products and services.

2. Top executives must get serious about grounding their firms in values of empathy and humanity. If they don't know how, they need to learn, not leave it to underlings.

3. Those values must be injected into every corner of an organization and its processes. Not once, via mottos or memos, but operationally, and continuously.

4. The way decisions are often made needs to change, as does who makes them. Even if this means having to rethink part of the business model.

5. Innovation can be applied in changing culture as well as in creating products. Isn't it time, for example, that we disrupt the HR department?

Unfortunately, even these steps are only half the job. The other half must come from stakeholders on the outside, which is why in the second part of this book, I also make suggestions for each stakeholder about how to place humanity front and center in tech innovation once more.

Now let me add a caveat: this is a fast-moving story, with the exploits and misdeeds of the tech giants rarely straying far from the news agenda. Given that the lag between finalizing a book and its eventual publication is usually several months, it's inevitable that some of the examples I focus on will have been overtaken by events. Nevertheless, they form part of a pattern of behavior and have helped shape my thinking about what must be done—by the tech giants themselves, by the authorities, and by the rest of us—to fix this crisis.

As technology hurtles relentlessly forward into murky areas such as machines learning for themselves, the moment to call time on what Apple's Tim Cook memorably termed the industry's "chaos factory"[5] is in danger of slipping away. That sense of urgency has been compounded by the COVID-19 crisis placing the global economy on the critical list, with the livelihoods and living standards of many hundreds of millions under threat. But in turbulent times there is also opportunity. As the virus rages, many of the tech giants I discuss in this book have shown how they can also be a force for good. Now they have the chance to address their failings and make that behavior the norm.

---

[5]2019 Commencement address by Apple CEO Tim Cook, June 2019, https://news.stanford.edu/2019/06/16/remarks-tim-cook-2019-stanford-commencement/

One

Monsters of Scale

CHAPTER 1

Making the World a Better Place

When I first began working for OZON, I fell instantly in love. What drew me was the ability for us to make seemingly minor changes that had tremendous real-world impact. Here we were, in the vastness of Russia, building a business that would soon deliver books to millions of people, some in places with hardly a road to speak of. We could make it possible, in these places at the ends of the Earth, for people to choose among hundreds of thousands of books. And, eventually, the same service would deliver equipment for their homes, toys for their children, parts for their cars—all shipped straight to their door.

This astonishing aspect of the work was what I found so exciting: what we did within the digital realm could so quickly alter the possibilities of the physical one. At massive scale and incredible speed. That is what I fell in love with. The benefits felt boundless. In many ways, they still do.

TECH AS DRIVER OF ECONOMIC AND SOCIAL PROGRESS

If we look more specifically at some of the key indicators of economic and social progress (GDP, poverty, life expectancy, literacy), the positive impact of digital technologies is evident across the board.

While there are debates on how to measure the impact of the digital economy on GDP due to the amount of free digital products created by the industry and the lack of clear definition of what the "digital economy" covers exactly, the OECD[1] assessed that in 2015 the information and communication technology sector accounted for 4.5 percent of total value added in OECD countries. Access to broadband internet is as clear a booster of economic development as anything. The World Bank estimates that an increase in fixed broadband penetration of 10 percentage points results in a

---

[1]OECD Economic Outlook 2017, https://www.oecd-ilibrary.org/science-and-technology/oecd-digital-economy-outlook-2017_9789264276284-en

1.35 percent increase in per capita GDP for developing countries and a 1.19 percent increase for developed countries.[2]

Digital innovation is improving the standards of living of millions of people thanks to greater efficiency and lower costs across industries, starting with agriculture and transportation. From better irrigation and pesticide and fertilizer use to more efficient agricultural supply chain management, there are countless examples around the world of technology improving the life of people. Mobile supercomputers in our pockets connect us with people virtually anywhere on the planet, play our music, and look up any fact. Smart homes, powered by personal digital assistants that learn our preferences as we use them, offer enhanced security monitoring, automated climate control, and shopping with a few voice commands. Augmented and virtual reality is available in our living rooms, offering new frontiers for entertainment and education. Plant-based meat is now served at fast-food restaurants. Drones and mini-cameras have revolutionized videography. And look at how 3D printers throughout the world helped manufacture the necessary parts for ventilators, as well as face masks and nasal swabs, to fight the COVID-19 pandemic.[3]

Technology is also helping to improve health and increase life expectancy. Living beyond 100 is likely going to become the norm for most children in the developed world before the end of this century. The British Office for National Statistics estimates that in 2043 in the UK, 20.8 percent of newborn boys and 26.1 percent of newborn girls are expected to live to at least 100 years of age.[4] Thanks to technology we will have a longer life and also a healthier one, with fewer diseases and side effects associated with old age. From Alzheimer's and Parkinson's to cancer, tech is making progress toward a future where they all might be curable.

Similar lines of research into faster cures via better drug delivery are seeing astonishing breakthroughs thanks to artificial intelligence. In February 2020, a team of researchers announced their AI program had invented a drug molecule that had gained approval for use in human trials—a first for machine learning. Typically, drug development takes about five years, often longer, before it gets to human trials. The AI developed drug took just 12 months.[5]

---

[2]Michael Minges, "Exploring the Relationship Between Broadband and Economic Growth," World Bank, 2016, http://pubdocs.worldbank.org/en/391452529895999/WDR16-BP-Exploring-the-Relationship-between-Broadband-and-Economic-Growth-Minges.pdf

[3]Macy Bayer, "3D printing community fighting coronavirus by making crucial medical parts," TechRepublic, April 3, 2020, https://www.techrepublic.com/article/how-3d-printing-can-be-used-for-coronavirus-testing-kits-masks-and-ventilator-parts/

[4]Office for National Statistics, "Past and projected period and cohort life tables, 2018-based, UK: 1981 to 2068," December 2, 2019, https://www.ons.gov.uk/peoplepopulationandcommunity/birthsdeathsandmarriages/lifeexpectancies/bulletins/pastandprojecteddatafromtheperiodandcohortlifetables/1981to2068

[5]Jane Wakefield, "Artificial intelligence-created medicine to be used on humans for first time," BBC, January 30, 2020, https://www.bbc.com/news/technology-51315462

COVID-19 social distancing requirements have boosted telemedicine services into everyday use, but long before the pandemic these services were complementing local health services in remote, rural communities. Data sharing and comprehensive meta-analyses have sped up the flow of information between health systems and hospitals, and mobile software applications are allowing both healthcare professionals and patients to check in and monitor situations constantly and remotely.

In one of the most heartwarming examples I have come across, a nonprofit called Living Goods provides digital tools and information via mobile phone for parents and community health workers in impoverished areas that have little access to doctors. "Thanks to technology, you can turn an ordinary person into someone who can diagnose and in most cases deliver a treatment that directly reduces child mortality," said CEO Nicola Crosta of Impact46, a social impact accelerator. After three years, the nonprofit demonstrated a 27 percent reduction in under-five mortality in Uganda. Infant and neonatal—under 1 month—mortality was also significantly reduced by 33 and 27 percent, respectively.[6]

The access that an increasing number of us have to seemingly infinite information is unlike anything to have happened before in human history. Massive Open Online Courses (MOOCs) reached 110 million people in 2019, with more than 13,500 courses available. And those numbers don't even include China, the largest nation with more people online than any other.[7] Tusome, a literacy platform in Kenya adopted by the Kenyan government, has benefited over 6.5 million children nationwide,[8] throughout 23,000 government-run primary schools as well as 1,500 private schools. It has increased literacy, as well as deepened and widened the impact of good teachers and teaching methods.[9] MindSpark, a program focused on STEM learning in India, improved students' performance in math by 38 percent in just five months. The program costs merely $2 a year per student when scaled up to more than 1,000 schools.[10]

And of course, technology has revolutionized the workplace, in ways too numerous to count. From software that puts data analysis on steroids to robots that make and package products, dramatic efficiencies have made businesses more competitive and profitable.

---

[6]https://livinggoods.org/what-we-do/results-evidence-and-research/research-initiatives/
[7]Dhawal Shah, "By the Numbers: MOOCs in 2019," Class Central, December 2, 2019, https://www.classcentral.com/report/mooc-stats-2019/
[8]Nathan Ochunge, "US government extends funding for Tusome program," *The Standard*, September 8, 2019, https://www.standardmedia.co.ke/article/2001341132/us-government-extends-funding-for-tusome-programme
[9]"In poor countries technology can make big improvements to education," *The Economist*, November 17, 2018, https://www.economist.com/international/2018/11/17/in-poor-countries-technology-can-make-big-improvements-to-education
[10]Stefan Dercon, "Is technology key to improving global health and education, or just an expensive distraction?" World Economic Forum, May 31, 2019, https://www.weforum.org/agenda/2019/05/technology-health-education-developing-countries/

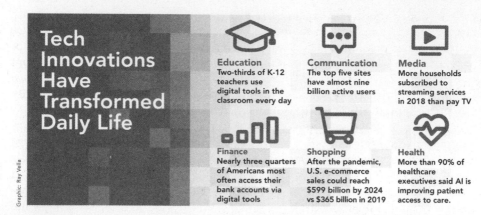

Graphic: Ray Vella

Source: Gallup, New Schools Venture Fund, Statista, Deloitte, KPMG, ABA/Morning Consult, eMarketer

FIGURE 1.1   Impact of tech innovation on daily life.
Source: Gallup, Statista, Deloitte, KPMG, ABA/Morning consult, eMarketer

Finally, digital technologies will also likely be what will help us with the next big challenge humanity is facing: the degradation of our environment and climate change. Solar and wind energy now produce electricity more cheaply than coal. The entire field of Climate Informatics, which is continuously deepening our understanding of the long-term and short-term impacts of climate change, could not exist without AI and the tools necessary to capture and analyze increasingly complex sets of climatic data.

These are remarkable accomplishments, worthy of praise and admiration. And tech companies receive both from us, overwhelmingly. A survey conducted by The Verge at the end of 2019 found that the vast majority of users—around 90 percent—view brands like Amazon and Google favorably, while around 70 percent of users believe that they remain a positive influence on society.[11] I know exactly how they all feel, because I still swoon over much of tech, too.

HIDDEN EFFECTS

So why is this book mainly focused on the problems tech is creating for humanity? For starters, because tech is now so deeply ingrained in everyday life, many of its

---

[11]Casey Newton, "The Verge Tech Survey 2020," The Verge, March 2, 2020, https://www.theverge.com/2020/3/2/21144680/verge-tech-survey-2020-trust-privacy-security-facebook-amazon-google-apple

more insidious effects also occur in the background, like some kind of white noise that is easy to ignore. Yet tech companies' influence over everything from the nature of work, to our privacy, to the contours of our cities, to the underlying fairness of our economies and the health of our democracies, is massive, and growing more so by the minute. As explained by William Davidow, author of *The Autonomous Revolution,* the technologies of the future (AI, robotics, Internet of Things) "not only make society more efficient and productive; they transform its structure."[12]

Moreover, I don't accept the oft-heard tropes of tech that these problems are necessary trade-offs to get us the many benefits technology brings us. In most cases, they are not. Or that these trade-offs are not worth public scrutiny due to their inevitability or their complexity. Or that disruption for disruption's sake is a good thing. Or that the negative effects of the tech revolution are similar to those of previous ones, and sort themselves out in the end. This book seeks to document how the staggering size and world-bending power of tech's unicorns is central to this particular revolution, and why that poses an existential threat that we must grapple with, and soon.

One of the many difficulties in addressing these issues is the "attention economy" that tech has created. When so much competes for our attention, and when we are trained to expect and demand instant gratification, it is hard to focus on the bigger picture.

Just think back to your first time using Facebook and marveling at the ability to connect with people around the world, before learning how it data-mines your posts and profile and tracks your every digital move. Or, if you have a small business, how Google drives big sales increases until you realize how dependent you are on them when suddenly the search giant tweaks its algorithm and kills your business. And there is nothing you can do. We often tend to think this way: very short-term, very self-centered. As long as we don't know about the sweatshops making our phones, or the trackers following our every move as we navigate through the internet, it's fine. Ignorance really is bliss, and tech is very good at keeping us distracted with an endless stream of shiny new toys and capabilities.

To be sure, it is difficult and complicated to directly measure tech's negative impact on our day-to-day life. A lot of the effects are not caused by the technology directly, as with previous waves of innovation (like a car generating carbon monoxide, which affects the atmosphere in ways we can measure objectively). Rather, these effects are often complex changes in human behavior that some technology provokes (we stop believing in facts; our attention span decreases) or secondary effects (increase of rents for locals because of the increase of short-term rentals for tourists).

---

[12]William Davidow, "Forget STEM, Study Sociology," LinkedIn, June 22, 2020, https://www.linkedin.com/pulse/forget-stem-study-sociology-william-davidow

This opacity is further compounded by:

- Massive scale and the network effects that build it making it hard to track how tens of millions of people are affected.
- The refusal of Big Tech to disclose data: we can't say how many people have decided to not vaccinate their children because they've been exposed to bogus claims on the side effects of vaccines. We don't really know how much the traffic has gotten worse because Uber and Lyft won't tell us how many cars they have on the street at any given time.
- The lack of ethics boards (like the ones universities have) to vet tech's behavioral experiments on people. A few engineers can decide to test something, change a few lines of code, and start experimenting right away. "Unlike academic social scientists, Facebook's employees have a short path from an idea to an experiment on hundreds of millions of people," noted a profile of Facebook's data team.[13]

Big Tech's scale is powered by the fact that a set of goods and services can be provided to a near infinite number of additional customers, all at the same time, at an incremental cost that is often close to zero. This, and the network effects that Big Tech enjoys—which means people have few alternatives to the platforms that all their friends and family use—help create near monopolies, enormous growth and profits, and unrivaled political power.

We are living in a period of historic, exponential growth and change. In the near term, that might be the best we can do: to begin to notice, and grapple with, technology's implications. So much of the technology that governs our world is opaque, hidden away from us under secretive algorithms and impenetrable code, like so many black boxes. Only there are people there, inside the boxes, writing the code. And people who lead them.

I am not arguing that all is lost. Instead, I am passionate about pushing tech to evolve, not only for the greater good but because it makes sound business sense, so that we can continue to enjoy the best that tech brings us without dystopian consequences that can be avoided, or at least minimized. So, let's open up the boxes. They aren't black, very often. Mostly they're quite glassy, airy, and based around the San Francisco Bay and other tech hubs. There's a bubble that surrounds them, cutting off the culture inside from the rest of the world.

---

[13] Kashmir Hill, "Facebook Manipulated 689,003 Users' Emotions for Science," *Forbes*, June 28, 2014, https://www.forbes.com/sites/kashmirhill/2014/06/28/facebook-manipulated-689003-users-emotions-for-science/

CHAPTER 2

Culture Bubble

I'm being given a tour of a tech giant in Silicon Valley by a kombucha-sipping senior engineer, probably making a couple of million bucks a year (including stock options), when our conversation takes an unexpected turn. As we pass a kitchenette area overflowing with Willy Wonka–style goodies, he declares that the 30-plus varieties of snacks on offer there are "making him fat." Later, as we pass one of several on-campus cafeterias, he tells me, without a hint of self-awareness, that the restaurant-quality chef-cooked meals, served on demand throughout the day, and late into the evening too, "can get a little repetitive." Then, he moves on to another topic.

It was the casual, throwaway nature of those remarks—uttered in the epicenter of global tech, just a few blocks away from people who don't know if they're going to eat at all that day, in counties where a staggering 27 percent of the population was categorized in one study as "food insecure"[1]—that most struck me. So brazen was his sense of entitlement (which I have found to be quite prevalent among people who have never experienced any other type of work environment) to free candy, potato chips, and gourmet food that he was complaining about it. Over the years as a tech executive, I've received or witnessed similarly tin-eared complaints on a bewildering range of topics, from the unlimited waistline-testing "fro-yo" to the "overcrowded meditation room," to those who demand to know why they "only" received a 10 percent pay raise that year (in an industry where the median Big Tech salary is already around $200,000).[2] There can be few more egregious illustrations of the disconnection between the gilded lives led by employees at many tech unicorns (and indeed smaller firms) and almost everyone else.

---

[1]Second Harvest Food Bank's Food Insecurity Study press release, December 2017, https://www.shfb.org/docs/news/release/20171212_FundingGap.pdf

[2]Marlize van Romburgh, "9 Major Bay Area tech employers pay a typical worker more than $200K a year," *Silicon Valley Business Journal*, June 12, 2019, https://www.bizjournals.com/sanjose/news/2019/06/12/median-pay-big-tech-aapl-fb-nflx-goog-intc-tsla.html

The unprecedented wealth of such companies has led to staff living and working in hyper-privileged bubbles where their every whim is catered to and every need anticipated. According to research by ABC News and others,[3] Google, for example, doesn't just offer free meals at the more than 30 cafés at its Mountain View HQ (co-founder Sergey Brin once reportedly said, "No one should be more than 200 feet away from food"), it also has nap pods, free massages, and a luxury hotel-style concierge service to run errands for staff. Reportedly, at Airbnb workers get paid to volunteer and can claim up to $2,000 a year to stay at locations listed on the platform around the world. Spotify staffers are treated to free lunch-hour concerts, while those workers planning to have a child can get fertility assistance (and money to freeze their eggs, if they're not planning to start a family anytime soon). Biotech firm Genentech reportedly offers workers on-site car washes, haircuts, spa treatments, and even a dentist. At VMware, staff can get two days off for pet bereavement. COVID-19 and the need to work remotely will likely create a new set of perks and benefits at all these companies.

Now let me be clear: my beef is certainly not with the benefits themselves. Most of the aforementioned perks are highly desirable and in an ideal world all companies, not just cash-rich tech firms, would be in a position to offer them. In fact, I personally supported a lot of these at Compass, from free lunch to extended maternity/paternity leave, free healthcare, and tuition subsidies. But that's fantasyland for the vast majority of businesses. Nor would I dismiss out of hand, ungrateful recipients notwithstanding, the underlying principle of offering them. Perks were introduced in an attempt to solve a set of very specific problems around talent recruitment and retention, as well as workplace efficiency, in an industry growing at an explosive rate. However, few who devised this benefits bonanza would have anticipated some of the more exotic examples we see today.

Opinion is divided on where exactly this perks culture originated. One highly plausible theory goes that it is simply the modern Valley's take on the traditional American "company town," like Hershey, Pennsylvania, where at the turn of the last century, founder Milton Hershey built a "town" for his chocolate factory employees, which included affordable housing, public schools, social clubs, an amusement park, and even a zoo.[4] It's widely assumed that perks culture in its most recent incarnation, in the Bay Area at least, was pioneered by Google. When it began as a research project, initially known as Backrub, in Menlo Park in 1996, Google's

---

[3]"Coolest employee perks at Silicon Valley tech companies," ABC7 News, July 24, 2018, https://abc7news.com/technology/coolest-employee-perks-at-silicon-valley-tech-companies /3816443/, and Mary Meisenzahl, "The most incredible perks Silicon Valley workers can take advantage of," Business Insider, September 15, 2019, https://www.businessinsider.com/ perks-that-silicon-valley-workers-can-take-advantage-of-2019-9
[4]Elizabeth Nix, "5 Famous Company Towns," History TV, August 22, 2018, https://www .history.com/news/5-famous-company-towns

founders Larry Page and Sergey Brin were still PhD students at Stanford University. In their early 20s and yet to emerge fully from the campus cocoon—with its dorm, laundry, dining room, and health services on tap—they ended up replicating the world they were familiar with when they came to start their company some two years later.[5] In the years that followed, and as the venture capital dam burst and cash began to flood into the Valley, a battle for scarce and highly prized engineering talent erupted among startups, eager to differentiate themselves, and the quality and variety of perks on offer began to ramp up.

And while primarily a weapon in the talent war, perks might have another more pernicious purpose too. According to Richard Walker, Professor Emeritus of Geography at the University of California, Berkeley, and a veteran Valley-watcher, the provision of "all these goodies in the workplace" was ultimately designed to keep everyone in the office. And to keep them productive. "If you don't have to run errands, and you can even get baby-care, then it just keeps you working all those extra hours, which has been the work culture anyway for a very long time," he says. "So this is also surveillance in a way, because they can keep track of you every minute of the day."

Furthermore, Professor Walker explains, the impact of this trend has been to bolster a "very male," almost infantilized culture. "By sheltering these guys in this little cocoon or womb, it kind of emphasizes that young male problem, where Mom takes care of everything; it's kind of magical, where food just appears, and 'If my treat isn't there it's because Mom forgot to provide it!'"

He continues: "In the late nineteenth century you see the bourgeoisie trying to deal with getting beyond Dickensian abstention and saving and hard work into a culture that allowed free time, get to the great outdoors, enjoy culture and so on. But now it's so extreme, it's like where's my Snickers bar? It's a kind of *reductio ad absurdum* of satisfying people's needs. But it's through *things*, it's through no effort, and it just appears magically. If it's not Mom, then it's your employer, it's the market, it's Amazon Prime, and all that."

The carousel of perks on offer at many tech unicorns further toxifies this culture. According to Deano Roberts, until recently VP Global Workplace and Real Estate at work collaboration unicorn Slack, now in a similar role at Samsara, the Valley has made a fundamental error by crossing the line from promoting employee well-being to breeding a sense of entitlement and cutting tech workers off from the surrounding community. A U.S. Army veteran who is still a colonel in the Army Reserves, Roberts explains that staff at Slack are provided with "one or two" free meals a week, largely for their team-building effect. "And then we'd tell our employees, 'We pay you well! You need to get out of this building. Go spend your money in these local

---

[5] Jordan Valinsky, "Google's Incredible Growth: A Timeline," CNN Business, December, 2018, https://edition.cnn.com/interactive/2018/12/business/google-history-timeline/index.html

mom and pop shops, there's great restaurants that are small businesses, go be part of the community. It's better for you and it's better for the community."

Besides, perks aren't the reason anybody chooses to do their job, Roberts continues. "No one says 'Man, I really hate my job and my boss, but I get free ribs on Thursday!' So yeah, the Valley's gotten this wrong—I think it's an insult to employees. And I don't think it's something [that is] sustainable. It creates a culture bubble which isn't healthy because you're literally looking out the window at folks that don't have that benefit."

While OZON never competed on this front—and it would certainly have made it easier to recruit against Yandex, Google, and others in Russia, if we could have—other companies at which I've had leadership or advisory roles have participated in this no-holds-barred approach to talent acquisition and retention. The result is tech workers becoming largely insulated from the lives of the overwhelming majority of the population, encouraging a flint-hearted belief that those who struggle and do not share in this bounty are somehow authors of their own fate who should simply "stop complaining," "make better choices," or "work harder."

"WHAT DO ENGINEERS KNOW ABOUT THE WORLD!"

In my own experience, backed by academic research,[6] many engineers are introverts, who—because of their somehow narrow training and their early experiences—have difficulties seeing the world from others' perspectives and the unintended consequences and side effects of technology on society. One study entitled *Personality Types in Software Engineering*,[7] from the University of Western Ontario, concluded:

> *When software engineers discuss how a task needs to be accomplished, the majority tend to be poor at verbalizing how the task affects the people involved. In fact, the greatest difference between software engineers and the general population is the percentage that takes action based on what they think rather than on what somebody else feels. That does not help bring the software engineers closer to the user.*

---

[6] Arif Raza, Zaka-ul-Mustafa, and Luiz Fernando Capretz, "Personality Dimensions and Temperaments of Engineering Professors and Students: A Survey," https://arxiv.org/ftp/arxiv/papers/1507/1507.06896.pdf
[7] Luis Fernando Capretz, "Personality types in software engineering," University of Western Ontario, February 22, 2002, https://www.researchgate.net/publication/222526030_Personality_types_in_software_engineering

Big Tech's Diversity Challenge

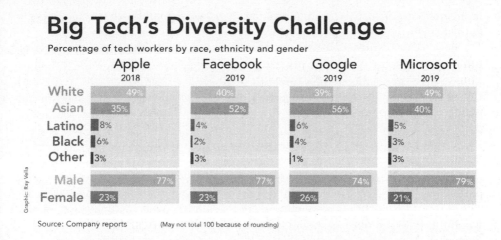

Percentage of tech workers by race, ethnicity and gender

	Apple 2018	Facebook 2019	Google 2019	Microsoft 2019
White	49%	40%	39%	49%
Asian	35%	52%	56%	40%
Latino	8%	4%	6%	5%
Black	6%	2%	4%	3%
Other	3%	3%	1%	3%
Male	77%	77%	74%	79%
Female	23%	23%	26%	21%

Graphic: Ray Vella

Source: Company reports　　(May not total 100 because of rounding)

FIGURE 2.1　Big Tech's racial and gender diversity challenge.
Source: Company reports

Engineers in the U.S. tend to emerge from a similar background anyway, says Berkeley's Professor Walker. "There's a whole history of the carefully sheltered, technically well prepared, but uneducated engineer. When I was a student at Stanford I was going to be an engineer, until I realized that 80–90 percent of all my courses were predetermined and that's to keep you from actually learning anything about society, so that you will build really good bridges or machines for the productive apparatus and never question it. So a lot of these guys are just socially underprepared."

Yes, he may be exaggerating for effect, but he is doing so to make a very serious point: we shouldn't be surprised that engineers, often unschooled in the humanities, then hothoused in the fraternity-style atmosphere of high-growth startups, largely in a corner of California or Seattle, filter bubbles themselves, should end up writing code with little intuitive understanding of its real-world impact.

And this effect is compounded by the fact that, despite its "woke" ideology and social justice warrior-style grandstanding, the Valley has always been, and still is, overwhelmingly male, white, or Asian (see Figure 2.1).

As for the lack of women, tech executives like to hide behind the excuse that not enough females enroll in the requisite science, technology, engineering, and math (STEM) classes in school. In fact, many women who enroll in those programs leave them, or go into other jobs, because the bro engineer culture is too often rife with harassment, misogyny, or just plain segregation. According to an MIT study of engineering students, "women often feel marginalized, especially during internships, other summer work opportunities, or team-based educational activities. In those situations, gender dynamics seem to generate more opportunities for men to work on the most challenging problems, while women tend to be assigned routine tasks or simple managerial duties."[8]

Women account for approximately 13 percent of the tech engineering workforce. Imagine how different software creation might be—and how much higher the empathy quotient would be—if those numbers were different.

When it comes to leadership (management) positions, the picture deteriorates further still:[9] just 3 percent of Facebook's leadership were of black heritage, while at Uber, Microsoft, and Google it was 2.8 percent, 2.2 percent, and 2 percent, respectively. Similarly, just 3 percent of leadership roles at Facebook were filled at that time by Latinx people. At Twitter, Google, and Uber, it was 2.3 percent, 2 percent, and 1.4 percent, respectively. Meanwhile women held just a third—or markedly fewer—leadership roles at Twitter (33 percent), Apple (29 percent), Facebook (28 percent), Amazon (25 percent), Google (25 percent), Uber (21 percent), Microsoft, Intel, and Pinterest (19 percent).

Although the situation is slowly improving, in certain areas at least, and a concerted effort is being made in some quarters, this longstanding lack of diversity, of both ethnicity and gender, is likely to be self-perpetuating until the number of computer science graduates better reflects the makeup of the wider population. For example, recent statistics show that in the U.S. the female share of computer science bachelor's degrees has declined slowly from a peak of approximatively 37 percent in 1984 to plateau at around 18 percent between 2007 and 2016.[10] The proportion of computer science majors by race/ethnicity between 2015 and 2016 was around 10 percent for those of black heritage, 12 percent for Hispanics, and 7 percent for Asians.[11]

Unsurprisingly this deeply entrenched underrepresentation of minorities has often resulted in an absence of diverse thinking, which has over the years led to disasters like Google's Photos app notoriously tagging black people as gorillas (and it was later revealed that, three years later, the only remedial action Google engineers took at the time was to block gorillas from its image labeling algorithms),[12] or even

---

[8]Peter Dizikes, "Why do women leave engineering?" MIT News, June 15, 2016, https://news.mit.edu/2016/why-do-women-leave-engineering-0615

[9]Rani Molla, "Tech diversity: How Facebook compares to other tech companies in diversity," recode, April 11, 2018, https://www.vox.com/2018/4/11/17225574/facebook-tech-diversity-women

[10]"Women in Computer Science: Getting involved in STEM," https://www.computerscience.org/resources/women-in-computer-science/

[11]Blanca Myers, "Women and Minorities in Tech, By the Numbers," *Wired*, March 27, 2018, https://www.wired.com/story/computer-science-graduates-diversity/

[12]Alistair Barr, "Google Mistakenly Tags Black People as 'Gorillas,' Showing Limits of Algorithms," *Wall Street Journal*, July 1, 2015, https://blogs.wsj.com/digits/2015/07/01/google-mistakenly-tags-black-people-as-gorillas-showing-limits-of-algorithms/

Google's autocomplete search tool, which has been caught promoting, among other delights, Holocaust denial, White Supremacy, Islamophobia, as well as a host of conspiracy theories, although that has since been fixed.[13]

"STEVE JOBS DIDN'T BUILD APPLE BY BEING HUMBLE AND CARING ABOUT PEOPLE"

This concentration of young white and Asian males with a narrow outlook helped a number of dangerous stereotypes to emerge.

An example of this is what I like to call "Steve Jobs Syndrome." Whether true or not, many have associated him with a belief that his undoubted genius excused any kind of behavior and his legacy has cultivated an indelible association between being a jerk and a genius, which has ballooned to the point where many people believe that a founder-CEO, in particular, actually *has* to be a jerk to be a genius. Having a cartoonishly overblown "get shit done" Type A personality (think Uber founder Travis Kalanick, serial unicorn founder Elon Musk, and Adam Neumann, former front man of WeWork) has for a long time been a source of pride for the tech community. And this "syndrome" isn't the exclusive preserve of men (although it seems to mostly affect men); just look at the behavior of Theranos founder Elizabeth Holmes, who even sported Jobs-style black turtlenecks while knowingly putting lives at risk, which would ultimately see her charged with criminal fraud.[14] The founder of one of the tech companies whose acquisitions I oversaw used to say every time I called him out on his lack of empathy and humility that led to many disastrous decisions: "Steve Jobs didn't build Apple by being humble and caring about people."

Then there's a mutation of the genius-jerk theory: the misunderstood lonely nerd who is quite brilliant yet socially awkward and abrasive in person—something we non-geniuses just have to accept. Think Gilfoyle in HBO's *Silicon Valley*, a character all too familiar to anyone who has worked in tech, whose misogyny and mean-spirited condescension are tolerated because of his ability to "change the world" through writing gravity-defying code.

The flourishing of this syndrome has helped cultivate another tech myth: that of "exceptionalism," in which unicorn founders, execs, early hires, and certain VCs, who have all drunk deeply from the Kool-Aid, believe that because the world is

---

[13]Carole Cadwalladr, "Google is not 'just' a platform. It frames, shapes and distorts how we see the world," *The Guardian,* December 11, 2016, https://www.theguardian.com/commentisfree/2016/dec/11/google-frames-shapes-and-distorts-how-we-see-world

[14]Reed Abelson, "Theranos Founder Elizabeth Holmes Indicted on Fraud Charges," *New York Times,* June 15, 2018, https://www.nytimes.com/2018/06/15/health/theranos-elizabeth-holmes-fraud.html

a meritocratic place, they and they alone are responsible for their success, due to the fact that they are smarter and work harder than anyone else. The trouble with that theory is that it is demonstrably untrue in the vast majority of cases, not least because while, yes, they may be smart and work hard, they are also the beneficiaries of a once-in-a-century alignment of circumstances, ranging from the development of the internet itself to the Wild West–style "lawlessness" of the Valley, which was left free to roam far ahead of governments, regulators, and tax codes, to today's unprecedented surfeit of venture capital and scale culture.

Meanwhile, if you genuinely believe that anyone has a shot at becoming a billionaire, and that Silicon Valley embodies the American Dream that anything is achievable, then it becomes easy to conclude that anyone who is not successful deserves their fate. This libertarian attitude helps explain the lack of empathy among a certain tech's elite, who consider their vast wealth "earned" and other people's failure the result of some version of laziness, are generally suspicious of governments, and believe they pay too much in taxes.

This has further spawned a number of self-interested beliefs that are closely and proudly held by the tech "tribe," including notions such as "as long as I produce outstanding results I won't be fired," that technology itself isn't good or bad, but neutral ("there is no bias in code"), tech "solutionism" ("tech will solve everything," "we just need better tech, more tech," etc.), gender/race-neutral approach ("we only hire the best"), and so on.

Together this hyper-protected world, lack of diversity, "tribal" mythologies, and hyper-specialization have had both positive and malign effects. On the one hand, all tribes have their customs and shibboleths and in many ways these myths have helped spur a fast-moving, solution-oriented culture, where people are unafraid of daunting challenges and pursuing bold targets, enabling small startups to take on the biggest monopolies and incumbents. That shouldn't be underestimated. It has given us any number of new tools and services. And personally, I would find it very difficult to return to working in traditional corporations, which I now find often painfully slow and bureaucratic.

But it also led to a flawed and troubling "tech bro" or simply bro culture. Corralling group of mostly young white and Asian male engineers, who tend to hire from their immediate circle, who spend long hours and often their downtime together, in an environment that pushes them to "move fast and break things" (while Facebook publicly abandoned that motto, it still very much captures the spirit in many tech startups), and creates an outlook in which everyone is judged based on young male behavior patterns. The types of things I witnessed over the years include the work hard/play hard attitude, epitomized by a culture of booze-fueled partying; people making loud, bold statements; recklessness; the prioritizing of hyper-growth over sustainable profits; and demeaning comments about women and minorities. Of course, other professions encourage similar cliques and behaviors, from Wall Street to certain law firms and elements of the sales, media, and advertising industries. Yet it is particularly embedded and hard to fix in tech, because it tends to take root at the early stages of a startup. CEOs often come from engineering backgrounds, everyone's focused on day-to-day survival, and by the time the team hires their first HR person, bro culture has often become the norm. This monochrome mindset once again means they are more likely to struggle to understand the impact of the products and services they help create.

* * * *

The myriad causes of the tech giants' issues are well documented. However, ultimately a key shift in the way the Valley (and by implication those giants based elsewhere) is perceived might have been down to something rather more nuanced, argues Russell Hancock, CEO and president of Joint Venture Silicon Valley, which for the past quarter of a century has been gathering data to track trends across the Valley, published annually in the *Silicon Valley Index*: Big Tech is no longer innovating chiefly to solve problems, but perversely is now the source of many of society's problems instead. "It used to be that the things [they] were bringing to market were universally hailed and badly wanted," he says. "Now tech companies . . . are [producing] tools that can be used to invade privacy, or tamper with democratic processes, or they're addictive—so they're not ameliorating the condition of mankind, they are actually making us worse. That's a really significant change."

Increasingly isolated from the wider world, the tech elite has gradually lost touch with the people they serve and, as a result, can no longer fully understand the societal impact they have.

CHAPTER 3

Emerald Cities

In July 2016, Cadence, a fine dining establishment located in the Mid-Market district of San Francisco, served its final meal. Its six months of operations were described by Sarah Fritsche, former food writer at the *San Francisco Chronicle*, as "a stunningly short life for a restaurant expected to be a blockbuster."[1] Unfortunately Cadence was far from the only restaurant to close its doors in the same neighborhood over a matter of months.

Four years earlier, Twitter had moved into the area. The social media firm was the first of several celebrated tech companies (including Zendesk, Yammer, Square, Spotify, and Uber) to open up in the city's then emerging Mid-Market district between mid-2012 and 2014,[2] alongside luxury apartment complexes, whose residents reportedly included large numbers of high-earning tech workers. Over the next few years, a wave of upscale restaurants followed, tempted by the area's evolving demographics as well as incentives from the city. Several failed; some, like Cadence, didn't last much beyond the appetizer.

While restaurants often misfire for a complex web of reasons—and in the Mid-Market district these included endemic homelessness—there was broad agreement among the neighborhood's restaurateurs that tech companies' free cafeterias made achieving profitability a struggle for many of them. The former chief executive of the Golden Gate Restaurant Association, Gwyneth Borden, reckons that, pre-COVID-19, there were as many as 50 free staff cafeterias in the city of San Francisco alone, primarily in the tech sector. "There was so much

---

[1] Sarah Fritsche, "Mid-Market dining seeks the right recipe," *San Francisco Chronicle,* July 14, 2016, https://www.sfchronicle.com/restaurants/article/Mid-Market-s-restaurant-scene-pending-boom-8376942.php
[2] Roland Li, "Tech cafeteria ban? A timeline of mid-Market's restaurant boom and bust," *San Francisco Chronicle,* July 24, 2018, https://www.sfchronicle.com/restaurants/article/Tech-cafeteria-ban-A-timeline-of-Mid-Market-s-13101484.php

conversation around how tech supports restaurants [at the time]," she recalls wryly. "There was even an instance in the Mid-Market, where a restaurateur had been lured by certain executives to open up a restaurant across the street with the promise that there'd be thousands of workers coming into the area. Unfortunately, what those executives failed to mention was that they would be putting in free cafeterias."

Over the course of the past two decades, free staff cafeterias—much like some of the other perks on offer that I have described, including dry cleaning and medical and dental services—have had the effect of cutting off many of the tech from their immediate community, often in sprawling, university-style campuses. Now while it is plainly nonsensical to pin all of the blame on tech companies for the impact of the Valley's extraordinary success, this has nevertheless triggered resentment from some local businesses. They believed they were promised rich pickings of potential new customers on their doorstep, but instead saw no meaningful uplift in trade, or worse.

"One of the reasons some of [the tech giants] are being vilified is because they create these bubbles that are hermetically sealed and inside the bubble is like the Emerald City of Oz—these amazing universes that they've created—and yet everything happens inside the bubble," says Russell Hancock, publisher of Valley trend-tracker *Silicon Valley Index*, who cites the example of the city of San Jose, California, whose downtown is home to Adobe's headquarters. "San Jose was so excited to have [Adobe's] investment in their city, but it hasn't panned out. When people go there, they drive in their cars, they go into a garage, they go up into the towers and stay inside until they leave. So the impact on San Jose has been really minimal and disappointing."

Some big-name tech firms, as well as a few city authorities, stung by criticism and in some cases a local backlash, are now taking active measures to address this disconnection between tech giants and the surrounding community. When Facebook—famous for its high-quality free food—announced that it was to open a new hub in the city of Mountain View, city officials effectively banned the social network from offering regular fully subsidized staff meals in an effort to drive customers to local restaurants.[3] The policy shift was as a direct result of Google, which is headquartered in Mountain View, having multiple free restaurants allegedly putting the squeeze on local businesses.[4]

Google has taken steps not to compound its missteps in Mountain View. Hancock points to the giant's proposed vast new development in San Jose named "Downtown West," which could ultimately house up to 25,000 employees in an open tech campus in the heart of the city's downtown, adjacent to a brand-new

---

[3]Wendy Lee and Roland Li, "Mountain View's unusual rule for Facebook: No free food," *San Francisco Chronicle,* July 23 2018, https://www.sfchronicle.com/business/article/Mountain-View-s-unusual-rule-for-Facebook-No-13096100.php
[4]Daniel Debolt, "Can't compete with free eats," *Mountain View Voice,* July 11 2013, https://www.mv-voice.com/news/2013/07/11/cant-compete-with-free-eats

multimodal train station.[5] "They've decided to turn that [fortress] model on its head," he says. "Now they don't want to be insular, they want to use the amenities of the city, they want to be integrated with them."

However, while Downtown West was awaiting official approval at the time of writing, a sizable anti–Big Tech backlash was in full swing in San Jose. "Since Google first announced its intention to build what would be the largest technology campus in all of Silicon Valley here in San Jose, it's really been the number one concern from the public—particularly for low-income working people, communities of color, and seniors," says Jeffrey Buchanan, director of policy at Working Partnerships USA, a grassroots campaign against inequality and poverty. "There's been a tremendous fear that this project and a number of other large-scale commercial office buildings that are trying to bring more tech companies into the city are going to be the straw that breaks the camel's back for folks that are already struggling to hang on here in the city." Buchanan says that despite a "really strong interest" in seeing Google making large-scale investments in affordable housing in San Jose, past experience of Big Tech building frenzies prompts wariness. "Typically we've seen companies expand and rents rise," he says. Time and again at public meetings about Downtown West, he heard people talking about their struggle to make rent. Tech campuses are entirely dependent on thousands of subcontracted service workers, including cleaners, security officers, food service workers, and corporate shuttle drivers, Buchanan continues. "These are largely low-wage jobs, and if they're not unionized, oftentimes they're not paid the kind of wages where they can afford to live here in the Bay Area. Google's certainly not the worst when it comes to these issues—and there's still the possibility we could have some positive outcomes from this project. But just because of its size and because of what the community has seen, as the tech industry has grown without taking responsibility for its impact, that's really what's spurred the enormous upswell of community interest in [Downtown West]."

At the time of this writing, COVID-19 is forcing tech companies to rethink remote working and office space. It is unlikely that they will go back in the foreseeable future to what existed pre-pandemic. At the same time, it is equally unlikely that office spaces will become completely unnecessary and that big tech hubs will empty themselves of all tech workers. As unemployment and inequality grow, it will continue to be critical for Big Tech to pay attention to the impact they have on their local communities.

"LANDLORDS POUNDING ON THE DOOR"

Over the past 25 years, Silicon Valley has seen seismic changes, including a population that has trebled to around 3 million people and the upending and

---

[5]George Avalos, "'Downtown West' plan: Google submits proposal for San Jose transit village," *Mercury News,* October 11, 2019, https://www.mercurynews.com/2019/10/11/google-submits-proposal-for-san-jose-transit-village-calls-it-downtown-west/

disappearance of entire industries, according to the *Silicon Valley Index*. And yet the biggest shift over that period, as far as Hancock is concerned, is what he describes as the "continued erosion and disappearance" of the middle class:

> *Silicon Valley has become a place of cleavages: extremely affluent people, highly skilled people who are filling out this tech economy, and the elimination of all those mid-range jobs—the accountants, the administrators, the assistants, the clerks, the archivists, the stenographers—a whole host of things that have been eliminated by the technologies that were invented here. And then our service sector... their wages have been stagnating over that period of time. So now we've become two valleys: An impoverished Valley and a wildly affluent, highly successful Valley. And we're looking at social stress, class tension and other things like that—and that's a new development.*

The Valley's jobs boom, which drew in hundreds of thousands of tech workers over the past decade, meant that demand skyrocketed to live in urban centers across the Bay Area so that they could be close to work, bars, restaurants, and entertainment. "The result of course is unbelievable pressure on real estate, it's just driven prices through the roof," says Professor Walker of UC Berkeley. "So you displace people, and landlords jump on the bandwagon... they have evicted tens of thousands of people in San Francisco and Oakland, and people have just been driven out by the market and by landlords pounding on the door."

Hancock says *Silicon Valley Index* data shows that for the first time since 1995, more people are leaving the region than are coming in, with people on lower incomes being driven farther afield. "These are people who still want to participate in this economy but can't afford it, and have to go further to find housing that's affordable. They're going to the far perimeter [of the Valley], to agricultural areas, and they're having to commute into Silicon Valley more than 90 minutes each way. Our region has about 100,000 of those now. That's creating harmful externalities: more carbon emissions into our atmosphere, the nation's worst traffic congestion, the quality of living just completely eroded."

The net effect of spiraling house prices and rents, driven in part by high-earning tech workers, has been a population shift that has seen the displacement of thousands of African Americans and Latinx households, according to the University of California at Berkeley's *Urban Displacement Project*.[6] This has led to what is in effect the "re-segregation of the Bay Area," says Anna Cash, until recently a program director at the project. "As housing prices shot up in many areas, many low-income

---

[6]UC Berkeley's Urban Displacement Project, "Rising Housing Costs and Re-Segregation in the San Francisco Bay Area," https://www.urbandisplacement.org/sites/default/files/images/bay_area_re-segregation_rising_housing_costs_report_2019.pdf

Silicon Valley's Struggling Minorities

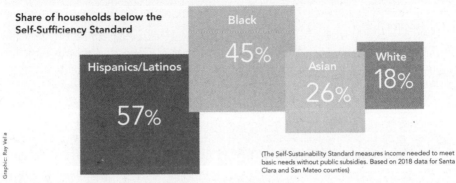

Share of households below the
Self-Sufficiency Standard

Black **45%**

Hispanics/Latinos **57%**

Asian **26%**

White **18%**

(The Self-Sustainability Standard measures income needed to meet basic needs without public subsidies. Based on 2018 data for Santa Clara and San Mateo counties)

Graphic: Ray Vella

Source: Silicon Valley Institute of Regional Studies, University of Washington

FIGURE 3.1   Racial income inequality.
Source: Silicon Valley Institute of Regional Studies, University of Washington.

people of color were moving outside of those core employment centers to places with lower housing prices but also fewer resources." This, she says, amounts to "shuffling poverty" and results in "a ruptured social fabric."

Displacement has a domino effect on families and individuals too, where those in work—as Hancock describes—are likely to have to commute farther to get there, with children being forced to move schools, says Lupe Arreola, executive director of Tenants Together, San Francisco, a statewide coalition of local tenant organizations. Physical social networks are stretched and broken, and need to be rebuilt in new, often unfamiliar locations. "People are having to recreate communities that they may have lived in for a long time," she says, "you're uprooting your life every single time you have to move."

Now that the middle classes feel the heat, they are reaching for their smartphones and voting, so the tides are turning. In October 2019, California Governor Gavin Newsom signed Assembly Bill 1482 into law. Known as the Tenant Protection Act of 2019, the legislation caps annual rent increases at 5 percent plus the rate of inflation for the next decade, while tenants will be protected from eviction without cause. It's estimated that 2.4 million households statewide will be affected by the new rent cap.[7]

---

[7] Laim Dillon, "California will limit rent increases under bill signed by Gov. Gavin Newsom," *LA Times,* October 8, 2019, https://www.latimes.com/california/story/2019-10-08/california-rent-cap-tenant-protections-signed

Yet there's frustration in Arreola's voice. "We should have had this level of urgency at the time when low-income and working-class people were getting evicted," she says ruefully, "instead of it reaching the point where families are living in cars."

"WE KNOW OUR RESPONSIBILITY TO HELP STARTS AT HOME"

Rent increases, evictions, growing inequalities—the unprecedented growth of the tech industry's workforce in the Valley has strongly intensified these problems, casting these entrenched issues into stark relief. Tech has played a similar role in cities like Seattle and neighborhoods like Venice Beach in Los Angeles. Yet it would be unfair to lay the blame solely on Big Tech. The severity of these issues would be very different if it wasn't for the poor land use, questionable housing policies, and political and economic choices made by local governments for decades. In an article published in July 2019, the consulting company McKinsey explained, "From 1999 to 2014, the Bay Area permitted construction of 61,000 fewer very-low-income affordable-housing units than recommended by the state and lost a substantial portion of existing housing inventory to market pressures—in San Francisco, for every two affordable housing units created, the city lost more than one from its existing inventory because of units being permanently withdrawn from the protection of rent control."[8] In the same way, while I understand the anger toward the private buses Big Tech started chartering for their employees that came to symbolize the housing crisis and the divide between rich and poor, I doubt that most of these buses would exist if the region had an extensive public transportation network. And in the meantime, the SFMTA said in a 2015 report that the shuttles remove nearly 4.3 million vehicle miles traveled from the region's streets each month.[9]

So far, at least two Valley giants have implicitly accepted their role in the housing crisis and pledged serious sums to help ease the situation on their own doorstep. In a carefully phrased blog post entitled "$1 billion for 20,000 Bay Area homes," published in June 2019, Google CEO Sundar Pichai wrote:[10] "As we work to build a more helpful Google, we know our responsibility to help starts

---

[8]Kate Anthony, "Homelessness in the San Francisco Bay Area: The crisis and a path forward," McKinsey & Company, July 11, 2019, https://www.mckinsey.com/industries/public-sector/our-insights/homelessness-in-the-san-francisco-bay-area-the-crisis-and-a-path-forward
[9]SFMTA, Municipal Transportation Agency, "Commuter Shuttle Pilot Program," October 5, 2015, https://www.sfmta.com/sites/default/files/projects/2015/Evaluation%20Report%20-%20Oct%205%202015.pdf
[10]Sundar Pichai, "$1 billion for 20,000 Bay Area homes," Google, Company Announcements, June 18, 2019, https://blog.google/inside-google/company-announcements/1-billion-investment-bay-area-housing/

at home.... The lack of new supply, combined with the rising cost of living, has resulted in a severe shortage of affordable housing options for long-time middle and low income residents," Pichai continued. "As Google grows throughout the Bay Area ... we've invested in developing housing that meets the needs of these communities." He then announced "an additional" $1 billion investment in Bay Area housing, which would lead to the development of at least 15,000 new homes at all income levels. Pichai went on to say that Google would also establish a $250 million investment fund "so that we can provide incentives to enable developers to build at least 5,000 affordable housing units across the market." The company also said that through Google.org, it would give a further $50 million in grants to nonprofits in the areas of homelessness and urban displacement, in effect acknowledging Big Tech's contribution to this crisis.

Apple went even further in its philanthropic efforts. In a press release published in November 2019,[11] the company announced that it was committing $2.5 billion to combat California's housing crisis. Sounding a bit like a government initiative, Apple announced a $1 billion affordable housing investment fund, which would offer the state and others "an open line of credit to develop and build additional new, very low-to-moderate-income housing," a $1 billion first-time homebuyer mortgage assistance fund, which would "provide aspiring homebuyers with financing and down payment assistance," and $300 million-worth of Apple-owned land in San Jose would be made available for affordable housing. Similarly, Facebook and other tech companies have committed hundreds of millions of dollars toward affordable housing in the Bay Area, while Microsoft is participating in a similar initiative in its hometown of Seattle.[12]

"SHOCKINGLY POOR VALUE FOR TAXPAYERS"

Despite these community-building efforts, the reality is that Big Tech is undermining cities and states by ruthlessly reducing its tax liabilities, money that governments could use to help solve some of the issues created by the very same companies.

With the promise of bringing jobs, tech companies are able to demand extraordinarily favorable terms from local and state governments. These kinds of arrangements are not particular to tech; many large corporations have been enticed

---

[11] Apple news release, "Apple commits $2.5 billion to combat housing crisis in California," November 4, 2019, https://www.apple.com/newsroom/2019/11/apple-commits-two-point-five-billion-to-combat-housing-crisis-in-california/

[12] Salvador Rodriguez, "Facebook and others pledge hundreds of millions of dollars toward affordable housing in Bay Area," CNBC, January 24, 2019, https://www.cnbc.com/2019/01/24/facebook-chan-zuckerberg-initiative-join-effort-to-expand-housing-in-the-san-francisco-bay-area.html

to locate plants or offices with subsidies and tax breaks. Perhaps most famously, sports teams will pick up and leave their hometown fans behind if another city offers the owners a sweeter deal on a taxpayer-financed stadium. Unfortunately, these deals frequently represent shockingly poor value for taxpayers. According to a *New York Times* investigation[13] in 2012, local incentives granted across America's states, counties, and cities amounted to an estimated annual $80 billion giveaway to companies.

But Big Tech, with its cachet of cutting-edge industry and well-paying jobs (for some), has demonstrated a particular talent for getting not only advantageous tax treatment, but other benefits that often are hidden from public view.

In 1997, on the brink of bankruptcy, Apple negotiated a deal with its hometown of Cupertino: in exchange for keeping its headquarters in the city, the company would get half of Cupertino's share of sales tax revenue generated when Apple sold to businesses in California for at least five years. That deal has been extended and continues today, but the terms are confidential.[14]

A $3 billion package to woo Foxconn, whose major customers include Apple, Google, HP, Microsoft, and many others, to Wisconsin in 2017 in an effort to create up to 13,000 jobs in the state, was reckoned to cost the state up to $19,000 per job *per year*.[15] Then, two years later, Wisconsin's governor announced that the Foxconn factory in Wisconsin would only create a tiny fraction (about 1,500) of the promised jobs.[16] At the time of the writing the innovation center buildings are still empty and the main factory hasn't yet opened.[17]

Amazon took it to an entirely new level when the trillion-dollar corporation launched a nationwide beauty pageant, wherein cities keen to host the e-commerce giant's secondary corporate headquarters tried to one-up one another with ever greater inducements consisting of tax incentives and grants, including $3.4 billion

---

[13]Louise Story, "As Companies Seek Tax Deals, Governments Pay High Price," *New York Times,* December 1, 2012, https://www.nytimes.com/2012/12/02/us/how-local-taxpayers-bankroll-corporations.html

[14]Laura Mahoney, "Apple's 22-Year Tax Break Part of Billions in California Bounty," Bloomberg Tax, April 24, 2019, https://news.bloombergtax.com/daily-tax-report-state/apples-22-year-tax-break-part-of-billions-in-california-bounty

[15]Julia Horowitz, "Foxconn's deal to create 13,000 jobs in Wisconsin: Where it stands," CNN Money, April 21, 2017, https://money.cnn.com/2017/08/21/news/foxconn-wisconsin-deal-updates/

[16]Nilay Patel, " Foxconn will only create 1,500 jobs, says Wisconsin governor," The Verge, July 10, 2019, https://www.theverge.com/2019/7/10/20689021/foxconn-wisconsin-governor-jobs-tony-evers-manufacturing

[17]Josh Dzieza and Nilay Patel, "Foxconn's buildings in Wisconsin are still empty, one year later," April 12, 2020, The Verge, https://www.theverge.com/2020/4/12/21217060/foxconn-wisconsin-innovation-centers-empty-buildings

offered by officials in New York and Virginia.[18] Amazon has proven particularly adept at hoovering up billions of dollars in state and local economic development subsidy deals over the years.[19]

In the end, Amazon canceled its plans to build its HQ2 in Long Island City, Queens, after political opposition.[20] Instead it chose the Arlington, Virginia, area across the Potomac River from Washington, D.C. Among the items allegedly demanded by the company: that officials are required to tell the company if any media organizations file public-records requests about any aspects of the deal, so that the company can seek to quash the request before information is released.[21]

$100 Billion Global Tax Gap

Subsidies and tax breaks are one thing. But Big Tech also has become a master at aggressively minimizing its tax obligations around the world. Airbnb is a case in point. While among the more trusted of the major tech brands, the short-term rentals marketplace is leveraging its digital platform status in two ways. First and most familiarly, thanks to its peer-to-peer model, it is able to sidestep most of the hotel industry's fixed costs, including staffing and employment protections. Second, and less well known, is Airbnb's "voluntary" tax arrangements that have allegedly short-changed state and city authorities across America and the wider world, eating into their budget.

In June 2019, Dan Bucks, a former director at the Montana Department of Revenue who spent the best part of two decades as executive director of the Multistate Tax Commission in Washington, D.C., found that Airbnb's "voluntary collection arrangements" have likely cost federal, state, and local governments in the U.S. an estimated $3.48 billion between 2013 and 2018. These are funds that could otherwise have been spent on public services, which in most U.S. cities are sorely needed.[22]

---

[18] Jacob Passy, "This is what Amazon's HQ2 was going to cost New York taxpayers," MarketWatch, February 16, 2019, https://www.marketwatch.com/story/what-amazons-hq2-means-for-taxpayers-in-new-york-and-virginia-2018-11-14

[19] Good Jobs First: Amazon Tracker, March, 2020, https://www.goodjobsfirst.org/amazon-tracker

[20] Amazon, "Update on plans for New York City headquarters," Day One: The Amazon Blog, February 14, 2019, https://blog.aboutamazon.com/company-news/update-on-plans-for-new-york-city-headquarters

[21] Marcus Baram, "Here are the most infuriating details of Amazon's HQ2 deals," FastCompany, November 13, 2018, https://www.fastcompany.com/90267287/here-are-the-most-infuriating-details-of-amazons-hq2-deals

[22] Dan Bucks, "Report: States and localities are losing money on Airbnb's tax deals," June 2019, https://www.ahla.com/sites/default/files/bucks_report_states_localities_losing_money_on_airbnb_tax_deals_june_2019.pdf

Bucks's report alleges that in offering entire homes and apartments converted from residential use to transient lodgings on its platform, Airbnb's "operations often violate local housing and zoning policies." To stop these "illegal" rentals from being shuttered, the startup "works to keep the identity and location of its lodging operations secret from public officials," Buck observed.

"That secrecy has also encouraged operators to avoid collecting sales and lodging taxes and paying income taxes and has shielded them from commercial property tax assessments," he writes. "Airbnb hardened the shield of secrecy for its lodging operators by offering to make payments, ostensibly for lodging and sales taxes, in return for highly questionable, special treatment by tax agencies—including being allowed to keep their lodging operators secret from all public authorities." According to the report, which was heavily promoted by the American Hotel & Lodging Association (AHLA), the Valley giant has secured these agreements in "over 35 states and several hundred localities."

Before I go any further, let's first remind ourselves, briefly, how we arrived at the current situation. Historically, companies have usually been taxed based on their physical presence. That of course didn't stop most businesses optimizing their tax affairs (known as "tax avoidance," rather than the illegal "tax evasion"), including sometimes going as far as changing the location of their HQ to a more beneficial jurisdiction.

The difference with tech companies is that their physical presence tends to be minimal, and with exceptions like Apple, and Amazon's foray into physical stores and fulfillment centers in the U.S., their production centers are mostly offices with engineers or sales and marketing folks, while their products and services (again with obvious caveats) are mostly virtual. Given all of the above, they have much more flexibility to decide where to declare their profits. An entirely legitimate process, known as transfer pricing, where two parts of the same international organization trade with one another (e.g., one company bills another for "services") has enabled Amazon, for example, between 2006 and 2014, to funnel around 75 percent of its EU revenue into a holding company, Amazon Europe Holding Technologies (AEHT) in Luxembourg. There, Amazon had received an agreement to operate tax-free. AEHT then made regular payments to Amazon U.S.[23] This led to a ruling from the European Commission in 2017 that Luxembourg had offered undue tax benefits to the U.S. giant of around €250 million. The commission considered this arrangement "illegal under E.U. state aid rules," as it enabled Amazon to pay "substantially less tax than other businesses."[24] At the time of writing, Amazon was continuing to "defend

---

[23]BBC News, "France tech tax: What's being done to make internet giants pay more?," July 11, 2019, https://www.bbc.co.uk/news/business-48928782

[24]European Commission, "EU Commission says Luxembourg aid to Amazon illegal," October 4, 2017, https://ec.europa.eu/ireland/news/eu-commission-says-luxembourg-aid-to-amazon-illegal_en

itself vigorously" against the commission's attempts to recover what it considers lost tax revenues.[25]

In December 2019, Fair Tax Mark, a UK nonprofit that launched a certification scheme in 2014 and campaigns for tax transparency and justice, published a report called "The Silicon Six and their $100 billion global tax gap."[26] The report found that there is "a significant difference between the cash taxes paid and both the expected [basic] rate of tax and, more significantly, the reported current tax provisions" of the six U.S. giants Facebook, Apple, Amazon, Netflix, Google, and Microsoft between 2010 and 2019.

The researchers identified that the gap between the expected rate of tax and the cash taxes actually paid by the six totaled $155.3 billion over that decade. It also revealed that the gap between the current tax provisions and the cash taxes actually paid was $100.2 billion, that the bulk of the shortfall arose outside the U.S., and that profits were shifted to tax havens such as Bermuda, Ireland, Luxembourg, and the Netherlands.

Overall, these companies, the report explains, "paid just 15.9% of corporation tax (cash) on their declared profits over the period 2010 to 2017 inclusive, at a time when the headline rate was 35%. The levels of tax paid are well below those paid by the majority of other businesses in the United States, which studies have found to be a mean of between 29.1% (1995–2004) and 26% (2008–2014)."

While none of the six giants emerged from the study with much credit for tax-paying responsibility to wider society, Amazon was deemed the worst offender. "The company is growing its market domination across the globe on the back of revenues that are largely untaxed, and can unfairly undercut local businesses that take a more responsible approach," wrote the authors of the Fair Tax Mark's report.

Amazon responded to the report with a blanket denial. In an emailed statement to tech website the Register[27] a spokesperson wrote, "Amazon represents about 1 percent of global retail with larger competitors everywhere we operate, and had a 24 per cent effective tax rate on profits from 2010-2018—neither 'dominant' or 'untaxed.' ... Governments write the tax laws and Amazon is doing the very thing they encourage companies to do—paying all taxes due while also investing many billions in creating jobs and infrastructure. Coupled with low margins, this investment will naturally result in a lower cash tax rate."

---

[25]Mark Sweney, "Amazon given €294m in tax credits as European revenues jump to €32bn," *The Guardian,* April 21, 2020, https://www.theguardian.com/technology/2020/apr/21/amazon-given-294m-in-tax-credits-as-european-revenues-jump-to-32bn
[26]Fair Tax Mark, "Tax gap of Silicon Six over $100 billion so far this decade," December 2, 2019, https://fairtaxmark.net/tax-gap-of-silicon-six-over-100-billion-so-far-this-decade/
[27]Thomas Claburn, "Silicon Valley Scrooges sidestep debt to society through tax avoidance to the tune of $100bn," *The Register,* December 4, 2019, https://www.theregister.co.uk/2019/12/04/silicon_valley_tax_sidestep/

When it comes to leveraging the tax laws, tech giants have indeed proven to be particularly skilled. They (along with others) feasted on the Trump administration's tax cut in 2017, according to a study by the Institute of Taxation and Economic Policy (ITEP). Amazon, for example, claimed a federal tax rebate of $129 billion on reported U.S. income of $11 billion, while "Netflix paid no federal income tax on $856 million of U.S. income."[28]

And in case you think this is just a broadside against the U.S. giants, research published by the European Commission[29] found European digital businesses were behaving similarly. "On average, domestic digitalised business models are subject to an effective tax rate of only 8.5%—less than half compared to traditional business models," the report found.

Like Margrethe Vestager, executive vice president of the European Commission for a "Europe Fit for the Digital Age," who as Competition Commissioner has been one of Big Tech's chief tormentors and a staunch defender of European-style public interest, I believe we've reached the stage where something has to give. "The thing is the situation is not sustainable," she said in an interview for this book. "The huge majority of businesses pay their taxes, they may do it joyfully [or] they may consider it a cost, but they pay their taxes. And it's not sustainable that they see their competitors for capital, for skilled employees, for customers, not pay their taxes, that [these competitors] don't contribute to the societies where they do their business."

The stifling effect this behavior has on startups and traditional competitors aside, systemic—albeit legal—corporate tax avoidance erodes governments' spending power for vital services. For companies who make much of their mission-oriented goals to improve the world around them (by connecting people, organizing the world's information, etc.), Big Tech's attitude to corporation tax chafes. Sure, the tech giants are far from alone in this regard, but they are particularly adept at it.

---

[28]Institute on Taxation and Economic Policy (ITEP), "Corporate Tax Avoidance Remains Rampant Under New Tax Law," April 11, 2019, https://itep.org/notadime/

[29]European Commission, "Communication from the Commission to the European parliament and the Council," September 21, 2017, https://ec.europa.eu/taxation_customs/sites/taxation/files/1_en_act_part1_v10_en.pdf

CHAPTER 4

The New Feudalism

Right now the jury is still out on whether the tech economy is ultimately a job creator or a job destroyer. As with many of the points in this book, that topic is complex, nuanced, and polarizing. As of today, while tech has upended some businesses, it has helped drive expansion in so many industries that the net effect is likely more jobs, even if there is disagreement over how to quantify it. Whether that will be true as automation driven by artificial intelligence expands throughout the economy is another matter. Either way, it is critical that we look deeper than simple employment numbers.

Tech defenders argue that the information revolution is no different from others in history. One can certainly draw parallels to the industrial revolution, for example: powered by relentless innovation, it, too, created new jobs while killing others. What is different is the degree to which tech companies, and unicorns in particular, have changed the nature and financial underpinnings of work, and the relationship between employers and workers. Whereas the industrial revolution paved the way for a new middle class and lifted overall prosperity, the tech revolution has helped to hollow out the middle class and catalyze a greater level of income inequality than at any time in modern history. And no matter what some tech executives, venture capitalists, and their investors claim, these trade-offs need not be the inevitable consequence of progress.

THE HUMAN IMPACT OF TECH DISRUPTION

Understanding how different the current revolution is starts with the underlying ethos of the tech industry, which—in the name of delivering more efficiency, more capabilities, and at lower cost—is to disrupt deeply entrenched legacy businesses and processes. And to be clear, if legacy businesses are bloated, delivering poor quality and bad service at high prices, they deserve all the disruption they get.

But to compete, tech early on identified the cost of labor as among the biggest inefficiencies of its targets. Thus, tech avoided unions at all cost. Compensation at

35

many startups was a mix of low salaries and stock options that might or might not ever attain significant value. The idea of pensions (at least in the United States) was relegated to the dustbin. And the widespread use of independent contractors and gig workers without any kind of social protection supported the economics of many Big Tech businesses.

In the early days of the tech boom, it was easy to be dazzled and distracted by all the new toys we were getting and by all the newly minted millionaires, some of whom were secretaries and cafeteria workers lucky enough to be hired at the right time by the right tech firms. But we are now seeing the bills come due, especially when it comes to the so-called gig economy.

Take Uber, a company closely associated with welcomed disruption. Ride-hailing apps are reckoned to account for about 75 percent of the ground transportation market in the U.S. for business travelers,[1] so it comes as little surprise that the overnight growth and popularity of Uber, Lyft, and similar services have sliced through the livelihoods of many traditional taxi, minicab, and private-hire drivers. To be sure, the old-school taxi business, especially in the major metropolitan centers like New York City and Chicago, was no paragon of virtue. It was notorious for its corruption and poor customer service and in dire need of reinvention. Yet the arrival of disruptive digital technology in the form of smartphone-enabled taxi apps has had a catastrophic effect on the incumbent industry's workers. Indeed, in New York the suicides of at least six drivers over a six-month period in 2018 may be attributable—at least in part—to the plunging value of taxi drivers' medallions and plummeting incomes due to the popularity of ride-share apps.[2]

In February 2018, a 61-year-old livery driver shot himself in front of City Hall in lower Manhattan.[3] Hours earlier Doug Schifter had written a Facebook post about his own perilous financial situation and how he was sometimes obliged to work more than 100 hours a week to make ends meet. Schifter blamed politicians for permitting the city's streets to be flooded with Uber's cars, which was also affecting traffic.

---

[1]Michael Cohn, "Lyft makes gains against Uber on expense reports," Accounting Today, April 30, 2018, https://www.accountingtoday.com/news/lyft-makes-gains-against-uber-on-business-travel-and-expense-reports

[2]Emma G. Fitzsimmons, "Why Are Taxi Drivers in New York Killing Themselves," *New York Times,* December 2, 2018, https://www.nytimes.com/2018/12/02/nyregion/taxi-drivers-suicide-nyc.html

[3]Jessica Bruder, "Drive to Despair," *New York Magazine,* May 24, 2018, https://nymag.com/intelligencer/2018/05/the-tragic-end-to-a-black-car-drivers-campaign-against-uber.html.
Ginia Bellafante, "A Driver's Suicide Reveals the Dark Side of the Gig Economy," *New York Times,* February 6, 2018, https://www.nytimes.com/2018/02/06/nyregion/livery-driver-taxi-uber.html

I will forever remember the reaction of two of my friends working at Uber at the time when, over dinner, I asked them how they felt about these suicides and the working conditions of Uber drivers that were starting to become public knowledge: "This is very sad but this is the cost of progress. The taxi industry needs to be disrupted and we're not forcing people to drive for us." Unfortunately, over the years, I've heard variations of these words abdicating any responsibility and justifying human pain in the name of technological progress so many times and from employees of so many different tech companies that I can't remember them all.

There's no doubt that the gig economy has offered new work opportunities, additional revenue sources, and much-needed flexibility to tens of millions. In the developing world it has some additional benefits too, such as in India, where *Foreign Policy* magazine reported "higher relative incomes, more jobs, less corruption, and, eventually, a formalization of the labor market."[4]

But there is also no doubt that, overall, gig work is short-term, insecure, high-pressure, low paid, and precarious, with few worker rights or protections. Indeed, the on-demand/freelance-labor model that companies such as Uber, Lyft, Instacart, Deliveroo, Postmates, and TaskRabbit favor—which poses as "flexible" and worker-friendly—leaves workers to fend for themselves or shifts the burden for retirement benefits, sick pay, parental leave, and healthcare back onto government in places where there is still a taxpayer-funded safety net. And while this new normal is increasingly being met with protests from workers[5]—and is being examined by regulators, policymakers, and in courtrooms around the world—the gig economy, in one form or another, is here to stay.

In effect, Big Tech has instituted the digital era's equivalent of feudalism, the hierarchical social system in medieval Europe of overlords, vassals, and serfs, only this time with fortunes built on data rather than land. In Valley terms the nobility and the clergy (founders and venture capitalists) are masters and owners of all they survey and generally mingle only with the royal ministers and powerful merchants (leadership team and top product and engineering employees). The vassals (non-engineering employees) are considered important but not critical and somewhat replaceable. At the bottom of the pyramid are the serfs and the peasants, who in this analogy, rather than working the land, drive for Uber or Lyft, or deliver packages for Amazon or meals for Deliveroo or DoorDash, or worse still work for paltry amounts in sweatshops (see Figure 4.1).

---

[4]Ravi Agrawal, "The Hidden Benefits of Uber," Foreign Policy, July 16, 2018, https://foreignpolicy.com/2018/07/16/why-india-gives-uber-5-stars-gig-economy-jobs/
[5]Simon Joyce, "A global struggle: worker protest in the platform economy," European Trade Union Institute, 2020, https://www.etui.org/Publications2/Policy-Briefs/European-Economic-Employment-and-Social-Policy/A-global-struggle-worker-protest-in-the-platform-economy

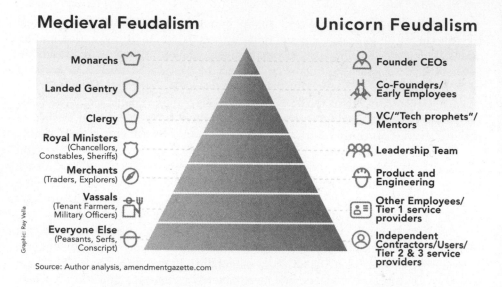

FIGURE 4.1   Medieval Feudalism versus Unicorn Feudalism.

In my experience, even when an executive at one of these firms brags that they "know what it's like" to drive for a ride-hailing app because they were a driver for a day a few months ago, in reality they have not the faintest clue about what it really means to be dependent on getting enough work on any given day to be sure they can feed their family or pay for next week's gas. The situation has been exacerbated by the spread of COVID-19, with many gig economy workers unable to afford to stop working despite a lack of coverage for sick pay or related benefits. (It should be noted that, as I write, Amazon, Instacart, DoorDash, Uber, and Lyft had all offered their gig workers up to two weeks of sick pay if they can show they have been diagnosed with or quarantined because of COVID-19.)

In this new era of relentless insecurity and volatility for tens of millions of people around the world stuck in this new feudalism, it is becoming harder not just to raise a family or buy a home, but simply to get by. Disturbing stories about life as a food delivery driver or next-day delivery courier or warehouse/fulfillment-center worker abound. If anything, the situation for manual workers is worse still. In 2019, the Vox Media–run tech website The Verge obtained documents that revealed that Amazon's automated system tracks fulfillment center employees and "automatically generates any warnings of terminations regarding quality or productivity."[6] More worrying still, it even tracks "time off task," known as TOT, where employees can be warned

---

[6]Colin Lecher, "How Amazon automatically tracks and fires warehouses workers for 'productivity,'" The Verge, April 25, 2019, https://www.theverge.com/2019/4/25/18516004/amazon-warehouse-fulfillment-centers-productivity-firing-terminations

or fired for taking too long between scanning individual packages. Some workers avoid bathroom breaks as a result, reported the site, which also revealed that an attorney representing Amazon admitted that the company had fired "hundreds" of employees in a single facility between August 2017 and September 2018 missing productivity targets.[7]

It doesn't stop there. A deep dive investigation by BuzzFeed, titled "The Cost of Next-day Delivery,"[8] paints a picture of the crushing pressure placed on contracted-out courier services working for Amazon, who are frequently expected "to deliver hundreds of packages each shift—for a flat rate of around $160-a-day—at the direction of dispatchers who often compel them to skip meals, bathroom breaks, and any other form of rest, discouraging them from going home until the very last box is delivered." The BuzzFeed feature discovered that drivers often have to deliver at least 250 packages a day, which works out as less than two minutes per package based on an eight-hour shift. "Amazon goes further than gig economy companies, which insist its drivers are independent contractors with no rights as employees," the piece reported. "By contracting instead with third-party companies, which in turn employ drivers, Amazon divorces itself from the people delivering its packages."

That allows it to avoid legal liability for accidents, as when one driver hit and killed an 84-year-old woman in Chicago, in the run-up to Christmas 2016. "The damages, if any, were caused, in whole or in part, by third parties not under the direction or control of Amazon.com," its lawyers said in a court filing.[9]

The story added that "public records document hundreds of road wrecks involving vehicles delivering Amazon packages in the past five years, with Amazon itself named as a defendant in at least 100 lawsuits . . . including at least six fatalities and numerous serious injuries." And that, it noted, is likely to be a significant underestimate because many accidents involving third-party contractors will not be reported in a way which would link them to Amazon.

"THEY DO A LOT MORE REVENUE WITH A LOT FEWER PEOPLE"

It's not as if many Big Tech companies can't afford to support their workers with increased benefits and protections. Google, Facebook, Apple, and Microsoft

---

[7]Amazon Termination Documents, https://cdn.vox-cdn.com/uploads/chorus_asset/file/16190209/amazon_terminations_documents.pdf
[8]Caroline O'Donovan, "The Cost of Next-day Delivery," BuzzFeed, August 31, 2019, https://www.buzzfeednews.com/article/carolineodonovan/amazon-next-day-delivery-deaths
[9]Amazon's Answer to Complaint, Escamilla v Inpax, filed March 24, 2017, https://www.documentcloud.org/documents/6368692-Amazon-s-Answer-to-Complaint-Escamilla-v-Inpax.html

are highly profitable, with cash holdings in the billions of dollars. (Amazon is profitable but shows lower margins by investing more back into the company.) One reason for their success is that unlike legacy industrial and financial services giants, who employ hundreds of thousands of people, Big Tech companies have lean payrolls. In the retail economy, the world's biggest private sector employer, Walmart, had some 2.2 million "associates" on its payroll in 2018.[10] By contrast, Amazon employed 650,000 that year.[11] The new information giants, touted as powerhouses of economic growth, can operate with far fewer people. Facebook, for example, had 48,268 full-time employees as of March 2020,[12] Alphabet, Google's parent, had 103,549 on its payroll April 2019[13]—a growth spurt largely reflective of the advertising giant's diversification into cloud computing, hardware, AI, and autonomous vehicles. When Facebook acquired WhatsApp for $19 billion in 2014, the messaging service reportedly had just 55 people on staff, including its founders.[14] "People think of [Google, Apple, Facebook, and Amazon] as job creators, they are actually job destroyers," declared author and academic at NYU's Stern School of Business, Scott Galloway, in his celebrated talk "Who Is the Fifth Horseman?" "They're not doing anything evil, but they just do more with less. Specifically, they do a lot more revenue with a lot fewer people."[15]

And that's not only true for the "big four," but for many of the emerging giants too, who are, among other things, having a serious and ongoing impact on existing employment ecosystems. Specifically, many of the jobs their businesses displace will not get replaced—just look at social media's impact on ad and subscription-supported traditional media, or e-commerce's carpet-bombing of bricks-and-mortar retail. (And this, of course, is a mere taste of what lies ahead with the coming automation/AI revolution. Services giant PricewaterhouseCoopers predicts that up to 30 percent of jobs will be vulnerable to automation by the mid-2030s.)[16] Meanwhile, the more secure jobs created by Big Tech usually require specialist skills, which makes retraining of displaced workers a long shot.

---

[10]Walmart, Company Facts, https://corporate.walmart.com/newsroom/company-facts
[11]https://www.macrotrends.net/stocks/charts/AMZN/amazon/number-of-employees
[12]Facebook, Company Info, About Facebook, https://about.fb.com/company-info/
[13]Seth Fiegerman, "Google's parent company now has more than 100,000 employees," CNN Business, April 29, 2019, https://edition.cnn.com/2019/04/29/tech/alphabet-q1-earnings/index.html
[14]Dominic Rushe, "WhatsApp: Facebook acquires messaging service in $19bn deal," *The Guardian,* February 20, 2014, https://www.theguardian.com/technology/2014/feb/19/facebook-buys-whatsapp-16bn-deal
[15]https://www.youtube.com/watch?v=XCvwCcEP74Q
[16]PWC, "Will robots really steal our jobs?," 2018, https://www.pwc.co.uk/economic-services/assets/international-impact-of-automation-feb-2018.pdf

$1.42 PER HOUR

Not to be forgotten is Big Tech's persistently patchy record when it comes to worker conditions at places such as Chinese supplier factories, where staff are not so much precariously employed as exploited. In June 2018, China Labor Watch (CLW), a New York City–based non-government organization that monitors Chinese workers' rights, investigated Hengyang Foxconn, a factory that makes Amazon Kindles, Echo Dots, and tablets.

According to the CLW report,[17] that investigation uncovered evidence that the factory had recruited an illegal number of so-called "dispatch workers"—agency workers who do not enjoy the same protections as those who are employed by the factory—and that all workers were subject to long hours and low wages. At the time, both Amazon and Foxconn responded by saying they would make improvements to the factory's working conditions.

But conditions deteriorated instead.

Little more than a year later, CLW's investigators found a catalogue of abuses at the same Amazon supplier plant, including workers doing more overtime hours, decreased wages, and the illegal hiring of a large number of both dispatch workers and 16- to 18-year-old "interns," who were allegedly obliged to work overtime and night shifts.[18] The use of interns is especially troubling for a company that, at the time of writing, had a market cap of about 1 trillion dollars and 2019 revenues roughly equivalent to the GDP of Finland or Vietnam. When the report was published, Foxconn had already recruited 1,581 interns from vocational schools, who earned the equivalent of $248 a month, or $1.42 an hour, when in 2018 they had earned $276 a month.

If interns were unwilling to work overtime or night shifts, the factory would arrange for teachers to pressure workers. If they refused to work overtime and night shifts, the factory allegedly requested teachers from their schools to fire them.

Under fire, Amazon said at the time: "If we find violations [of our supplier code of conduct], we take appropriate steps, including requesting immediate corrective action." Unsurprisingly, Elaine Lu, program officer at CLW, sounded skeptical about that claim. "When we released our report last year, Amazon and Foxconn said they were going to address the issues [raised]," she said. "But one year later we're still finding these same issues."

Two months after the follow-up investigation at Hengyang, CLW separately exposed similar violations at Apple's so-called "iPhone City," Zhengzhou Foxconn,

---

[17]China Labor Watch, "Amazon profits from secretly oppressing its supplier workers: An investigative report on Hengyang Foxconn," June 10, 2018, http://www.chinalaborwatch.org/report/132

[18]China Labor Watch, "Amazon's supplier factory Foxconn recruits illegally: Interns forced to work overtime," August 8, 2019, http://www.chinalaborwatch.org/report/143

the largest iPhone factory in the world.[19] "Apple and Amazon have their own codes of conduct and a lot of the issues we find are in violation of [those]," said Lu. "They have the capacity to make the improvements. If we, as such a small organization, are able to find these issues, given the profits they make, the question is why can't Apple or Amazon find these same issues in their supply chain?" She left the question hanging.

From many conversations I've had over the years, I can say that no one I've encountered at companies like Amazon and Apple would be remotely comfortable with factory workers being exploited in this way, let alone with the disgrace of child labor. (And it's worth pointing out that tech companies are far from alone in their use of sweatshop labor; from fast fashion to toy manufacturing, it has, over the years, been rife.) Whatever the cause—and my guess would be a combination of "out of sight out of mind" and of "silo mentality" at many of these giants, with hardware manufacturing particularly cloaked in secrecy, meaning that few employees would ever be permitted onto the factory floor, have access to any substantial information about labor costs and working conditions, or be part of any decision relative to them—they genuinely perceive themselves to be ethical outfits. However, the facts once again suggest a different story, laying Big Tech's lack of empathy painfully bare.

---

[19]China Labour Watch, "iPhone 11 illegally produced in China: Apple allows supplier factory Foxconn to violate labor laws," September 8, 2019, http://www.chinalaborwatch.org/report/144

CHAPTER 5

Anti-Social Networks

What a difference a decade makes. While still in their infancy, plat-forms such as Facebook and Twitter were hailed for their—albeit hotly contested—galvanizing roles in Iran's Green Movement in 2009 and the Arab Spring, which started less than two years later. Indeed, so fired up was he by the possibilities of social media that, writing in July 2009, Bush-era deputy national security advisor Mark Pfeifle called for Twitter and its creators to be considered for the Nobel Peace Prize.[1] "When traditional journalists were forced to leave the country, Twitter became a window for the world to view hope, heroism, and horror," he wrote giddily. "It became the assignment desk, the reporter, and the producer... Without Twitter, the people of Iran would not have felt empowered and confident to stand up for freedom and democracy. They did so because they knew the world was watching. With Twitter, they now shout hope with a passion and dedication that resonates not just with those on their street, but with millions across the globe."

There were notable skeptics of course, celebrated author Malcolm Gladwell among them. He dismissed what he characterized as the exaggerated claims, which largely emanated from the Valley and breathless media cheerleaders, writing, "Inno-vators tend to be solipsists. They often want to cram every stray fact and experience into their new model."[2]

Still, few would dispute the early 2010s were certainly something of a golden era for social media, in the West at least. These platforms, we were told, would help reinvigorate democracy by connecting people, giving ordinary people a voice, and making all information accessible.

---

[1]Mark Pfeifle, "A Nobel Peace Prize for Twitter?" *Christian Science Monitor,* July 6, 2009, https://www.csmonitor.com/Commentary/Opinion/2009/0706/p09s02-coop.html
[2]Malcolm Gladwell, "Small Change: Why the revolution will not be tweeted," *New Yorker,* September 27, 2010, https://www.newyorker.com/magazine/2010/10/04/small-change-malcolm-gladwell

As we now know all too well, it didn't pan out like that. At a time when 68 percent of Americans say they get news at least occasionally from social media,[3] these networks have had largely the opposite effect: Western-style democracy is in its most perilous state since the Second World War. Public votes have been hijacked, the well of political discourse poisoned, disinformation has been weaponized, while data mining, heavily resourced bot farms, and trolls have run amok. Social media firms are now confronting a whirlwind of their own making and—chillingly, as shown by Facebook's inability (or unwillingness) to quash its fake news problem—they have created a monster they can no longer control.

The latest Pew Research Center survey conducted in January 2020[4] found that "nearly three-quarters of Americans (74 percent) express little or no confidence in technology companies like Facebook, Twitter and Google to prevent the misuse of their platforms to influence the 2020 presidential election [...] At the same time, 78 percent say these companies have a responsibility to prevent such misuse." It's not hard to see why.

UNDERMINING FACTS AND SCIENCE

Anti-vaxxers—people who refuse to vaccinate their children due to junk science or conspiracy theories about "Big Pharma"—have been turbo-charged by social media, and especially Facebook. Simon Stevens, chief executive of England's National Health Service (NHS), even blamed "fake news" by anti-vaxxers on social media platforms like Instagram and YouTube for the tripling of measles cases in the UK.[5] Speaking in March 2019 at the Nuffield Trust, an independent health think tank, Stevens spoke of a "steady decline" in the uptake of the measles vaccine over the past five years, which he specifically linked to social media.

Stevens's assessment jibes with the high-profile case of Ethan Lindenberger, a then-18-year-old from Ohio, who got himself vaccinated behind his mother's back, and blamed Facebook for fostering her anti-vaxxer ideology. Lindenberger told the

---

[3]Elisa Shearer, "News Use Across Social Media Platforms 2018," Pew Research Center, September 10, 2018, https://www.journalism.org/2018/09/10/news-use-across-social-media-platforms-2018/

[4]Hannah Gilberstadt, "Few Americans are confident in tech companies to prevent misuse of their platforms in the 2020 election," Pew Research Center, February 24, 2020, https://www.pewresearch.org/fact-tank/2020/02/24/few-americans-are-confident-in-tech-companies-to-prevent-misuse-of-their-platforms-in-the-2020-election/

[5]Laura Donnelly, "Anti-vaccination fake news on social media fuels tripling in measles cases, head of NHS says," *The Telegraph,* March 1, 2019, https://www.telegraph.co.uk/global-health/science-and-disease/anti-vaccination-fake-news-social-media-fuels-tripling-measles/

Washington Post that Facebook, or websites that were linked to the platform, were essentially the only source his mother ever relied on for her anti-vaccine information.[6] (In contrast, his mother told the AP that her son had been made "the poster child for the pharmaceutical industry.")[7] Facebook conceded that it knew it had more to do and said that it was considering reducing the appearance of anti-vaccination material in search results and "Groups you should join."[8]

The social media giant was also in the firing line after an investigation in November 2019 by *The Telegraph* found the platform was allegedly profiting from allowing advertisers to target new parents with homeopathic "vaccine alternatives."[9] The newspaper reported that Facebook was auctioning off advertising space for up to 18 pence (around 23 cents) per click to companies selling homeopathic remedies. Against a backdrop of declining vaccination rates for measles, mumps, and rubella (MMR), advertisers were able to ensure their material was directed to parents of young children, who also may not previously have shown interest in alternatives to medically supported immunizations.

This stream of monetized misinformation has taken on a whole new—and even darker—resonance amid the rise of COVID-19 and the complex role played by, among others, Twitter, Facebook, and YouTube. Like many millions of others, I found the direct access to information these platforms offered to be a lifeline at a time of deep disquiet. And I'm not only talking about trusted news media sources, but as I live in New York City, updates that came directly from the Twitter accounts of the Governor's Office, the NYPD, and the NYCT Subway were invaluable too. Then there's the flipside. With the United States, as I write, facing a large proportion of the world's COVID-19 cases and a rapidly rising death toll, social media platforms have enabled a torrent of anti-science misinformation (see Figure 5.1).

Despite the giants, including Facebook, Google, LinkedIn, Twitter, Microsoft, YouTube, and Reddit issuing a joint statement vowing collectively to stem the tide, while elevating authoritative content,[10] researchers continued to uncover social

---

[6]Michael Brice-Saddler, "Teen who defied anti-vax mom says she got false information from one *Source:* Facebook," *Washington Post,* March 6, 2019, https://www.washingtonpost.com/health/2019/03/06/ethan-lindenberger-mom-anti-vax-facebook-groups/

[7]Lauran Neergaard, "Teen tells Senate why he defied his mom to get vaccinated," AP, March 6, 2019, https://apnews.com/3e8f6df82ebf40b3a4884f7a8d0da463

[8]Facebook, "Combatting Vaccine Misinformation," March 7, 2019, https://about.fb.com/news/2019/03/combatting-vaccine-misinformation/

[9]Katherine Rushton, "Facebook making money from firms targeting new parents with homeopathic 'vaccine alternatives,' investigation finds," *The Telegraph,* November 3, 2019, https://www.telegraph.co.uk/news/2019/11/03/facebook-making-money-firms-targeting-new-parents-homeopathic/

[10]https://twitter.com/reddit/status/1239703084110098434

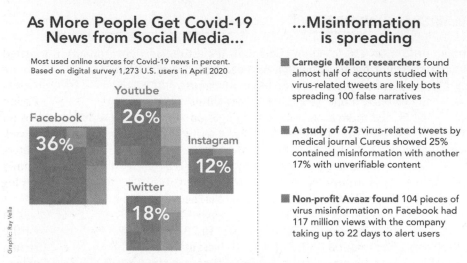

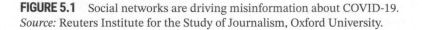

FIGURE 5.1   Social networks are driving misinformation about COVID-19.
Source: Reuters Institute for the Study of Journalism, Oxford University.

media posts and videos riddled with lies and deliberate misinformation. "We've found Facebook groups amassing hundreds of thousands of members and YouTube channels with millions of subscribers, awash with fake 'cures' and conspiracy theories about everything from COVID-19 being caused by 5G towers to false flag theories about a New World Order," wrote Imran Ahmed, CEO of UK nonprofit the Center for Countering Digital Hate (CCDH).[11] Among the CCDH's revelations was a YouTube account belonging to an American chiropractor, with more than a million views, advocating using essential oils and vitamin C to treat the disease. BuzzFeed reported that in another video the same individual claims that hand sanitizer causes hormone disorders, cancer, heart disease, and diabetes.[12]

Yet social media's role in scaremongering and sowing fake information over COVID-19 is merely the latest manifestation of a problem that has been simmering for years.

---

[11]Imran Ahmed, "Covid-19 misinformation can be as dangerous as the virus itself—we must mobilise to stop its spread," *The Telegraph,* March 27, 2020, https://www.telegraph.co.uk/global-health/science-and-disease/covid-19-misinformation-can-dangerous-virus-must-mobilise/

[12]Joey D'Urso, "YouTube Is Letting Millions of People Watch Videos Promoting Misinformation About the Coronavirus," BuzzFeed, March 19, 2020, https://www.buzzfeed.com/joeydurso/youtube-coronavirus-misinformation

DEMOCRACY UNDER ATTACK

During the 2016 U.S. election campaign, it's estimated that a precision-targeted Russian disinformation campaign on Facebook, intended to churn the electorate and largely support the election of Donald Trump, reached some 126 million users through Facebook alone. Additionally, according to the *New York Times*, Russian agents published more than 131,000 messages on Twitter and over 1,000 videos on YouTube.[13] Amid the choreographed hand-wringing and anguish that followed, Facebook's Mark Zuckerberg—who had in 2016 dismissed the notion that voters were manipulated in Trump's favor on his platform as "a crazy idea"[14]—solemnly vowed to fix this unprecedented electoral interference, one of the most complex problems modern Western democracy has ever faced.

In a 3,000-word blog post entitled "Preparing for Elections,"[15] published in September 2018, Facebook's CEO declared: "In 2016 we were not prepared for the coordinated information operations we now regularly face. But we have learned a lot since then and have developed sophisticated systems that combine technology and people to prevent election interference on our services." He concluded: "One of the important lessons I've learned is that when you build services that connect billions of people across countries and cultures, you're going to see all of the good humanity is capable of, and you're also going to see people try to abuse those services in every way possible. As we evolve, our adversaries are evolving too. We will all need to continue improving and working together to stay ahead and protect our democracy."

Two years on from that post, all the evidence shows that so far he has failed. Fast-forward to the European elections held in May 2019, and history was on the brink of repeating itself. In the run-up to that election, the campaign group Avaaz launched a Europe-wide investigation "Far Right Networks of Deception"[16] on Facebook, and the research team were shocked by what they discovered: well-organized far right and anti-EU groups were weaponizing social media on an industrial scale to spread hateful content and disinformation that garnered an estimated 762 million views over the three months in advance of the election.

---

[13]Mike Isaac, "Russian Influence Reached 126 Million Through Facebook Alone," *New York Times,* October 30, 2017, https://www.nytimes.com/2017/10/30/technology/facebook-google-russia.html

[14]Adrienne Jane Burke, "Facebook Influenced Election? Crazy Idea, Says Zuckerberg," Techonomy, November 11, 2016, https://techonomy.com/2016/11/28196/

[15]Mark Zuckerberg, "Preparing for Elections," Facebook notes, September 12, 2018, https://www.facebook.com/notes/mark-zuckerberg/preparing-for-elections/10156300047606634/

[16]Avaaz, "Far Right Networks of Deception," May 22, 2019, https://secure.avaaz.org/campaign/en/disinfo_network_report/.

The 2016 U.S. race for the White House had proved to be a wakeup call for Avaaz, which first assembled a team to dig into electoral manipulation on Facebook ahead of the Brazilian general election held in October 2018, which saw right wing populist Jair Bolsonaro emerge victorious. "Right before the Brazilian elections, fake news was running wild and we were just shocked with the amount of disinformation going on in Brazil that was really going viral," recalls Brazilian-born Flora Rebello Arduini, who went on to lead the EU networks "takedown" operation for Avaaz the following spring. "The political debate was being driven by disinformation as a political tactic, by not going to mainstream media, but using social media [instead]." So Avaaz assembled a small team of researchers, data analysts, and investigative journalists to try to flag the fake news before it went viral and map the intricate networks that lay behind it. Using a social media monitoring tool called CrowdTangle, Rebello Arduini and her coworkers would identify a Facebook page that was sharing fake news. They would then click through to the similar pages Facebook recommended on the first page, and check the content against fact-checking sites. Patterns would start to emerge; a number of pages would coordinate by posting the same or similar content simultaneously, while also cross-promoting one another. Once they had mapped 28 pages, the team wrote an article for a leading Brazilian newspaper. Facebook was apparently jolted into action, responding by not only removing the 28 mapped pages but more than 40 other pages and 43 profiles too.

The Brazilian election acted as both proof of concept for Avaaz's approach and a dress rehearsal for the then fast-approaching Europe-wide elections of 2019. After running a fundraising campaign among the group's more than 60 million members globally,[17] Avaaz set up a team of 30 people, including journalists, data analysts, and researchers across Europe, with a "war room" later established in Brussels in the month of the vote itself. Overall Avaaz reported almost 700 "suspect pages and groups" to Facebook, which were followed by a total of about 35 million people and generated over 76 million "interactions" (comments, likes, and shares) over a three-month period prior to the election. Facebook removed 132 of the pages and groups reported, accounting for almost 30 percent of all interactions across the networks in question.

The way these groups were able to manipulate Facebook's safeguards, particularly in light of Zuckerberg's assurances that the platform had "developed sophisticated systems that combine technology and people to prevent election interference on our services," should ring alarm bells. In Italy, for example, Avaaz's investigation prompted Facebook to take down 24 Italian pages with over 3.9 million followers for breaching the platform's policies. The offending pages, many of which were supportive of Matteo Salvini's hardline League or the populist Five Star Movement, peddled false information and "divisive anti-migration" content. One tactic employed by

---

[17]https://secure.avaaz.org/page/en/

those behind the groups was to slowly but steadily change a page's name, turning an apparently nonpolitical group into a partisan one, while retaining all the likes and followers it had already accrued over the months and years. A page that started with the title "Calcio Passione" (literally Football Passion), apparently for football fans, for example, had its name changed eight times, including to "Music on the World," before ending up as "Noi siamo a 5 Stelle" ("We are the Five Star Movement").

Avaaz reckoned that, in Italy alone, it had identified 14 main networks in apparent breach of Facebook's guidelines, including 104 pages and eight groups with a total of 18.26 million followers over the three months before the EU elections—enough, perhaps, to have an impact on a closely fought campaign in a divided country. Similar cases were discovered in Germany, Spain, and Poland.

While Facebook apparently "welcomed" Avaaz's efforts, it was also clear they were not doing anything sufficient to combat a problem on this scale with such far-reaching implications for democracy. "They were basically outsourcing to a crowd-funded organization like [Avaaz] to do the work they were supposed to be doing," says Rebello Arduini. "It seemed they were relying on 30 people from Avaaz, and other small anti-disinformation organizations, to do what 30,000 people [i.e. the mix of full-time employees, and mostly third-party contractors and companies Facebook uses to moderate its platform] didn't." While she wouldn't discuss the behind-closed-doors conversations they had with Facebook, Arduini said that when her organization threatened to go to the press, "action [was] taken faster."

It gets even worse for Facebook. A report on how the manipulation of public opinion on social media (chiefly on Facebook, "the platform of choice") has become a global issue, published in September 2019 by the Oxford Internet Institute (part of the University of Oxford) detailed an array of abuses by government agencies and political parties on the platform.[18]

Styled as "the only regular inventory of its kind to look at the use of algorithms, automation and big data to shape public life," the report found that organized manipulation via social media platforms had more than doubled since 2017 (although this is partly due to researchers getting better at detecting it). A staggering 70 countries—including politicians and political parties from 45 democracies—have deployed so-called "computational propaganda," which the authors describe as "including the use of 'political bots' to amplify hate speech or other forms of manipulated content, the illegal harvesting of data or micro-targeting, or deploying an army of 'trolls' to bully or harass political dissidents or journalists online," to covertly mold public opinion.

---

[18] Oxford Internet Institute press release, "Use of social media to manipulate public opinion now a global problem, says new report," September 26, 2019, https://www.oii.ox.ac.uk/news/releases/use-of-social-media-to-manipulate-public-opinion-now-a-global-problem-says-new-report/

"Traditional gatekeeping used to be done by human editors," explains co-author Samantha Bradshaw, "but now there are complex mathematical equations that are making these decisions about who wins and who loses and what is visible and what isn't." The report also found that in 26 authoritarian states, governments have used computational propaganda as a tool of information control, while a small number of sophisticated state actors use the same techniques for "foreign influence operations, primarily over Facebook and Twitter." The platforms themselves attributed this "cyber troop activity" to just seven countries, mostly the usual suspects: China, India, Iran, Pakistan, Russia, Saudi Arabia, and Venezuela.

"We use the term 'troops' because they're organised groups of people, in many cases this is their job," Bradshaw explains. "They show up to an office building. They work nine-to-five, they get benefits, there's probably air conditioning in their offices and things like that. So it's not just a lone wolf hacker or a kind of collective of people who are coming together and trying to use the tools of computational propaganda for their own purposes. There's actually some kind of organized coordinated activity behind what you see on the content layer."

While Bradshaw concedes that Facebook and other platforms have introduced a number of policy changes over the past three years, so far they are failing to meaningfully protect democracies. "Most of the changes have had to do with adjusting algorithms and affecting ways that information is prioritised, maybe downgrading stuff that has been fact-checked as false and promoting content that has been fact-checked as true by the third-party fact-checkers that come online."

And yet, a whole presidential election cycle later, the platforms are still plagued with electoral interference. In late March 2020, the *New York Times* revealed[19] a number of examples of how, while they have spent billions in a bid to stop a repeat of 2016's Russian-backed meddling, the nature of the threat tech giants like Facebook, Google, and Twitter faced has evolved. "Russia and other foreign governments once conducted online influence operations in plain sight, buying Facebook ads in rubles and tweeting in broken English, but they are now using more sophisticated tactics such as bots that are nearly impossible to distinguish from hyperpartisan Americans," reported the newspaper.

UNRELENTING HATE

One unpalatable truth among many is, if you're in the outrage industry, trolls are good for business. Luciana Berger, a Jewish MP formerly of the UK's Labour party

---

[19]Kevin Roose, "Tech Giants Prepared for 2016-Style Meddling. But the Threat Has Changed," *New York Times,* March 29, 2020, https://www.nytimes.com/2020/03/29/technology/facebook-google-twitter-november-election.html

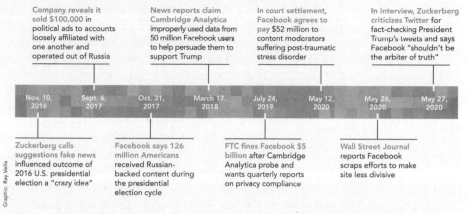

The Saga of Facebook and Fake News A timeline of events

Company reveals it sold $100,000 in political ads to accounts loosely affiliated with one another and operated out of Russia	News reports claim Cambridge Analytica improperly used data from 50 million Facebook users to help persuade them to support Trump	In court settlement, Facebook agrees to pay $52 million to content moderators suffering post-traumatic stress disorder	In interview, Zuckerberg criticizes Twitter for fact-checking President Trump's tweets and says Facebook "shouldn't be the arbiter of truth"

Nov. 10, 2016	Sept. 6, 2017	Oct. 31, 2017	March 17, 2018	July 24, 2019	May 12, 2020	May 26, 2020	May 27, 2020

Zuckerberg calls suggestions fake news influenced outcome of 2016 U.S. presidential election a "crazy idea"	Facebook says 126 million Americans received Russian-backed content during the presidential election cycle	FTC fines Facebook $5 billion after Cambridge Analytica probe and wants quarterly reports on privacy compliance	Wall Street Journal reports Facebook scraps efforts to make site less divisive

Graphic: Ray Vella

Source: New York Times, Washington Post, Wall Street Journal, Guardian, CNN, NBC News, Fox News, NPR, Reuters

FIGURE 5.2 A short history of fake news on Facebook.
Source: New York Times, Washington Post, Wall Street Journal, Guardian, CNN, NBC News, Fox News, NPR, Reuters.

(who has since joined the Liberal Democrats), was on the receiving end of such a vitriolic and unrelenting campaign of bigotry between 2013 and 2019, in one case chiefly over Twitter, that it resulted in the criminal conviction of six individuals. Two were jailed. Abuse included the photo-shopping of her face onto rats and victims of the Holocaust, a yellow star was superimposed onto her forehead with the hashtag #HitlerWasRight, rape and death threats were routinely made, while Berger was also a target of U.S. white supremacist site the Daily Stormer's "Filthy Jew Bitch" campaign, which according to the Metropolitan Police saw over 2,500 venomous Tweets directed at her over a three-day period alone. Unsurprisingly it took a considerable toll on her. "This isn't just someone 'having a go,'" she told the BBC, after one particularly single-minded aggressor was jailed.[20] "I felt unsafe because some of the people involved in that campaign . . . it inspired others to post messages that told me to watch my back, referred to where I lived and made physical threats against me."

Berger maintains that while the authorities, including the police, were supportive, for many years Twitter, like other social media platforms, was largely unhelpful and noncommittal, in effect falling back on the familiar "We're just a platform, not a publisher" excuse. She firmly believes that there is still a lot more these platforms

---

[20] BBC News, Liverpool, "Man jailed for harassing Labour MP Luciana Berger," December 8, 2016, https://www.bbc.co.uk/news/uk-england-merseyside-38249351

should be doing, including handing over evidence to the police in different jurisdictions when it is requested, she says over email.

When asked about Berger's experience, Twitter board member Martha Lane Fox, a "first wave" internet pioneer with LastMinute.com and a baroness in the UK's upper house, the House of Lords, conceded that too much of the onus to report abuse still falls on the victims of social media hate crime. "It's not fair and it's not right that it's Luciana's responsibility to deal with people who are giving her shit online," she says. "That just feels wrong."

"There's still a lot more that can be done in terms of giving people more options and filters [on social media platforms to protect against abuse]. Progress has been made, it's just not been fast enough. I can speak for Twitter, as [CEO] Jack [Dorsey]'s probably said it 100 times: This is absolutely a top priority."

And while the online abuse she faced was on the most extreme end of the spectrum, Luciana Berger was far from alone. In the runup to December 2019's UK general election, an investigation by the BBC and Demos, a liberal UK think tank, found a surge in abuse and death threats on Twitter directed at parliamentary candidates running for reelection.[21] Focusing on Tweets sent a fortnight or so up to around the midpoint of the campaign, the team trained an algorithm to sift through millions of Tweets and separate the genuinely abusive from legitimate, if unduly harsh and personal, criticism. Around 7 percent of the Tweets—some 334,000—received by candidates was categorized as abusive, which worked out as 10 for every single minute of the campaign up to that point. Once the data had been crunched, it was revealed that—among other findings—white candidates were four times more likely to be accused of "treachery," British South Asian candidates four times more likely to be told to "shut up," and black candidates 25 percent more likely to have their intelligence called into question. A prominent black Labour politician, David Lammy, said he was "staggered by just how toxic things had become" on social media. "Most of the abusive Tweets directed at me are really pushing deeply racist stereo-typical tropes—tropes about being stupid, tropes about being lazy, there are tropes which involved the 'N-word,'" he said. The BBC emphasized that while they focused on Twitter for purposes of this exercise, the abuse was certainly not confined to Twitter, nor was it even primarily targeted at politicians.

(And it must be said the U.S. giants aren't the only culprits here—China's social media video app TikTok, for example, was recently at the center of a caste-based hate speech storm in India, among many other incidents.)

For his part, Damian Collins MP, until recently the influential chair of the UK House of Commons Digital, Culture, Media and Sport (DCMS) Committee, argues that the problem is larger still.

---

[21] https://www.bbc.co.uk/iplayer/episode/m000c8cz/click-the-outrage-election

"My biggest concern is about the wider impact it has: It normalizes that sort of hate speech and encourages more of the same. If you allow people to dehumanize others in what they say about them [on social media], then that has a wider negative impact on society as well."

Indeed, social media invective is directed overwhelmingly at people who aren't in the public eye and therefore far less able to defend themselves.

"WHEN SHE SHOWED ME THE MESSAGES, I JUST FELT SICK"

Using Freedom of Information requests to obtain data from 43 police forces across England and Wales, UK charity the National Society for the Prevention of Cruelty to Children (NSPCC) discovered that online sexual "grooming" offenses against kids had risen by a third over the past year (4,373 recorded offences of sexual communication with a child in the year to April 2019, compared with 3,217 a year earlier).[22] Appallingly, 20 percent of the victims were 11 years of age or younger.

The charity revealed that over the last two years, "Facebook-owned apps (Facebook, Messenger, Instagram, and WhatsApp) and Snapchat were used in more than 70 percent of the instances where police recorded and provided the communication method, while Instagram was used in more than a quarter of them."

The NSPCC cited the case of "Freya" (not her real name), who was 12 when her Instagram account was flooded with explicit messages and videos sent by a stranger, while she was staying at a friend's house. "When she showed me the messages, I just felt sick," said her mother. "It was such a violation and he was so persistent. He knew she was 12... Freya didn't even understand what she was looking at. There were pages and pages of messages, he just didn't give up."

The NSPCC has been campaigning for a change in the law, which would require social networks to proactively identify and prevent grooming on their sites by, among other things, using AI to detect suspicious behavior; sharing data with other apps to better understand the methods offenders use and flag suspicious accounts; and turning off friend suggestion algorithms for children and young people. It is also calling for tough sanctions for tech firms that fail to protect their young users. These include steep fines, boardroom bans for directors, and the creation of a new criminal offense for platforms that commit gross breaches of their duty of care (which will finally form part of the UK government's forthcoming Online Harms bill).

---

[22] N.S.P.C.C., press release, "Recorded online sexual grooming crimes rise by a third," September 11, 2019, https://www.nspcc.org.uk/what-we-do/news-opinion/recorded-online-sexual-grooming/

While clearly no system is going to successfully stamp out all predatory pedophilic behavior on social media and messaging apps, providing enhanced protection for kids is surely a baseline ethical requirement for platforms to fulfill themselves. As the technology exists to greatly limit this blight, failure to do so is an indication of skewed priorities.

"#NEWZEALANDMOSQUEATTACK"

The dissemination of terrorist images, video, and propaganda, including school shootings, gun rampages, and beheadings, was an outrage mainstream social media firms had supposedly all but banished from their platforms. Indeed, Facebook itself, which boasts an impressive-sounding "counter terrorist unit"[23] chiefly focused on Islamist terrorist factions ISIS and Al Qaeda, claimed in its November 2019 Community Standards report that the rate at which it "proactively detects content affiliated with any terrorist organization on Facebook was 98.5 percent and 92.2 percent on Instagram."[24]

Yet in March 2019, when a white nationalist went on a murderous rampage in Christchurch, New Zealand, slaughtering 51 Muslim worshippers and injuring scores more, he was able to livestream his attack on Facebook Live. Critically, the video was not automatically detected. It was a user who first flagged the video, 29 minutes after it had started, and 12 minutes after the live broadcast ended.

According to a blog post from Chris Sonderby, VP and Deputy General Counsel at Facebook, live footage of the mass shooting was viewed just 200 times in real time, and 4,000 times in total before it was removed.[25] However, before the platform had been alerted to the video, a user on 8chan (an online message board linked to white supremacism, neo-Nazism, the alt-right, racism and anti-Semitism, hate crimes, child pornography, and, yes, multiple mass shootings) posted a link to a copy of it on a file-sharing site. Sonderby wrote that in the first 24 hours, the company "removed about 1.5 million videos of the attack globally. More than 1.2 million of these videos were blocked at upload, and were therefore prevented from being seen on our services."

---

[23]David Uberti, "Facebook Went to War Against White Supremacist Terror After Christchurch. Will It Work?," Vice News, October 3, 2019, https://www.vice.com/en_us/article/vb5yk3/facebook-went-to-war-against-white-supremacist-terror-after-christchurch-will-it-work

[24]https://about.fb.com/news/2019/11/community-standards-enforcement-report-nov-2019/

[25]Chris Sonderby, "Update on New Zealand," Facebook News, March 18, 2019, https://about.fb.com/news/2019/03/update-on-new-zealand/

Writing in the *New York Times*, opinion writer Charlie Warzel described the choice by Facebook—and YouTube—to "pull back the curtain" to share this data on views, block attempted uploads, and remove the Christchurch video as "a careful bit of corporate messaging" too: "It's less an open book and more of an attempt to show their work and assuage critics that, despite claims of negligence, the tech giants are, in fact, 'on it,'" he wrote.[26]

He didn't stop there. "Most troubling, it's also a bid to reframe the conversation toward content moderation rather than addressing the role the platforms play in fostering and emboldening online extremism." He also quoted Joan Donovan, the director of the Technology and Social Change Research Project at Harvard, who had told him, "if platform companies are going to provide the broadcast tools for sharing hateful ideologies, they are going to share the blame for normalizing them."

In the aftermath of the atrocity, Facebook—but also Twitter, YouTube, and Reddit—came under intense scrutiny, as well as pressure to remove harmful content with far greater rigor. Two months after the massacre, as part of its response, Facebook announced that it would restrict who would be able to livestream video on the platform, by introducing a "one strike" policy to Facebook Live that would ban users who violate the platform's community standards.[27] This applies to content posted elsewhere on Facebook, not just streamed on Facebook Live.

One would be forgiven for assuming that with new measures in place, alongside rigorous detection algorithms, teams of crack moderators, including "counterterrorism" specialists, and assurances that the platform was "working around the clock" (Chris Sonderby again), it would have been impossible to view footage from the Christchurch atrocity on Facebook weeks, let alone months, later.

Astonishingly, you'd be wrong.

A full six months later, in fact, the supposedly scrubbed footage was still found on the platform with only a "Violent or graphic content" warning. In September, NBC News reported that "more than a dozen videos" taken from the gunman's livestream of the mass murder were still searchable on the platform, and some of them had apparently been on Facebook since the incident itself.[28] "It's literally the same footage," Eric Feinberg, an internet security researcher and founding partner of deep web monitoring firm GIPEC Worldwide, which discovered the

---

[26]Warzel, Charlie, "We're Asking the Wrong Questions of YouTube and Facebook After New Zealand," *New York Times,* March 19, 2019, https://www.nytimes.com/2019/03/19/opinion/facebook-youtube-new-zealand.html

[27]Makena Kelly, "Facebook imposes restrictions on live-streaming to prevent future abuse," The Verge, May 14, 2019, https://www.theverge.com/2019/5/14/18623892/facebook-restrictions-live-streaming-prevent-future-abuse-christchurch-new-zealand

[28]Olivia Solon, "Six months after Christchurch shootings, videos of attack are still on Facebook," NBC News, September 20, 2019, https://www.nbcnews.com/tech/tech-news/six-months-after-christchurch-shootings-videos-attack-are-still-facebook-n1056691

videos, told the network. His software had identified between 300 and 400 versions of the video on Facebook and Instagram in the six months following the attack. In an interview for this book, Feinberg explained that within hours of the attack itself, as past experience had taught him, Islamic State and other radical Islamist groups would be seizing on the footage to recruit or radicalize for similar attacks against Christian or Jewish targets. So he created code containing hashtags in Arabic—such as "#Christchurchvideo," "#NewZealandmosqueattack," and the name of the mosque—and he found the videos.

In November 2019, Feinberg, who is also VP of the Coalition for a Safer Web, carried out research that contributed to another story, this time in advertising industry bible *Ad Age*,[29] in which he exposed that Islamic State videos on Facebook-owned Instagram were appearing alongside top brands, leading to the removal of at least 28 accounts. He alleges that both Facebook's moderators and AI do a "very poor job" of scouring for terrorist and extremist content, especially in non-Western languages: "What my system does is pick up on the hashtags and keywords that are used by nefarious actors. We do it in multiple languages, a lot in Arabic because we're tracking ISIS and radical Islamist groups. I call them hashtags of terror."

He alleges that while Facebook—and the other major platforms—are making the right noises when it comes to cracking down on terrorist content, this is largely for public consumption. "It's all B.S., it's all rhetoric, it's not true," he says. "How much evidence do you want? Don't believe anything they say." He grows angrier still. "Silicon Valley is a sick culture. And they're exporting this sickness around the world. Look what happened in Myanmar," he adds, referencing Facebook's admitted role in Myanmar's persecution of Rohingya Muslims.[30]

And let's be in no doubt that manipulation and lies on social media are no abstract concept. The ability to spread disinformation can have fatal consequences. Analysis by the BBC of millions of English-language reports discovered that, over a two-year period ending in November 2018, at least 31 people were killed in India by mob attacks fueled by false rumors and lies disseminated on Facebook-owned WhatsApp and other social media.[31] One video clip that went viral on WhatsApp in India in 2018 featured a man riding pillion on a motorbike who apparently snatches

---

[29]Garett Sloane, "Instagram takes down 28 terrorist accounts in cases that demonstrate perils for brands on social," Ad Age, November 22, 2019, https://adage.com/article/digital/instagram-takes-down-28-terrorist-accounts-cases-demonstrate-perils-brands-social/2218246

[30]Alexandra Stevenson, "Facebook Admits It Was Used to Incite Violence in Myanmar," *New York Times,* November 6, 2018, https://www.nytimes.com/2018/11/06/technology/myanmar-facebook.html

[31]Shadab Nazmi, "Social media rumours in India: counting the dead," BBC News, November 13, 2018, https://www.bbc.co.uk/news/resources/idt-e5043092-f7f0-42e9-9848-5274ac896e6d

a child from a roadside—but was in fact a staged public information video from Pakistan—ultimately led to vigilantes killing an estimated 10 people in Bangalore, including one man who was beaten to death and dragged through the streets.[32]

The public information portion of the clip had been deliberately edited out.

"THE UGLY"

So why is it that despite the tech giants frequently making the right noises in public, apparently taking many of the right steps—and despite near-limitless financial resources—their platforms still bristle with universally reviled content, hate speech, and disinformation?

A leaked Facebook memo from 2016, published by BuzzFeed some two years later, rather let the cat out of the bag.[33] Entitled "The Ugly" and circulated internally—with a depressing and notable lack of awareness—just days after the murder of a Chicagoan was streamed on Facebook Live,[34] one of the platform's VPs, Andrew Bosworth, described by the publisher as "one of Zuckerberg's longest-serving deputies," wrote of Facebook's mission:

> *We connect people. That can be good if they make it positive. Maybe someone finds love. Maybe it even saves the life of someone on the brink of suicide. So we connect more people. That can be bad if they make it negative. Maybe it costs a life by exposing someone to bullies. Maybe someone dies in a terrorist attack coordinated on our tools. And still we connect people. The ugly truth is that we believe in connecting people so deeply that anything that allows us to connect more people more often is* **de facto** *good ... We connect people. Period. That's why all the work we do in growth is justified. All the questionable contact importing practices. All the subtle language that helps people stay searchable by friends. All of the work we do to bring more communication in. The work we will likely have to do in China some day. All of it.*

Naturally, as soon as the memo hit the public domain, Facebook's spin operation purred into action. Distancing himself from Bosworth, Zuckerberg himself wrote:

---

[32] BBC News, India, "How WhatsApp helped turn an Indian village into a lynch mob," July 19, 2018, https://www.bbc.co.uk/news/world-asia-india-44856910

[33] Ryan Mac, "Growth At Any Cost: Top Facebook Executive Defended Data Collection in 2016 Memo," BuzzFeed News, March 29, 2018, https://www.buzzfeednews.com/article/ryanmac/growth-at-any-cost-top-facebook-executive-defended-data#.um626xwvE

[34] Laurie Segall, "Shooting death of Chicago man captured live on Facebook," CNN Business, June 20, 2016, https://money.cnn.com/2016/06/17/technology/facebook-live-shooting-death/index.html

"Boz is a talented leader who says many provocative things. This was one that most people at Facebook including myself disagreed with strongly. We've never believed the ends justify the means."

Yet as BuzzFeed noted, "The Bosworth memo reveals the extent to which Facebook's leadership understood the physical and social risks the platform's products carried—even as the company downplayed those risks in public."

As it turns out, Facebook's top executives not only downplayed the risks, they shut down their own concerned researchers. As reported by the *Wall Street Journal,* a slide in a 2018 internal presentation read: "Our algorithms exploit the human brain's attraction to divisiveness."[35] Without a change, the researchers said, Facebook would be offering up "more and more divisive content in an effort to gain user attention & increase time on the platform." In a 2016 internal report, researchers noted that 64 percent of people who joined extremist groups on Facebook in Germany did so as a result of its recommendation algorithms. The findings, according to the *Journal,* were shelved.

YOUTUBE RECOMMENDED ALEX JONES 15 BILLION TIMES

Every product and feature the social media giants build is designed to optimize retention or "product stickiness." Indeed, it's been revealed by YouTube's chief product officer, for example, that the company's recommendation algorithms drive 70 percent of what we view on the platform.[36] As Google engineers described in an academic paper published in 2016,[37] YouTube's recommendations are powered by Google Brain, which uses machine learning to sift through and identify the videos a particular user is likely to want to watch next. "Candidate videos" are then funneled from the ever-expanding deluge of content on the platform, and ranked, before a handful of videos are served up to the individual user.

To get a sense of just how powerful, manipulative, and indeed destructive this process is, research by Guillaume Chaslot, an ex-YouTube recommendations engineer himself, revealed that "Infowars" conspiracy theorist Alex Jones—who has since been banned from mainstream platforms including Apple, Facebook,

---

[35] Jeff Horwitz, Deepa Seetharaman, "Facebook executives shut down efforts to make the site less divisive," May 26, 2020, *Wall Street Journal,* https://www.wsj.com/articles/facebook-knows-it-encourages-division-top-executives-nixed-solutions-11590507499
[36] Ashley Rodriguez, "YouTube's recommendations drive 70% of what we watch," Quartz, January 13, 2018, https://qz.com/1178125/youtubes-recommendations-drive-70-of-what-we-watch/
[37] Paul Covington, "Deep Neural Networks for YouTube Recommendations," http://static.googleusercontent.com/media/research.google.com/en//pubs/archive/45530.pdf

YouTube, and Spotify[38]—was recommended on YouTube 15 billion times.[39] "My goal [in revealing this piece of information]: breaking a deadlock," Chaslot tweeted. "I talked about it to friends at Google for years. They thought 'if users don't complain, they must be happy.' But users didn't know that the most powerful AI [in] the world was being divisive for the sake of watch time. Now they know."

That same AI has also been harnessed by predatory pedophiles. A *New York Times* investigation revealed that researchers found that YouTube's recommendation algorithm was serving up innocent family videos featuring "prepubescent, partially clothed children" to users who had watched similar videos.[40] "YouTube had curated the videos from across its archives, at times plucking out the otherwise innocuous home movies of unwitting families," its reporters wrote. "In many cases, its algorithm referred users to the videos after they watched sexually themed content." The disturbing result amounted to a visual treasure trove for pedophiles. Jonas Kaiser, one of the researchers at Harvard's Berkman Klein Center for Internet and Society, who stumbled onto the videos, told the paper: "It's YouTube's algorithm that connects these channels."

Embarrassingly for YouTube, the *Times* story came just months after *Wired* magazine revealed that pedophiles "were hiding in plain sight" on the video-sharing platform.[41] That article, published in February 2019, reported that videos of children exposing themselves or posing provocatively were being viewed millions of times on YouTube, and appearing alongside advertising from major international brands. Meanwhile, comments posted beneath the videos appear to show pedophiles sharing timestamps for when provocative moments or exposed genitals can be seen, according to the magazine, which also reported that some of the children "appear to be as young as five" and that "Many of the videos have hundreds of thousands, if not millions of views, with hundreds of comments."

Wired alerted YouTube, which claims to be 99 percent effective at ensuring that advertisements only appear on appropriate content. But the reporter found that "with a blank YouTube account, and a couple of quick searches, hundreds of videos that are seemingly popular with pedophiles are surfaced by YouTube's recommendation system. Worse still, YouTube doesn't just recommend you watch more videos of children innocently playing, its algorithm specifically suggests videos

---

[38]Alex Hern, "Facebook, Apple, YouTube and Spotify ban Infowars' Alex Jones," *The Guardian,* August 6, 2018, https://www.theguardian.com/technology/2018/aug/06/apple-removes-podcasts-infowars-alex-jones

[39]https://twitter.com/gchaslot/status/967585220001058816

[40]Max Fisher, "On YouTube's Digital Playground, an Open Gate for Pedophiles," *New York Times,* June 3, 2019, https://www.nytimes.com/2019/06/03/world/americas/youtube-pedophiles.html

[41]K.G. Orphanides, "On YouTube, a network of paedophiles is hiding in plain sight," *Wired,* February 20, 2019, https://www.wired.co.uk/article/youtube-pedophile-videos-advertising

that are seemingly popular with other [pedophiles], most of which have hundreds of thousands of views and dozens of disturbing comments. Many include pre-roll advertising."

Over the summer of 2019, the platform sought to stem the drip-feed of corrosive PR by announcing that it would be "removing more hateful and supremacist" content[42] by "specifically prohibiting videos alleging that a group is superior in order to justify discrimination, segregation or exclusion based on qualities like age, gender, race, caste, religion, sexual orientation or veteran status. This would include, for example, videos that promote or glorify Nazi ideology, which is inherently discriminatory. Finally, we will remove content denying that well-documented violent events, like the Holocaust or the shooting at Sandy Hook Elementary, took place."

SECTION 230

One thing that has become ever-clearer in this attention economy is that it involves the deliberate abdication of moral responsibility. Usually the leaders of unicorns in this space, draping themselves in the flag of "free speech," justify and absolve themselves by relying on Section 230 of the U.S. Communications Decency Act, which offers protective cover every bit as powerful as Harry Potter's invisibility cloak. In the words of *Wired*'s Matt Reynolds, Section 230 set the goalposts of the internet we have today.[43] "Zuckerberg's dream of a global town square is right there in embryonic form in Section 230," he wrote. "It gave internet startups and their investors the confidence that they could fill their platforms with content from ordinary users, without attracting any legal liability for anything those users might write."

Nevertheless, according to a research paper from Rutgers Law School,[44] this highly controversial piece of legislation "protects online intermediaries like social media platforms from being sued for transmitting problematic third-party content. It also lets them remove, label, or hide those messages without being sued for their choices. The law is thus simultaneously a shield from liability—encouraging platforms to transmit problematic content—and a sword—allowing platforms to manage that content as they like. Section 230 has been credited with creating a boisterous

---

[42]YouTube Official blog, "Our ongoing work to tackle hate," June 5, 2019, https://youtube.googleblog.com/2019/06/our-ongoing-work-to-tackle-hate.html
[43]Matt Reynolds, "The strange story of Section 230, the obscure law that created our flawed, broken internet," *Wired UK,* March 24, 2019, https://www.wired.co.uk/article/section-230-communications-decency-act
[44]Ellen P. Goodman, "Section 230 of the Communications Decency Act and the Future of Online Speech," Rutgers Law School Research Paper, October 16, 2019, https://papers.ssrn.com/sol3/papers.cfm?abstract_id=3458442

and wide-open Internet ecosystem. It has also been blamed for allowing platforms to profit from toxic speech."

Meanwhile in the UK, which of course isn't covered by Section 230 and has seen individuals sued for libel on social media platforms (though not, yet, the platforms themselves) resistance is ramping up. The new Conservative majority government, which won a landslide victory in December 2019, included an online harms bill[45] in its raft of proposed new legislation, which will place a statutory duty of care on internet companies to take responsibility for the safety of their users, including for tackling terrorism, child sexual exploitation and abuse, and inciting or assisting suicide. The legislation will be policed by regulator Ofcom (officially the Office of Communications), which will have the power to fine the tech giants significant sums.

"The online harms bill finally made it clear once and for all that platforms actually do have a reasonable duty of care to the people who use their services. It was an absolute travesty that it took so long to achieve this," says Saul Klein, a London-based investor at LocalGlobe, and a former co-founder of DVD delivery service LoveFilm, which was acquired by Amazon. "The notion that [social media giants] get a free pass because they are a common carrier or dumb pipe is the worst 'Look-no-hands' approach to building businesses. That they do have a duty of care is just common sense, given the role they play in today's society. It's just ridiculous to think otherwise at this point."

Nevertheless, in America the Section 230 status quo remains firmly in place for now, and with Big Tech spending more than $64 million on lobbying in 2018 alone,[46] few would bet on that changing anytime soon.

"YOU'RE ARGUING ABOUT WHETHER THE BABY'S DEAD"

Back in 2016, I witnessed the Valley's ethical contortions first-hand. In a private conversation with two (male) social media executives, I described the harassment and bullying of women in my own (real-life) social circle on Twitter, Facebook, and other platforms. These friends, I told them, were starting to avoid social media because they found them too aggressive. I was met with a well-worn response: "Oh, that sucks, but..." followed by protestations of "It's not our job to filter content," and "We're just a platform, not a publisher," and "Hate speech, proportionately, is such a small part of our output. A necessary evil to protecting free speech," and so on.

---

[45] https://www.gov.uk/government/consultations/online-harms-white-paper/online-harms-white-paper

[46] AJ Dellinger, "Tech companies spent more than $64 million on lobbying in 2018," Engadget, January 23, 2019, https://www.engadget.com/2019-01-23-tech-companies-lobbying-2018-google-facebook-amazon.html

I countered that, even setting the argument for showing decisive moral leadership to one side, going all-out to solve this problem makes clear business sense too: In the end, if my friends are feeling this way, then it's highly likely that many others around the world are having a similar reaction. And if tens of millions of female (and perhaps as many male) users tire of the relentless toxicity, they will eventually quit these platforms in droves. That, in time, would present an existential threat. The answer, I argued, was and remains, at least in significant part, ramped up human moderation.

Their response (and, remember, this was 2016)? "Artificial intelligence will solve it for us," parroting the Zuckerberg party line. Yes, I agreed, AI will be part of the solution. But let's not kid ourselves here. It won't be anything like enough on its own—we're nowhere near the point, even today—and in the meantime this issue will only fester.

Finally, they conceded that human moderators would indeed play a role, as they already do—and they would be hiring more. Yet it turned out that the numbers they had in mind at the time—certainly fewer than 10,000—would be wholly inadequate for the scale of the task at hand. I told them they were going to need many times that for a user base of their size to tackle a crisis on this scale, in a variety of languages to boot.

"Yeah," came the reply, "that's probably not going to fly."

Jump forward two years, however, and a strategic about-face had taken place. Facebook, for example, had plainly concluded that the tsunami of vitriol, violence, and fake news on its platform could no longer be kept in check by a relatively small number of moderators and machine learning alone. By the end of 2018 the company had expanded its "safety and security" team to around 30,000 people—half of whom are "content reviewers."[47] A mix of full-time employees, contractors, and third-partner companies, between them they cover every time zone and about 50 languages.

Unsurprisingly, however, policing the deluge of extreme content ranging from the dissemination of fake information to the violent, hard-core pornographic, and everything in between, has taken a severe toll on moderators, who are nonetheless destined to play an important role in fixing this mess. During every shift, these individuals have to view many hundreds of videos and images, often plumbing the depths of human depravity. In a deep dive investigation into the twilight world of content moderation entitled "The Trauma Floor: The secret lives of Facebook moderators in America," The Verge reporter Casey Newton spent months interviewing a dozen current and former staffers at third-party company Cognizant, which reviews

---

[47]Ellen Silver, "Hard Questions: Who Reviews Objectionable Content on Facebook—And Is the Company Doing Enough to Support Them?," Facebook News, July 26, 2018, https://about .fb.com/news/2018/07/hard-questions-content-reviewers/

content on behalf of Facebook.[48] Unable to be identified due to being obliged to sign nondisclosure agreements (NDAs), the staffers were "pressured not to discuss the emotional toll that their job takes on them, even with loved ones, leading to increased feelings of isolation and anxiety." Of the Cognizant workplace, Newton alleged:

> *It's a place where, in stark contrast to the perks lavished on Facebook employees, team leaders micromanage content moderators' every bathroom and prayer break; where employees, desperate for a dopamine rush amid the misery, have been found having sex inside stairwells and a room reserved for lactating mothers; where people develop severe anxiety while still in training, and continue to struggle with trauma symptoms long after they leave; and where the counselling that Cognizant offers them ends the moment they quit—or are simply let go.*

In a now infamous leaked audio recording of a "Q&A with the CEO" session at Facebook's Menlo Park HQ in October 2019,[49] among many other issues, Mark Zuckerberg discussed content moderation in the wake of The Verge exposé, saying, intriguingly, that the company works with outside firms so that "we can scale up and down and work quickly and be more flexible." To his credit, of the "challenges" individual moderators face, his words implied empathy: " . . . we want to make sure that these folks who are affiliated with the company and very much part of our family as a company are treated well and have the same kind of support that employees would have when dealing with difficult jobs which a lot of people here have."

However, he then described some of the reporting (including, by implication The Verge's investigation) as "a little overdramatic." "From digging into them and understanding what's going on," he said, "it's not that most people are just looking at just terrible things all day long. But there are really bad things that people have to deal with, and making sure that people get the right counseling and space and ability to take breaks and get the mental health support that they need is a really important thing."

He continued: "I think we have more than 30,000 people who are doing content moderation. It's a huge effort. If you look across all the different types of content that people share on our services, including messaging, it's more than 100 billion

---

[48] Casey Newton, "The Trauma Floor: The secret lives of Facebook moderators in America," The Verge, February 25, 2019, https://www.theverge.com/2019/2/25/18229714/cognizant-facebook-content-moderator-interviews-trauma-working-conditions-arizona

[49] Casey Newton, "Read the Full Transcript of Mark Zuckerberg's Leaked Internal Facebook Meetings," The Verge, October 1, 2019, https://www.theverge.com/2019/10/1/20892354/mark-zuckerberg-full-transcript-leaked-facebook-meetings

pieces of content a day. . . . Within a population of 30,000 people, there's going to be a distribution of experiences that people have."

Chris Gray, who worked for CPL, a Dublin-based outsourced company that moderates content for Facebook, had an experience on the darker end of the spectrum Zuckerberg refers to. When he worked for the contractor between 2017 and 2018, while he went through training he began by reviewing images and video that users had reported for being pornographic. It was to prove a relatively gentle introduction. From an initial focus on policing pornography, his role then shifted into moderating what he terms "the high-priority" content, for the UK and Ireland, including bullying, threats of violence, hate speech, and graphic violence—"just all the nasty stuff, and all the worst you can imagine of the world," Gray recalls. After that he was viewing Islamic State executions, beatings, murder, torture, a woman stoned to death, child exploitation, the torture of animals including video footage of dogs being cooked alive. He was later diagnosed with PTSD and is now suing Facebook in Ireland.[50]

But the material he was viewing wasn't the only problem. Getting decisions right on whether to take a particular video or image down was also stressful—particularly as moderators are constantly being audited by supervisors. "Someone is double-checking what you're doing, they're taking a representative sample of your work and you have to reach this 98 percent quality score," he explains. "And you never do at the first round, you always get these mistakes and you have to appeal your mistakes. After a while your big preoccupation is arguing the point that you're right."

He mentions the time he was viewing images of a massacre of Rohingya Muslims in Myanmar. "There was an image of a baby with somebody's foot on its chest. I had decided that was a dead baby because it wasn't fighting back, and its eyes were closed. And my auditor had responded, 'There's nothing to indicate that the baby is dead, so you've made the wrong decision.' Can you imagine that you're arguing about whether the baby's dead because you don't want to get your quality score down? All you care about is getting the point back, not whether the baby is dead.

"So it's dehumanizing. You're distancing yourself from what you're seeing, and at the same time you wake up in the middle of the night and suddenly you'll sit up and say did I miss a nipple? Was that a naked breast? Or was there a terrorist flag in the background of that mass murder that I witnessed? Because if there was then I've deleted it for the wrong reason and therefore I've made a quality mistake and I could get in trouble."

---

[50] Alex Hern, "Ex-Facebook worker claims disturbing content led to PTSD," *The Guardian,* December 4, 2019, https://www.theguardian.com/technology/2019/dec/04/ex-facebook-worker-claims-disturbing-content-led-to-ptsd

"I'M GOING TO SHOW YOU MORE CAR CRASHES"

Technology's ability to overpower and overwhelm humanity is no longer even in question. And yet, according to Aza Raskin, co-founder of the Center for Human Technology and formerly creative lead at Mozilla, as a society we have been caught off guard. Why? Because it turns out we focused on the wrong thing all along. "Technologists and culture has fixated on the point when technology takes control by overwhelming human strengths—the so-called 'singularity'—but has entirely missed the point where technology takes control by exploiting human weakness. That's the true singularity and perhaps we are already there."

Tech wasn't even the first industry to figure out that attention could be monetized and that "time on site" (literally the amount of time visitors spend on your website or app) was the metric that mattered most; in fact it was Las Vegas casinos, and slot machines in particular, he says. "They were the first industry to integrate real-time A/B testing into their product. Slot machines are very effective, persuasive technology. They are now so effective that some adults choose to wear a diaper to keep playing instead of using the restroom. Normally, when you think of a slot machine you think large levers and loud noises, but that's not what modern slot machines are like. They're very quiet. Casinos create special zoned spaces to play in, fine-tuned to keep you in a hypnotic state of mind, the ceiling height and lights are just so, the wins and the losses are both accompanied with similar hushed happy melodies and are calculatingly dosed at just the right rate to keep you there. It's not a fair fight. The casinos have A/B tested their way to a powerful human-nature trap," he says. "And Silicon Valley companies have done the exact same thing. Do you recognize that hypnotic, auto-pilot state from using your phone? We all do. The soft animal underbelly of our minds is increasingly vulnerable to increasingly powerful technology."

We first experienced this as "information overload," when the human ability to process information, our natural curiosity, was surpassed, Raskin tells me. Next came "tech addiction," where we've lost the ability to self-regulate because technology is overwhelming our vulnerabilities. The next phase was the polarization caused by what he describes as "the hacking of moral outrage."

"It's not that [the platforms] are showing people what they want, they're showing people what they can't help but look at," he says. He develops his point further. "If you drive past a car crash, you can't help but look at the car crash because it's surprising; and there's a little AI now that's watching you and [concluding] 'Oh, I guess you like car crashes, that's your true revealed preference. I'm going to show you more car crashes.' And then you're living in a world of car crashes. That's very explanatory of the way the world feels."

The platforms have built a giant lever for changing beliefs, behaviors, and attitudes and hooked it up to their supercomputers' "voodoo doll" model of every individual user, Raskin explains. "It starts as a little bit generic and then our meta data is collected—our hair, our toenail clippings, our click trails. When I give talks now I ask how many people think that Facebook listens to all of their conversations, because they've talked about some specific product with their friend and then it shows up in the news feed the next day and it's just too eerie? Half to two-thirds of the hands go up in the room. And to me the truth is much creepier. It's not that they are listening and hence know what we say because then we can just ban that practice. It is that the models about us are getting so good that it can predict things that we think about.

"Imagine playing chess against someone who could predict all of your moves before you made them. You would be irrevocably dominated. As technology is increasingly able to predict our behaviors and beliefs—and what will change them—will our agency and 'free will' also be irrevocably dominated?"

CHAPTER 6

Venture Capital and the Holy Grail of Scale

I f it wasn't for venture capital (VC), Silicon Valley and the tech industry at large—at least as we know it today—wouldn't exist. VC is indispensable to innovation, the lifeblood coursing through the ecosystem's veins. Yet simultaneously it has been one of the key factors in Big Tech's nosedive into an ethical quagmire.

VC has been especially critical to the fortunes of tech's herd of unicorns in the Valley and increasingly around the world. As described in 2009 by authors Michel Ferrary and Mark Granovetter in their paper "The Role of Venture Capital Firms in Silicon Valley's Complex Innovation Network,"[1] VC investors bring five elements to the table, and only the first is usually understood. They are financing, selection, signaling, collective learning, and embedding. Financing, of course, refers to venture capitalists' role in funding startups. Without access to early-stage finance there would probably be no Big Tech: Google, Apple, Facebook, and Amazon all took on VC investment. (Not to mention Twitter, Airbnb, WhatsApp, Pinterest, Uber, Deliveroo, WeWork, and just about any other post-2010 internet-enabled startup you care to name.)

Venture investing is a high-stakes, high-risk/high-reward endeavor: as many as three in every four startups fail to return money to their backers, according to a study by Harvard Business School.[2] That's why "selection" is so important. As the authors note: "Venture capitalists can often judge the potential of an innovation better than entrepreneurs. VC firms eliminate startups by refusing to invest in some of them at the seed stage."

---

[1] Michel Ferrary, "The Role of Venture Capital Firms in Silicon Valley's Complex Innovation Network," May 2009, https://www.researchgate.net/publication/249006197_The_Role_of_Venture_Capital_Firms_in_Silicon_Valley's_Complex_Innovation_Network
[2] Shikhar Ghosh, "The Venture Capital Secret: 3 Out of 4 Startups Fail," Harvard Business School, September 19, 2012, https://www.hbs.edu/news/Pages/item.aspx?num=487

Next comes "signaling," which is about the way VC funding, particularly from a prominent Valley firm like Sequoia, Kleiner Perkins, Benchmark or Andreessen Horowitz, confers credibility on a startup to the rest of the ecosystem. "Collective learning," meanwhile, refers to the way, once funded, a startup is immediately plugged into the deep and hard-won knowledge gained over years by VCs, who—as Ferrary and Granovetter point out—"have evaluated thousands of projects and funded and accompanied dozens of startups," accumulating "deep understanding of industrial, technological legal and managerial issues." The last of the five elements that VCs offer is "embedding," where "the embeddedness [sic] of entrepreneurs in the complex networks of Silicon Valley is a major factor determining the success of startups."

Without all of the above, therefore, the Valley and other leading tech clusters would almost certainly not have flourished to the point of producing the sorts of global success stories we see today.

As for venture's wider impact, a separate study, this time by Stanford Graduate School of Business,[3] found that over the past three decades VC has had an outsized impact on the economy, by fueling some of the world's most innovative businesses. "Of the currently public U.S. companies we have founding dates for, approximately 1,330 were founded between 1979 and 2013. Of those, 574, or 43%, are VC-backed," wrote authors Ilya A. Strebulaev and Will Gornall. "These companies comprise 57% of the market capitalization and 38% of the employees of all such 'new' public companies. Moreover, their R&D expenditure constitutes an overwhelming 82% of the total R&D of new public companies."

The lack of a mature venture capital ecosystem with deep roots, meanwhile, is one of the key reasons why European tech startups lag their American counterparts. The fragmentation of the European market and less flexible regulation have also contributed to the fact that there are far fewer unicorns in Europe, but the venture capital gap is a critical factor (see Figure 6.1).

While the European ecosystem has been improving steadily over the past few years, it wasn't so long ago that raising VC money in Europe was a tall order. Gillian Tans, former CEO of Booking.com, my former employer, revealed to Bloomberg[4] that Booking sold to Priceline because it was desperate for money to keep growing. "Maybe if at that time there would have been more funding available, Booking would have made different choices," she said in the interview.

---

[3]Ilya A. Strebulaev and Will Gornall, "How Much Does Venture Capital Drive the U.S. Economy?," Insights by Stanford Business, October 21 2015, https://www.gsb.stanford.edu/insights/how-much-does-venture-capital-drive-us-economy

[4]Jeremy Khan, "Why can't Europe do tech?," Bloomberg, August 16, 2018, https://www.bloomberg.com/news/features/2018-08-16/inside-europe-s-struggle-to-build-a-truly-global-tech-giant

Europe's Lagging VC Market

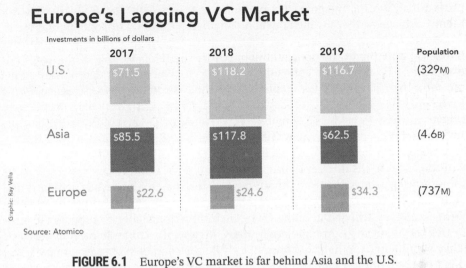

Investments in billions of dollars

	2017	2018	2019	Population
U.S.	$71.5	$118.2	$116.7	(329M)
Asia	$85.5	$117.8	$62.5	(4.6B)
Europe	$22.6	$24.6	$34.3	(737M)

Graphic: Ray Vella

Source: Atomico

FIGURE 6.1   Europe's VC market is far behind Asia and the U.S.
Source: Atomico.

Founder of fashion-tech unicorn Farfetch, Jose Neves, told *Wired*[5] that European founders, until recently, were not taken seriously by American VCs. "There was this perception that great tech businesses were only born in Silicon Valley," he said.

And it's precisely because of its vital role in the tech ecosystem that venture capital bears so much responsibility for the shape of the wider industry, for good and for bad.

THE GOOD, THE BAD, AND THE UGLY

Venture capital leadership tends to share many of the same traits as the tech executives they fund: overwhelmingly white or Asian male, often sexist, obsessed with getting impossibly rich, messianic about the benefits of disruption, and convinced they are smarter than most. The symbiosis doesn't end at the writing of investment checks. VC firms with large investments take board seats at their portfolio companies. Yet rather than being a potential leavening influence on bro culture, or a governor on the hype and excess of many tech firms, VCs too often look away, or celebrate the young founders who create that environment, and participate in talking up the companies and their technologies regardless of whether they have yet

---

[5] James Silver, "The story of London's tech scene, as told by those who built it," *Wired UK*, April 24, 2019, https://www.wired.co.uk/article/oral-history-london-tech-scene

proved their worth. The goal is to maximize the "exit," the payoff for their investments, achieved either through the company being acquired or going public.

As is the case with tech executives, venture capitalists are not monolithic. Since the bursting of the dot.com bubble in the early 2000s, the VC industry has evolved and become more competitive and more diverse in its approaches. Some are more hands-on with the companies in their portfolios, others less so. Some prefer early-stage investing, others later. Some prefer consumer-facing businesses, others business-to-business. Some are very attuned to issues of diversity, battling sexism and taking a longer view. Others definitely less so.

In my experience, 5 to 10 percent of VCs are outstanding. They help you take your business to the next level, because of the type of connections they can enable for recruiting or business, and the strategic vision they have for your company and your industry. They push you to see around the corners—both short term and long term—and they will go out of their way, including financially, to support the businesses they believe in through tough times. Meanwhile, 20 to 30 percent are good (they genuinely try to help and once in a while they succeed; they are available, yet don't distract you too much; they do their homework and ask relevant questions in board meetings). Around 40 to 50 percent are mediocre (neither fundamentally good nor bad; they give you a check but they don't really do much more than that), and 15 to 20 percent are bad or really bad (this is where you find the misogynists, the know-it-alls who never have time to follow up on any promise they make, the ones who invest in your competitors, or who screw you with complex special terms or last-minute conditions when you're trying to close a round).

Despite these differences, the underlying system of venture funding helps to drive a common culture of seeking hypergrowth (usually defined as 40 percent average annual growth maintained for more than a year), sometimes at any cost and without regard for the consequences. And manic drive for growth contributes to the lack of empathy and some of the biggest ethical and moral lapses in the industry.

"IT'S ALL ABOUT SCALE"

There are different factors, all working in concert, to explain this intense focus on hypergrowth.

To start, it is important to understand how venture funding works. Venture firms channel pools of money given to them by wealthy investors looking for outsized returns, usually charging them between 2 percent and 2.5 percent of the money invested for the privilege. In addition, in return for funding a company, VC firms get a share of the profits generated by their investments, often in the range of 20 to 30 percent (otherwise called carried interest or carry). This only gets paid off at the exit. When the latter pays off it is both game-changing and name-making for a firm and more than makes up for the investments that never make it, which is the majority.

Sequoia, for example, saw its $60 million investment in WhatsApp turn into $3 billion.[6] Sequoia and Kleiner Perkins backed Google to the tune of $12.5 million in 1999. A year after Google's IPO in 2004, their stakes were worth $4.3 billion each.[7]

This race to maximum payoff gets supercharged by other factors that result in even more disproportionate weight placed on hypergrowth at (almost) any cost.

The size and certainty of the management fees, combined with the relative ease with which VC firms can raise large sums of money for new funds, have led VCs to increase the size of their new funds. The median fund size increased to $78.5 million in 2019, the highest in the past decade. Firms raising follow-on funds closed vehicles that were 55 percent larger at the median than their previous fund.[8] As the number of funds and money allocated to VCs increased, the competition to invest in the best startups increased proportionally, leading to inflation around valuations as founders shop for the least dilution/loss of control. And thus the pressure to deliver high growth—to "grow into" the valuation—increases.

Meanwhile, each new, eye-popping valuation creates priceless hype and buzz around a company, which helps its chances of getting more money later at more inflated valuations, and confers credibility on its VC backers, who are looking to raise more cash to deploy. And so, growth becomes even more critical to help justify the hype.

In fact, one of the dirty secrets of venture funding is that a company's valuation has often little or nothing to do with its performance as a business. Especially in the early startup stage, when a company might not even be an established business yet, valuing the company is arbitrary, based on educated guesswork, negotiation with the founders, and hope.

In his post "Venture Capital: It is a pricing, not a value, game!,"[9] New York University finance professor Aswath Damodaran explains why "VCs don't value companies, they price them." The vast majority of VCs tend to value startups based on what other people are willing to pay for that kind of business (the pricing approach) rather than the business's ability to generate earnings and cash flow (the value approach; which, to be fair, is particularly hard to do with young, innovative, and fast-paced companies). The result is that startup valuations can be widely decorrelated from

[6]Sarah McBride, "With WhatsApp deal, Sequoia Capital burnishes reputation," Reuters, February 21, 2014, https://www.reuters.com/article/us-whatsapp-facebook-sequoia-idUSBREA1K04720140221

[7]CB Insights, "From Alibaba to Zynga: 40 of the Best VC Bets of All Time," January 4, 2019, https://www.cbinsights.com/research/best-venture-capital-investments/#Goo

[8]Q4 2019 Venture Monitor, PitchBook-NVCA, https://nvca.org/wp-content/uploads/2020/01/Q4_2019_PitchBook_NVCA_Venture_Monitor.pdf

[9]Aswath Damodaran, "Venture Capital: It is a pricing, not a value, game!," Musings on Markets, October 2, 2016, https://aswathdamodaran.blogspot.com/2016/10/venture-capital-it-is-pricing-not-value.html

their actual or even future ability to generate cash (with the attendant problems with which we've become all too familiar once these companies go public).

Damodaran also notes that VCs often "invest in companies who aim to dominate markets, choosing business with monopolistic tendencies because those are easy heuristics to discover, with clear patterns for scale." In other words, VCs look for "winner-take-all" types of markets, because the chance for a large exit is higher. Particularly in these markets, the push for rapid growth can be extreme, sometimes known as "blitz scaling." Uber is a poster child for this approach, taking in round after round of financing—at ever-escalating valuations—as it sought to rapidly spend its way to ride-share dominance around the world. Restaurant delivery service DoorDash is another classic case of using a war chest of venture capital to buy scale regardless of how much money it loses. Like others in its industry, it has been caught listing restaurants on its site for delivery without the restaurant's consent, and with lower prices listed. In a now infamous example, a restaurateur demonstrated how he could place a large order of his own pizza, paying DoorDash $16 per piece, only to be paid $24 per piece by DoorDash. To top it off, the restaurateur soon realized he didn't even need to make the pizzas at all, saving all the production costs, since the DoorDash delivery person who paid full price was then handing the boxes back to the restaurant for $16.[10]

To be sure, a lot of VC and entrepreneurs have gotten smarter about all this over the years. But many of them continue to keep the pressure on. As recently as 2019 I heard a venture capitalist state, "Public markets will reward you for top line (i.e. revenue) growth and give you little credit for profitability. If you're able to deliver more than 50 percent growth annually, you won't have any problem raising more money to finance your losses. It's all about scale," he said. "Just focus on scale. The rest will take care of itself."

"YOU DON'T SCALE FAST IF YOU TRY TO GET EVERYTHING PERFECT"

The results of all this can be perverse. Desperate for growth, companies might spend more money to add customers than those customers yield in revenue, meaning they are just burning their investors' money. In effect, they spend $10 to acquire revenue worth $5. Or they might cut corners, or ignore regulators. Small, nagging problems are left to accumulate and fester. And in the frenzy to grow, they are less likely to focus on building empathetic, durable cultures, to treat their employees well, and to be good corporate citizens. All of these things damage the chances of long-term

---

[10]Ranjan Roy, "Doordash and Pizza Arbitrage," The Margins, May 17, 2020, https://themargins.substack.com/p/doordash-and-pizza-arbitrage

success. "Whenever you scale aggressively you end up with some error, which leads to a mess that you might have to then clean up later," says Hussein Kanji, founding partner at London's Hoxton Ventures, backers of three unicorns: Deliveroo, Babylon Health, and cyber-security firm Darktrace. "But you don't scale fast if you try to get everything perfect."

Significantly, it also means that many of these companies never end up working out a sustainable business model and keep talking about future viability instead. In extreme cases, it incentivizes VCs to convince founders to say no to an exit offer and wait for a billion-dollar exit that never materializes.

There are other effects: As pricing is quite subjective, inflated valuations of one company can lead to skyrocketing valuations of other startups in a similar space. But as soon as one of them encounters problems, it can become harder for all firms in the space to fundraise, and valuations start to drop.

Indeed, VCs can inflate a valuation in numerous ways throughout the funding lifecycle of a startup, further divorcing the number from the performance or prospects of the company. In negotiating deal terms, for example, a VC can demand preferential treatment in recouping some or all of its investment, relative to other investors, if the company fails. This happens when the VC might be squeamish about investing more money at a higher valuation, but the company does not want the negative publicity and potential dilution of a down round (financing at a lower valuation than the previous round).

In another scenario, a down round can be made to look like an up round because the company issues more shares to the VC in exchange for a higher valuation. This dilutes the value of existing investors' shares, but looks to the media and the world like the company is getting hotter and hotter.

All of this can lead founders to be much more bullish about the future of their company than they should be. On too many occasions, I've heard things like, "We doubled our valuation in less than xx months, so there's no reason why we can't double it again!" So they take even more risks and cut even more corners, further increasing their burn rate.

FOMO

When you have very little objective data with which to assess a startup, let alone any credible evidence upon which to base a valuation, the simple answer is to wait to follow the herd: "If x and y invested in that company, then I don't want to miss out." I've lost track of the number of times I heard friends, when in fundraising mode, describe the excruciating process where you technically have promises from enough investors to close your round, but not a single one of them is ready to make the decisive move of actually providing a binding term sheet that sets a valuation.

This happened to me when I was CEO of Ozon.ru and seeking to raise $100 million (a large sum at the time). We were able to close the round only because, by pure chance, while I was visiting my brother in Japan, I got introduced to Mikitani-san, the CEO of Rakuten. I hadn't even been planning to talk to him about fundraising, but right at the end of our conversation I mentioned the ongoing process. By some miracle, he told me on the spot that he wanted to invest $5 million, and back in Russia a few weeks later, a term sheet arrived. The investment was for a relatively small amount, but crucially it came with a valuation attached. And from there, closing everyone else was (almost) a cakewalk.

But when everyone is waiting to follow someone else, there is less diversity in the types of startups that get funded. It can also result in dubious businesses getting funded, with nowhere near the appropriate quality of due diligence or, later on, oversight required given the level of investment. One VC takes the plunge, and others pile in as groupthink takes over. This can sometimes be good for companies that end up being successful, high-quality investments, but it can also lead to disasters like Theranos, Juicero, Zenefits, Secret, and too many others to mention.

HARVARD OR STANFORD?

Considering the homogenous nature of the VC community, groupthink is hardly surprising. VC's diversity problem is well documented (see Figure 6.2).

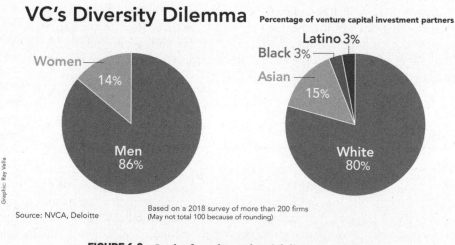

FIGURE 6.2   Lack of gender and racial diversity in VC.
Source: NVCA, Deloitte.

Not surprisingly, these numbers correspond with how venture capital has been allocated. According to one recent study,[11] 77.1 percent of founders receiving VC-backed deals over the past five years were white. One percent were black, just under 2 percent were Latino, and female-led startups got only 9 percent. It is no wonder, then, that there is a sameness to the types of investments VCs make. Many good ideas are being left on the table, or killed before they even get into the room. "We see thousands of promising underrepresented startup founders seeking capital every year, and the opportunity to tap into a more diverse pool of founders is real," said Brittany Davis, director of deal flow at Backstage Capital, a rare VC firm that looks to invest in founders who are women, people of color, and gay.[12]

There has been enough pushback recently, culminating with the Black Lives Matter movement, that many VC firms are talking a good game of seeking to invest in minority-led or female-led firms, and in trying to increase diversity in the VC firms themselves. So far, the numbers have not moved significantly. Even more insidious is when female founders either get rejected or walk away from potential investment because they would not sleep with the VC they pitched.[13]

On top of the diversity issue, the lack of operational experience of most VC partners (again, there are exceptions) means that VCs tend to be disconnected from the reality of the business. I have personally spent hours (and I do mean hours) trying to get an investor to understand that the difficulties around scaling a warehouse or a call center have less to do with capital or hardware and more with humans and the complex processes required to hire and manage large groups of people in small spaces. (I remember having to explain that while I could certainly extend lunch hours from, let's say, 11 am until 2:30 pm, I couldn't reasonably ask employees to eat at 4 pm, on the pretext that this would allow us to spread lunch over a longer period and thus the canteen/kitchen could take up less space.) Or why (when I was recently helping a friend put a new business plan together in the early stages of the COVID-19 outbreak) asking for endless dashboards and updates during a pandemic is not only selfish, it's actually dangerous for the business you invested in and thus for your investment.

This operational inexperience and naivete leads to certain types of companies—and therefore founders—being financed, while others are routinely ignored. It can also mean the boards become overloaded with directors who similarly lack the experience of having grown a company through turbulent times

---

[11] Diversity in U.S. startup, RateMyInvestor, https://ratemyinvestor.com/diversity_report
[12] Mary Ann Azevedo, "Untapped Opportunity: Minority Founders Still Being Overlooked," February 27, 2019, https://news.crunchbase.com/news/untapped-opportunity-minority-founders-still-being-overlooked/
[13] Paris Martineau, "Female Founders Still Face Sexual Harassment from Investors," *Wired*, November 15, 2018, https://www.wired.com/story/female-founders-still-face-sexual-harassment-from-investors/

as well as calmer ones, and who are ill equipped to offer counsel to a founder caught in an ethical bind or dealing with a tricky people issue.

A NEW INVESTOR CLASS?

Due to many of the problems just outlined, VCs are no longer universally regarded as holding the necessary golden tickets for entrepreneurs. Founders have grown weary, and wary, of being pushed into unfavorable deal terms, or partnering with VCs who—depending on the size of their stake—have later elbowed founders out of the way. Or who are simply not providing the support the founder needs.

As a result, new funding sources have emerged. Angel investing has grown, and become more sophisticated, for companies not seeking giant investments. Private equity firms have jumped into the fray, as have some investment banks. And a more diverse set of VC firms, which think differently and in some cases are located outside of Silicon Valley, are increasingly dotting the landscape.

Still, for entrepreneurs who have unicorn dreams, the top tier of VC firms remains in high demand. They still wield enormous power and influence, have the most money to deploy, and still provide the guidance and support that can mint billionaires. They also (though not exclusively) still help perpetuate many of the problems discussed in this chapter, from the push for hypergrowth to a bro culture to self-aggrandizement, alongside a lack of empathy for users and the wider world.

While there are some signs that this era is finally drawing to a close (Uber's CEO Dara Khosrowshahi said in an earnings announcement in February 2020, "The era of growth at all costs is over"),[14] it really is a case of "only time will tell." With $121 billion of unspent cash as of midyear 2019, as per data provider Pitchbook,[15] the likelihood that this money will ultimately be spent on hypergrowth is going to be high. COVID-19 is certainly making investors and founders conscious of startups' bottom lines and resetting valuations, but whether that remains the case when the outbreak finally eases is anyone's bet.

The reality is, the drive for dominance is part of venture capital's DNA. "Monopoly is the condition of every successful business," venture capitalist Peter Thiel famously wrote in his controversial book *Zero to One*. His definition of monopoly is more nuanced than our image of the rapacious mega-corporation, but

---

[14]Sara Ashley O'Brien, "Uber CEO says 'era of growth at all costs is over' after losing $8.5 billion last year," CNN Business, February 7, 2020, https://edition.cnn.com/2020/02/06/tech/uber-q4-earnings/index.html

[15]Alexander Davis, "Facing disaster, corporate venture capital to undergo key stress test," March 24, 2020, PitchBook, https://pitchbook.com/news/articles/facing-disaster-corporate-venture-capital-to-undergo-key-stress-test

the core value is similar: Own whatever market you are in, no matter how big that market might be. And then expand from there.

As I'll explore in the following chapter, if inexperienced young founders with psychopathic personality traits are then thrown into the mix, the results should surprise exactly nobody. As celebrated entrepreneur turned VC Marc Andreessen said a long time ago[16] (although he later distanced himself from the remark), "We tend to be pro-megalomania."

---

[16]Michael Liedtke, "Netscape co-founder making leap to venture capital," ABC News, July 6, 2009, https://abcnews.go.com/Technology/story?id=8011518s

CHAPTER 7

Psychos of the Valley

I n December 2018, Twitter's charismatic co-founder and CEO Jack Dorsey went on "a 10-day silent vipassana meditation" retreat in Pyin Oo Lwin, Myanmar, to mark his 42nd birthday.[1] The entrepreneur, who also happens to be founder and CEO of mobile payment unicorn Square, detailed his experience in a series of tweets[2] to his more than 4 million followers, noting, among other things, that "Vipassana is a technique and practice to 'know thyself.' Understanding the inner nature as a way to understand . . . everything" and that "Vipassana's singular objective is to hack the deepest layer of the mind and reprogram it: instead of unconsciously reacting to feelings of pain or pleasure, consciously observe that all pain and pleasure aren't permanent, and will ultimately pass and dissolve away."

So far, so Silicon Valley. Yet while extolling the virtues of meditation and praising his host country ("Myanmar is an absolutely beautiful country. The people are full of joy and the food is amazing. . . . We visited and meditated at many monasteries around the country"), Dorsey's tone-deaf tweets studiously neglected to mention Myanmar's brutal repression and persecution—including mass murder, infanticide, and rape—of Rohingya Muslims, which to date has driven some 700,000 from their homes into neighboring Bangladesh[3] and has seen former Nobel Peace Prize winner

---

[1] Alexandra Topping, "Twitter CEO accused of ignoring plight of Rohingya in tweets promoting Myanmar," *The Guardian,* December 9, 2018, https://www.theguardian.com/technology/2018/dec/09/twitter-ceo-jack-dorsey-accused-of-ignoring-plight-of-rohingya-in-tweets-promoting-myanmar
[2] https://twitter.com/jack/status/1071575088695140353
[3] Simon Lewis, "Tip of the Spear: The shock troops who expelled the Rohingya from Myanmar," Reuters, June 26, 2018, https://www.reuters.com/investigates/special-report/myanmar-rohingya-battalions/

and Myanmar leader Aung San Suu Kyi defend her country against accusations of genocide at The Hague.[4]

"If meditation is meant to make practitioners more aware and compassionate," noted Quartz writer Ephrat Livni wryly, "Dorsey's practice appears to have failed on that front."[5] Meanwhile Catherine Shu of TechCrunch apparently spoke for many when she observed, "Even though the crimes against Rohingya people have been well-documented in articles by major media outlets around the world, not once did Dorsey mention them in the more than a dozen tweets he wrote about his trip."[6]

Dorsey soon found himself on the wrong side of the kind of flaming that has become so commonplace on his and other platforms. "Go meditate in Syria next," tweeted one wag. Another tweeted a picture from HBO's *Silicon Valley*, in which the character of Gavin Belson—the founder of a spoof tech giant allegedly based on Google—is seen dressed as a monk while on a Buddhist retreat, with this caption: "You really couldn't be more of a big fat techbro [sic] stereotype, could you?"

Beating a hasty retreat, Dorsey responded gravely, with carefully measured humility, "I'm aware of the human rights atrocities and suffering in Myanmar. I don't view visiting, practicing, or talking with the people, as endorsement. I didn't intend to diminish by not raising the issue, but could have acknowledged that I don't know enough and need to learn more."[7]

Missing from the apology was any acknowledgment that social media played a significant role—as deployed by the military and government—in instigating violence against the Rohingya minority. It is that failure to even consider, let alone take responsibility for, the potentially devastating effects that technology enables which too often defines Silicon Valley.

Dorsey is one of the more enlightened of the many Valley founders who suffer from this shortcoming. As technological visionaries, they often come from an engineering culture that is long on the hubris that they alone have the answers, and short on empathy and compassion. In the name of greater efficiency, the default setting for many is to take people out of the equation whenever possible, and to put their faith in code and machines. They are in turn encouraged by an ecosystem of venture capitalists and others who prize these qualities as keys to business success.

---

[4]James Griffiths, "The West turned Aung San Suu Kyi into a saint. She was always going to disappoint," CNN, December 14, 2019, https://edition.cnn.com/2019/12/13/asia/rohingya-suu-kyi-myanmar-hague-intl-hnk/index.html
[5]Ephrat Livni, "Jack Dorsey missed the point of meditation on his Myanmar retreat," Quartz, December 10, 2018, https://qz.com/1489982/jack-dorsey-missed-the-point-of-meditation-on-his-myanmar-retreat/
[6]Catherine Shu, "Some things Jack Dorsey didn't mention in his Myanmar meditation travelogue," TechCrunch, December 10, 2018, https://techcrunch.com/2018/12/09/some-things-jack-dorsey-didnt-mention-in-his-myanmar-meditation-travelogue/
[7]https://twitter.com/jack/status/1072611908828708865

To his credit, Dorsey pledged $1 billion in equity (around 28 percent of his fortune) to a pandemic relief[8] fund during the COVID-19 crisis. And after listening to some of Twitter's staff, the company has been more aggressive than others in policing its platform and trying to eliminate its worst elements.

Being largely oblivious to the sometimes devastating unintended consequences of new technology demands a particular type of personality. CEOs as a category have topped the list of professional roles to which "psychopaths" are drawn.[9] In my experience this is accentuated in tech because of the self-selection process and nurturing environment for this type of behavior, in which excess is often actively encouraged. Given the mythology of "founder infallibility" that is so prevalent among large tech companies, in the Valley and beyond, psychopathic traits tend to trickle down through entire organizations, in effect creating "psychopathic" companies.

Among the 20 personality traits itemized in the widely accepted Hare Psychopathy Checklist (Revised)[10] are a grandiose sense of self-worth, poor behavioral controls, shallow affect (i.e., reduced emotional responses), pathological lying, a lack of remorse or guilt, a failure to accept responsibility for one's own actions, callousness and lack of empathy, and juvenile delinquency. These eight in particular, as well as many of the others, are absolutely rife across Big Tech. (And it's worth emphasizing that an individual doesn't need to exhibit all 20 of the traits to be considered a psychopath; rather they are measured across all 20, and scored from zero ["does not apply"] to two ["fully applies"] against each of them, with the bar for clinical psychopathy being a total of 30 or more.)[11]

A GRANDIOSE SENSE OF SELF-WORTH AND POOR BEHAVIORAL CONTROLS

Self-worth tends not to be in short supply in alpha-male tech giant bosses or their businesses, but even among Big Tech's parade of preening egos, the excesses of

[8]Mike Isaac, "Jack Dorsey Vows to Donate $1 Billion to Fight the Coronavirus," *New York Times,* April 7, 2020, https://www.nytimes.com/2020/04/07/technology/jack-dorsey-donate-1-billion-coronavirus.html

[9]Eric Barker, "Which Professions Have the Most Psychopaths? The Fewest?" *Time,* March 21, 2014, https://time.com/32647/which-professions-have-the-most-psychopaths-the-fewest/; Tomas Chamorro-Premuzic, "1 in 5 business leaders may have psychopathic tendencies—here's why, according to a psychology professor," CNBC, April 8, 2019, https://www.cnbc.com/2019/04/08/the-science-behind-why-so-many-successful-millionaires-are-psychopaths-and-why-it-doesnt-have-to-be-a-bad-thing.html

[10]Kristopher J. Brazil, "Hare Psychopathy Checklist (PCL)," November 2016, https://www.researchgate.net/publication/318596156_Hare_Psychopathy_Checklist_PCL#pf5

[11]*Psychology Today,* "Psychopathy," https://www.psychologytoday.com/gb/basics/psychopathy

the We Company's Adam Neumann are hard to beat. His fondness for walking New York's sidewalks shoeless, for top-of-the-range tequila, and smoking weed on private jets are well documented. As were his operatic ambitions for the company—according to the *New York Times*, Neumann "has said he wants to become the world's first trillionaire and president of the world," and how the company acquired a Gulfstream G650 for $60 million, "about the sum that the company was losing every two weeks."[12] It was also reported that he installed an infrared sauna and cold plunge pool in his Manhattan office, "made millions leasing buildings he partly owned back to WeWork," while its IPO filing revealed that Neumann had acted to trademark "We," which he then proceeded to charge the company $5.9 million for using—money he later returned.

When it comes to poor behavioral controls, Tesla and SpaceX CEO Elon Musk would top many lists. Musk deserves much credit for his bold visions of everything from colonizing space to hyperloop high-speed transit to alleviating climate change, and for his focus on tackling problems that matter for humanity no matter how large or difficult. But his antics have included smoking a joint on a video podcast (causing a 10 percent drop Tesla's stock price), using Twitter to telegraph business decisions,[13] or reopening Tesla's factory in Fremont, California, despite county shelter-in-place orders, while calling quarantine measures "fascist" and going on an expletive-laden rant during a Q1 earning call. (At the time of this writing several workers had tested positive for COVID-19 following the reopening.)[14]

In late 2018, Musk settled with the SEC for tweeting that he was planning to take Tesla private at $420 per share, pending a shareholder vote. Not only did the move never occur, but his breach of market disclosure rules earned him and Tesla fines of $20 million each.[15] In addition, he was required to step down as Tesla chairman, add two independent board members, and install additional corporate controls on his communications with the public.

"The total package of remedies and relief announced today are specifically designed to address the misconduct at issue by strengthening Tesla's corporate

---

[12]Amy Chozick, "Adam Neumann and the Art of Failing Up," *New York Times*, November 2, 2019, https://www.nytimes.com/2019/11/02/business/adam-neumann-wework-exit-package.html?action=click&module=Top%20Stories&pgtype=Homepage

[13]Paul A. Eisenstein, "Tesla stock plummets after Elon Musk smokes weed on live show and two execs quit in one day," NBC News, September 7, 2018, https://www.nbcnews.com/tech/tech-news/tesla-stock-plummets-after-elon-musk-smokes-weed-live-show-n907476

[14]Faiz Siddiqui, "Tesla defied county orders so it could restart production. Days later, workers tested positive for the coronavirus," *Washington Post*, June 9, 2020, https://www.washingtonpost.com/technology/2020/06/09/tesla-factory-coronavirus/

[15]Michael Wayland, "Tesla's chaotic year after Musk's 'funding secured' tweet," CNBC, August 8, 2019, https://www.cnbc.com/2019/08/08/teslas-chaotic-year-after-musks-funding-secured-tweet.html

governance and oversight in order to protect investors," said Stephanie Avakian, co-director of the SEC's Enforcement Division in its statement announcing the settlement.[16] The following year, the SEC asked that Musk be held in contempt of court for violating the settlement for tweeting production numbers that differed from the company's official statistics.

Musk, who made his fortune at PayPal, often makes grand pronouncements, such as when he said in 2016 that Tesla was only a year away from a fully autonomous vehicle that could traverse the country from Los Angeles to New York.[17] As with several other such statements, Musk was forced to walk it back. And in one of the most celebrated incidents, Musk took to Twitter to call a British cave diver a "pedo guy" after the diver said that a mini-sub that Musk was sending to Thailand to help rescue 12 trapped children in a flooded cave would not work. The mini-sub was never used.[18]

SHALLOW AFFECT (SUPERFICIAL EMOTIONAL RESPONSES)

Another symptom of psychopathy commonly found in larger-than-life unicorn founders is a trait termed "shallow affect," which we might liken to emotional illiteracy or reduced emotional responses to a given set of circumstances.

Exhibit A could be Travis Kalanick, Uber's testosterone-fueled co-founder. No incident captured the public's attention more than in February 2017, when Kalanick was caught in a dash-cam video, leaked to Bloomberg, in which he berates one of his platform's drivers who complained to him about fare cuts while Kalanick was riding in his car with two women on Super Bowl weekend.[19] After an exchange at the end of the ride, which began cordially enough, the volatile Uber boss grew impatient and then angry as the driver, Fawzi Kamel, told him that the firm had dropped its prices and that he was "bankrupt" as a result. "You know what? Some people don't like to take responsibility for their own shit," Kalanick barked back, his notoriously

---

[16]SEC, press release, "Elon Musk Settles SEC Fraud Charges," September 29, 2018, https://www.sec.gov/news/press-release/2018-226

[17]Dave Smith, "Elon Musk said a Tesla car would be able to drive itself across the country by the end of 2017—but it's 2019, and that still hasn't happened," Business Insider, March 13, 2019, https://www.businessinsider.com/elon-musk-tesla-car-drive-itself-across-the-country-2019-3

[18]Lora Kolodny, "Elon Musk found not liable in 'pedo guy' defamation trial," CNBC, December 6, 2019, https://www.cnbc.com/2019/12/06/unsworth-vs-musk-pedo-guy-defamation-trial-verdict.html

[19]Eric Newcomer, "In video, Uber CEO argues with driver over falling fares," February 28, 2017, Bloomberg, https://www.bloomberg.com/news/articles/2017-02-28/in-video-uber-ceo-argues-with-driver-over-falling-fares

short fuse caught for posterity on a dashboard camera. "They blame everything in their life on somebody else!"

While those words garnered headlines, it was Kalanick's reaction when shown the leaked video months later by fellow executives in a hotel conference room in San Francisco, described brilliantly in Bloomberg Businessweek, in an article entitled "The Fall of Travis Kalanick Was a Lot Weirder and Darker Than You Thought,"[20] which truly captured his shallow affect:

> *The executives were armed that day with something unusual for Uber Technologies Inc: the results of a survey. . . . About half the respondents had a positive impression of Uber and its convenient ride-hailing app. But if respondents knew anything about Kalanick, an inveterate flouter of both workplace conventions and local transportation laws, they had a decidedly negative view.*
>
> *As usual with Kalanick, the discussion grew contentious. [Uber president] Jones and his deputies argued that Uber's riders and drivers viewed the company as made up of a bunch of greedy, self-centered jerks. And as usual, Kalanick retorted that the company had a public-relations problem, not a cultural one.*

Then one of the executives took an urgent phone call. Bloomberg had just posted the dashcam clip of Kalanick's row with Kamal. Kalanick watched it with two executives. As reported in Bloomberg Businessweek:

> *As the clip ended, the three stood in stunned silence. Kalanick seemed to understand that his behavior required some form of contrition. According to a person who was there, he literally got down on his hands and knees and began squirming on the floor. 'This is bad,' he muttered. 'I'm terrible.' Then, contrition period over, he got up, called a board member, demanded a new PR strategy and embarked on a yearlong starring role as the villain who gets his comeuppance in the most gripping startup drama since the dot-com bubble.*

Ultimately, not even Uber's biggest VC could stomach his antics, and Kalanick was forced out.

---

[20]Eric Newcomer, Brad Stone, "The Fall of Travis Kalanick Was a Lot Weirder and Darker Than You Thought," Bloomberg Businessweek, January 18, 2018, https://www.bloomberg .com/news/features/2018-01-18/the-fall-of-travis-kalanick-was-a-lot-weirder-and-darker-than-you-thought

PATHOLOGICAL LYING

Now I must tread carefully with this next trait, so rather than "pathological lying," let me instead say that certain individuals in tech have an "economical" relationship with the truth and are prone to "distorting reality." Indeed, Steve Jobs himself became associated with the phrase "reality distortion field." According to a former colleague,[21] a manager in the Mac project named Bud Tribble claimed, back in 1981, "Steve has a reality distortion field.... In his presence, reality is malleable. He can convince anyone of practically anything." Jobs wasn't the only tech leader to persuade people to believe he was a prophet even when he was wrong. Theranos CEO Elizabeth Holmes convinced many (including veteran investors and politicians) of her "messianic vision" to defy reality with her "miracle" blood-testing kit.[22]

Most of us who work in the industry, or read media coverage about it, are sick of words like "revolutionize" or "innovative" or indeed the mother of all tech world clichés: "disruption," commonly used in relation to a new startup's (often workaday) product or service. Sure PR, by its very nature, has its own particular phraseology, but in relation to technology, the overuse of such words—alongside sometimes grotesquely exaggerated claims and the Valley's fake-it-'til-you-make-it culture[23]—essentially distorts reality. In addition, founders, especially in the early days of a new company, frequently make outlandish and grandiose claims for their startup's mission, or misrepresent their progress. Just think of Magic Leap, a secretive, Florida-based company promising to revolutionize the personal use of augmented "mixed" reality. Unlike virtual reality, in which everything is experienced inside a headset, mixed reality makes the animation appear in front of you while you are still seeing the rest of the world around you. One of the most hyped tech firms of the past several years, the company has attracted investment of more than $2.5 billion for a product that has yet to be released despite years of development and tantalizing promises and demonstrations from the company.[24]

As it turns out, some of those demonstrations were, essentially, faked. Former employees, according to a report by The Information, say videos showing various

[21] Andy Hertzfeld, "Reality distortion field," Folklore.org, February 1981, https://www .folklore.org/StoryView.py?story=Reality_Distortion_Field.txt
[22] Douglas Heaven, "Elizabeth Holmes: The hypnotic tale of the rise and fall of Theranos," *New Scientist,* March 21, 2019, https://www.newscientist.com/article/2197299-elizabeth-holmes-the-hypnotic-tale-of-the-rise-and-fall-of-theranos/
[23] Erin Griffith, "Theranos and Silicon Valley's 'Fake It Till You Make It' Culture," *Wired,* March 14, 2018, https://www.wired.com/story/theranos-and-silicon-valleys-fake-it-till-you-make-it-culture/
[24] Alex Heath, "Magic Leap Raises $350 Million, Withdraws Layoff Notices," The Information, May 21, 2020, https://www.theinformation.com/briefings/8879ae

capabilities in action were actually produced by third-party special effects companies without using Magic Leap products.[25]

A LACK OF REMORSE OR GUILT AND A FAILURE TO ACCEPT RESPONSIBILITY FOR ONE'S OWN ACTIONS

As founders push their companies through uncharted territory at a furious pace, naturally enough mistakes are made, some with serious consequences. And whether or not these are honest mistakes (the type we all make from time to time) or the intentional variety (because sometimes in tech, the end justifies the means), what strikes me is how few genuinely heartfelt apologies I've actually heard over the years. I've witnessed long, rambling explanations of what happened, half-hearted apologies that were carefully rehearsed by a PR team, accompanied by a vague list of solutions. But I can count on one hand the times I've heard a tech leader say something like "I'm so sorry. We screwed up. Badly. We really need to do better. Here are the steps we're going to take next. And we'll keep you updated on progress." One recent occasion that springs to mind was Zoom's CEO apologizing for recent security problems.[26] Another was back in 2016, when Airbnb CEO Brian Chesky apologized for racial discrimination on his platform.[27] ("I take responsibility for any pain or frustration this has caused members of our community. We will not only make this right; we will work to set an example that other companies can follow.")

But woeful, insipid, insincere apologies? Our cup overfloweth. To name just a couple of classics of the genre: YouTube boss Susan Wojcicki's non-apology to the LBGTQ community after the company failed to take decisive action over homophobic harassment on the platform ("I know that the decision we made was very hurtful to the LGBTQ community and that wasn't our intention at all.").[28] Or Mark Zuckerberg's statement after Facebook's unprecedented $5 billion fine, announced by the FTC in July 2019 following years of highly damaging revelations about the social media giant's privacy practices, including the exposure of up to 87 million

---

[25]Reed Albergotti, "The reality behind Magic Leap," December 8, 2016, The Information, https://www.theinformation.com/articles/the-reality-behind-magic-leap

[26]Russell Brandom, "Zoom CEO apologizes for security problems on public live stream," April 8, 2020, The Verge, https://www.theverge.com/2020/4/8/21213847/zoom-ceo-security-privacy-apology-fix-china-videoconference

[27]Brentin Mock, "As Black Travelers Turn Away, Airbnb Creates New Anti-Bias Policies," CityLab, September 8, 2016, https://www.citylab.com/equity/2016/09/as-black-travelers-turn-away-airbnb-creates-new-anti-bias-policies/499169/

[28]Julia Alexander, "YouTube CEO apologizes to LGBTQ community after outcry," The Verge, July 10, 2019, https://www.theverge.com/2019/6/10/18660473/youtube-lgbtq-susan-wojcicki-carlos-maza-steven-crowder

users' information in the Cambridge Analytica scandal.[29] ("We've agreed to pay a historic fine, but even more important, we're going to make some major structural changes to how we build products and run this company. We have a responsibility to protect people's privacy. We already work hard to live up to this responsibility, but now we're going to set a completely new standard for our industry.") Absent from both remarks: the word "sorry."

Sometimes, tech and other industry executives are instructed by their lawyers to not apologize for fear that it might be construed as admissions of guilt in the event of lawsuits. Unfortunately, these same executives often studiously avoid asking their lawyers for advice on other potential improprieties before it happens.

CALLOUSNESS AND LACK OF EMPATHY

Once again, there are rich pickings to be had. Take former Google CEO (and current Alphabet technical advisor) Eric Schmidt's spine-chilling dismissal of concerns over user privacy—words that have grown no less shocking over time. "If you have something that you don't want anyone to know, maybe you shouldn't be doing it in the first place," he told CNBC in 2009.[30] "But if you really need that kind of privacy, the reality is that search engines including Google do retain this information for some time. . . . And . . . we are all subject, in the United States, to the Patriot Act. It is possible that that information could be made available to the authorities."

Meanwhile, when it comes to Jeff Bezos, you can take your pick from gems including (after an engineer's presentation): "Why are you wasting my life?" And "I'm sorry, did I take my stupid pills today?" And let's not forget this one: "Do I need to go down and get the certificate that says I'm CEO of the company to get you to stop challenging me on this?"[31]

The social media giants routinely exhibit these traits, tolerating torrents of cruelty, trolling, and extremism. I have already covered myriad examples of Big Tech's callousness and lack of empathy toward some of society's most vulnerable. Although many CEOs and founders cling to the tired mantra that they are ultimately trying to make the world a better place—and most unicorn workers genuinely believe that—the dark side of growth at all costs is that it exacts a human toll. It frequently

---

[29]Cecilia Kang, "Facebook Says Cambridge Analytica Harvested Data of Up to 87 Million Users," *New York Times,* April 4, 2018, https://www.nytimes.com/2018/04/04/technology/mark-zuckerberg-testify-congress.html

[30]CNN, "Google CEO Eric Schmidt on privacy," YouTube, December 8, 2009, https://www.youtube.com/watch?v=Rpfa4sH4Dpk

[31]Joan E. Solsman, "'Why are you wasting my life?' And other Jeff Bezos gems," October 10, 2013, CNET, https://www.cnet.com/news/why-are-you-wasting-my-life-and-other-jeff-bezos-gems/

disregards those flesh-and-blood humans who might be disrupted, victimized, or displaced.

JUVENILE DELINQUENCY

High-growth tech giants, on a trajectory from startup to some of the biggest corporations in history in the matter of a couple of decades (or less), have undoubtedly and unavoidably committed acts of "juvenile delinquency" along the way. A singular and narrow focus on upending entire industries often leads young companies—and their founders/leadership, who are often quite young—to develop a low bar for tolerating aggressive behavior. Who could forget the senior Uber executive, for example, who came up with the idea that the company should splash a million dollars on hiring a team of opposition researchers and journalists to dig up dirt on its media critics to give them "a taste of their own medicine."[32]

In its early days, Uber fell afoul of regulators, and faced a criminal probe over its use of software that allegedly helped drivers evade local regulators.[33] As Laurence Dodds elegantly phrased in *The Telegraph,* "Those are the actions of a company ardent to establish market presence before it can be dislodged; less feudal knight, more Mongolian horse archer."[34] Over the past few years (and pre-COVID-19), venture-backed e-scooter companies like Bird and Lime have clogged city streets and endangered and injured pedestrians in pursuit of first-mover advantage in a cutthroat and quickly saturated marketplace.[35]

Meanwhile, the approach of the tech giants—with their huge cash positions and market caps—to any potential competitor is often one of "Sell to us, or we'll crush you." Some might call that old-fashioned extortion. In 2009, for example, Amazon sent a senior executive to speak with the leadership at Quidsi, the parent of online retailer Diapers.com. Amazon, Quidsi was told, was going to get into the diaper selling business and "suggested" that the company think of selling itself to

---

[32]Ben Smith, "Uber executive suggests digging up dirt on journalists," BuzzFeed, November 17, 2014, https://www.buzzfeednews.com/article/bensmith/uber-executive-suggests-digging-up-dirt-on-journalists

[33]Mike Isaac, "Justice Department expands its inquiry into Uber's Greyball tool," *New York Times,* May 5, 2017, https://www.nytimes.com/2017/05/05/technology/uber-greyball-investigation-expands.html

[34]Laurence Dodds, "Rivals see opportunity in Uber's London troubles," *The Telegraph,* November 27, 2019, https://mytonyst.blogspot.com/2020/02/londons-taxi-hailing-game-of-thrones.html

[35]Rachel Becker, "Scooter injuries are a thing, and they're sending people to the ER," The Verge, January 25, 2019, https://www.theverge.com/2019/1/25/18197523/scooter-injuries-bird-lime-la-california-emergency-room-concussion-helmet

the retailing giant. Quidsi demurred, at which point, according to *Businessweek,*[36] "Quidsi noticed Amazon dropping prices up to 30 percent on diapers and other baby products. As an experiment, Quidsi executives manipulated their prices and then watched as Amazon's website changed its prices accordingly. Amazon's pricing bots—software that carefully monitors other companies' prices and adjusts Amazon's to match—were tracking Diapers.com."

Quidsi saw its revenues plummet, and also calculated that Amazon would also have to be losing money in the price war, to the tune of more than $100 million. But Amazon could afford it. Soon, Quidsi entered into talks to sell Diapers.com to Walmart, which incensed Amazon further.

"When Bezos's lieutenants learned of Wal-Mart's counterbid, they ratcheted up the pressure, telling the Quidsi founders that [Bezos] was such a furious competitor that he would drive diaper prices to zero if they sold to Bentonville," according to Bloomberg journalist Brad Stone's book about Amazon, *The Everything Store.* "The Quidsi board convened to discuss the possibility of letting the Amazon deal expire and then resuming negotiations with Wal-Mart. But by then, Bezos's Khrushchev-like willingness to use the thermonuclear option had had its intended effect. The Quidsi executives stuck with Amazon, largely out of fear. The deal was announced Nov. 8, 2010."

***

Of the remaining traits among the Hare Psychopathy Checklist of 20, it isn't hard to find examples of the conduct of celebrated Big Tech founders and/or the companies they shape among the following: glib and superficial charm, constant need for stimulation, cunning and manipulative, parasitic lifestyle, sexual promiscuity, early behavior problems, lack of realistic long term goals, impulsivity, irresponsibility, and criminal versatility. Only the legalistic "revocation of conditional release," which specifically reflects the use of the test in the judicial system, draws a blank. Otherwise, the checklist suggests,[37] somewhat chillingly, that tech is indeed rife with psychopathy, which surely explains much about the fallout I have catalogued so far in these pages.

---

[36]Will Oremus, "The Time Jeff Bezos Went Thermonuclear on Diapers.com," Slate, October 10, 2013, https://slate.com/technology/2013/10/amazon-book-how-jeff-bezos-went-thermonuclear-on-diapers-com.html

[37]*Psychology Today*, Psychopathy, https://www.psychologytoday.com/gb/basics/psychopathy

CHAPTER 8

Between Scylla and Charybdis: What Happens If We Do Nothing

Before I start exploring solutions, and what all stakeholders, including each of us, can do to address the crisis, I want to take a moment to consider what will happen if nothing changes and current trends in tech continue. What will our lives—and the world around us—look like ten years from now, if convenience and, yes, our collective apathy mean the issues I've described so far aren't confronted and fixed?

I've heard people in the tech industry, and beyond, claim that there's nothing we can do, that "privacy is already dead," that the situation won't ever deteriorate to the doomsday scenario envisioned by some commentators, and, anyway, government "meddling" never works and it's surely best to allow Big Tech to course-correct and heal itself. To them, I reply that given the copious evidence we have from the past decade, and the last five years in particular, if we think things are bad today, just wait. . . .

In his seminal book *Amusing Ourselves to Death* (1985), the late academic Neil Postman wrote about the George Orwell versus Aldous Huxley versions of the future.[1] Postman—and I'm paraphrasing here—argued that while Americans were congratulating themselves that Orwell's grim vision of the future, as depicted in his dystopian classic *1984*, didn't come to pass, and that "the roots of liberal democracy held," we had forgotten the other "slightly less well known, equally chilling" version: Aldous Huxley's *Brave New World*.

---

[1] Neil Postman, *Amusing Ourselves to Death* (Penguin Books, 1985), https://quote.ucsd.edu/childhood/files/2013/05/postman-amusing.pdf

Huxley and Orwell, wrote Postman, did not predict the same future. "Orwell warns that we will be overcome by an externally imposed oppression. But in Huxley's vision, no Big Brother is required to deprive people of their autonomy, maturity, and history. As he saw it, people will come to love their oppression, to adore the technologies that undo their capacities to think," As Postman explained:

What Orwell feared were those who would ban books. What Huxley feared was that there would be no reason to ban a book, for there would be no one who wanted to read one. Orwell feared those who would deprive us of information. Huxley feared those who would give us so much that we would be reduced to passivity and egotism. Orwell feared that the truth would be concealed from us. Huxley feared the truth would be drowned in a sea of irrelevance. Orwell feared we would become a captive culture. Huxley feared we would become a trivial culture, preoccupied with some equivalent of the feelies, the orgy porgy, and the centrifugal bumblepuppy. As Huxley remarked in Brave New World Revisited, the civil libertarians and rationalists who are ever on the alert to oppose tyranny 'failed to take into account man's almost infinite appetite for distractions.' In 1984, Orwell added, people are controlled by inflicting pain. In Brave New World, they are controlled by inflicting pleasure.

I am not the first person to see clear parallels between these versions of the future and our current tech-fueled predicament. Yet I believe it is becoming ever clearer that if we do not act quickly and decisively to curb Big Tech's excesses, one of these two entirely plausible yet increasingly convergent scenarios might play out.

THE ORWELL SCENARIO

In the first, authoritarian vision—and we are already some way along this road—Big Tech, by chipping away at the public discourse, amplifying "alternative truths" and disinformation, as well as undermining our public institutions and increasing inequalities, helps to open the door to a new generation of populist and authoritarian leaders. Once these new leaders are in power, they use technology to strengthen and expand their authority. They start to whip up discontented citizens by stigmatizing immigration, vilifying opponents—including the free press—ignoring convention, trampling over legal precedent, nationalizing businesses (if they're left-wing populists), and expanding surveillance. Tech companies, which earn considerable business from government contracts, become de facto partners, releasing private data, creating back doors with which to spy on citizens, and monitoring communications "in the public interest."

The revelation in August 2019 that Ring, the smart doorbell-camera company owned by Amazon, had developed video-sharing partnerships with more than

400 police forces across America, is one early example. As the *Washington Post* reported:[2] "The partnerships let police request the video recorded by homeowners' cameras within a specific time and area, helping officers see footage from the company's millions of Internet-connected cameras installed nationwide." Although it's opt-in—homeowners can decline access—and officers do not get ongoing or live access to the video feeds, the sheer scale and growth of the project, which only began in spring 2018, and has since soared to more than 500 partnerships with law enforcement,[3] set off alarm bells among privacy campaigners and civil liberties groups, who view them as ad hoc surveillance networks.

Over 30 civil rights groups published a joint letter[4] in the wake of the *Post*'s revelations, arguing that the program had the effect of turning "police officers into salespeople for Amazon." The letter continued: "Amazon provides officers with talking points to promote their technology and products to residents,[5] and requests departments market the products at city events.... In some municipalities taxpayer money has been used to subsidize Amazon surveillance products for residents' use.[6] On the back end, Amazon carefully scripts everything that authorities say about the program,[7] and coaches police on the best talking points to get customers to hand over their footage."

Ring is of course far from the only tech company to forge close links with U.S. law enforcement and share critical information with the authorities. The role Big

---

[2]Drew Harwell, "Doorbell-camera firm Ring has partnered with 400 police forces, extending surveillance concerns," *Washington Post*, August 28, 2019, https://www.washingtonpost.com/technology/2019/08/28/doorbell-camera-firm-ring-has-partnered-with-police-forces-extending-surveillance-reach/

[3]Active Agency Map, https://www.google.com/maps/d/u/0/viewer?mid=1eYVDPh5itXq5acDT9b0BVeQwmESBa4cB&ll=36.19459170250789%2C-103.96982876449249&z=4

[4]Fight for the Future, "Open letter calling on elected officials to stop Amazon's doorbell surveillance partnerships with police," October 7, 2019, https://www.fightforthefuture.org/news/2019-10-07-open-letter-calling-on-elected-officials-to-stop/

[5]Caroline Haskins, "Amazon Is Coaching Cops on How to Obtain Surveillance Footage Without a Warrant," Vice Motherboard, August 5, 2019, https://www.vice.com/en_us/article/43kga3/amazon-is-coaching-cops-on-how-to-obtain-surveillance-footage-without-a-warrant

[6]Caroline Haskins, "US Cities Are Helping People Buy Amazon Surveillance Cameras Using Taxpayer Money," Vice Motherboard, August 2, 2019, https://www.vice.com/en_us/article/d3ag37/us-cities-are-helping-people-buy-amazon-surveillance-cameras-using-taxpayer-money

[7]Caroline Haskins, "Revealed: The Secret Scripts Amazon Gives to Cops to Promote Ring Surveillance Cameras," Vice Motherboard, August 6, 2019, https://www.vice.com/en_us/article/wjwea4/revealed-the-secret-scripts-amazon-give-to-cops-to-promote-ring-surveillance-cameras

Data analytics firm Palantir has played in Immigration and Customs Enforcement (ICE) operations has proved highly controversial.[8] Its FALCON Tipline software was recently used in what's been described as the decade's largest immigration raid, when 680 people were arrested by ICE agents who blitzed Mississippi workplaces. "The raids led to the arrest, prosecution, and deportation of hundreds of workers, separating them from their families, and terrorizing the immigrant community at large," according to grassroots Latinx activist group Mijente.[9]

Once society sets off down the slippery slope of gathering data on its citizens, it becomes far from a stretch to envisage the gradual phasing in of an industrial-scale surveillance system similar to China's social credit system,[10] where citizens are routinely monitored, "good behavior" is rewarded, and "'bad" can lead to blacklisting, which means people are, for example, denied credit or access to high-speed train tickets.

Yet this form of algorithmic surveillance has far deeper ramifications. It is widely believed that the Chinese government's ultimate goal is to actively change and remold its citizens' behavior. One way it is doing this is via an app known as "[President] Xi Study Strong Nation," through which the Communist Party of China "can assert its ideological and intellectual authority over Party members and employees of Party-run institutions, including schools and media," reported the China Media Project[11] in 2019. This isn't about old-school Party messaging, but rather the app "commands engagement" through awarding "Xi Study Points": "Once engagement with the app is enforced by administrative demands that it be installed and used, something that is already happening, the messages of the Party become inescapable.

"The platform has been designed with a built-in 'Xi Study Points' system that allows users to accumulate points on the basis of habitual use of the platform, from reading and viewing of content to the posting of comments and other forms of engagement. It has been widely promoted by local governments and ministries and departments across China, and *there have also been reports that some work units*

---

[8]Edward Ongweso Jr., "Activists Explain How Palantir's Tech Is Used in ICE Raids." Vice Motherboard, October 15, 2019, https://www.vice.com/en_us/article/9kegq8/activists-explain-how-palantirs-tech-is-used-in-ice-raids

[9]Mijente, "Breaking: Palantir's technology used in Mississippi raids where 680 were arrested," October 4, 2019, https://mijente.net/2019/10/palantirpowersraids/

[10]Alexandra Ma, "China has started ranking citizens with a creepy 'social credit' system—here's what you can do wrong, and the embarrassing, demeaning ways they can punish you," Business Insider, October 29, 2018, https://www.businessinsider.com/china-social-credit-system-punishments-and-rewards-explained-2018-4

[11]David Bandurski, "The dawn of the little red phone," China Media Project, February 13, 2019, http://chinamediaproject.org/2019/02/13/the-dawn-of-the-little-red-phone/

have ordered employees to attain specified point levels, with disciplinary measures to be imposed for those who fail to comply."

Not only is individual behavior thus being manipulated, but scores will also depend on a person's social network—the friends, family members, and associates with whom they spend their time, and what opinions they hold. However it is presented by the Chinese government, this amounts to a truly Orwellian nightmare: a digital version of the isolation of dissidents from their friends and family as practiced by the ugliest and most autocratic regimes of the past. In the not-so-distant future, this points-based system could even make it possible for the state to decide who should marry whom, and who is allowed to have children. Ultimately, through "selective breeding," it could gradually erase critical and independent thinking from its population.

Anyone who thinks the West currently lacks the infrastructure or willingness to deploy, say, Big Tech–created facial recognition technology under, perhaps, a future populist or authoritarian leader, unseen and almost overnight, should consider how widely we are already being monitored, particularly in the centers of Western power. Statistics uncovered by the Brookings Institution in 2017 found that although Beijing has a total of 470,000 CCTV cameras monitoring its citizens, ahead of London (with 420,000) and third-placed Washington D.C. (with just 30,000), when calculated as CCTV-cameras-per-1,000-people, London (with 48.4 per 1,000) and Washington (with 44.6) have proportionately far more than the Chinese capital (which has 21.9).[12] The numbers have likely gone way up since then.

Meanwhile, the speed at which some governments tried to introduce mass surveillance techniques at the height of the COVID-19 pandemic to limit the spread of the disease should also give us pause for thought. While China was fastest out of the blocks—by monitoring citizens' smartphones, deploying its hundreds of millions of FRT-enabled cameras and checking body temperatures in every public building, it was able to track the virus's spread—it was no outlier. In Israel, the government took the unprecedented step of empowering the nation's domestic intelligence agency to track coronavirus patients, while South Korea used mobile phone data for contact tracing, Taiwan used it for quarantine enforcement, and at the time of writing Reuters reported[13] on "a German-led effort . . . to rally other European countries behind a technology platform that could support contact tracing apps across the 27-member EU."

---

[12]Darrell M. West, "Benefits and Best Practices of Safe City Innovation," Center for Technology Innovation at Brookings, https://www.brookings.edu/wp-content/uploads/2017/10/safe-city-innovation_final.pdf

[13]Paresh Dave, "Explainer: How smartphone apps can help 'contact trace' the new coronavirus," Reuters, April 14, 2020, https://www.reuters.com/article/us-health-coronavirus-tracing-apps-expla/explainer-how-smartphone-apps-can-help-contact-trace-the-new-coronavirus-idUSKCN21W2I8

The author Yuval Noah Harari, writing in the *Financial Times*,[14] pointed out that the decisions taken by people and governments in the early weeks of the pandemic will probably shape the world for years to come. "We must act quickly and decisively. We should also take into account the long-term consequences of our actions. When choosing between alternatives, we should ask ourselves not only how to overcome the immediate threat, but also what kind of world we will inhabit once the storm passes."

THE HUXLEY SCENARIO

In *Brave New World,* Aldous Huxley paints a nightmarish genetically engineered future society where life is pain-free but essentially trivial and meaningless. The world Huxley envisioned has one goal: technological progress ("Progress is lovely"). Family and love don't matter. The economy, tech innovation, and growth do. Consumerism and productivism are the life's goal of every citizen. The parallels with Big Tech's world of venture-fueled innovation and growth-at-all-costs are striking. I'll cite three examples. First, Huxley's world is made up of a caste system, and at the bottom of the heap are "Epsilons," serf-workers who are conditioned to be satisfied with their meager lot in life. As described in chapter 4, it doesn't take a huge leap of imagination to think of gig economy workers, who are stuck in a precarious world, while being told that they should be happy to scratch a "flexible" living.

Second, in Huxley's depiction of a society controlled by a centralized power thanks to "man's almost infinite appetite for distraction," in many ways we have a precursor to Big Tech's attention economy, which hijacks people's minds and preys on our willingness to be perpetually entertained. Then there's the author's imagined world where liberty or individuality are expendable, and commercial companies are in the ascendant. While this is admittedly more of a stretch, the announcement at the time of writing that Google and Apple are teaming up to support contact tracing of COVID-19 carriers for governments around the world is an example of how immensely powerful tech companies are. While they should be commended for their contribution to pandemic management and for ensuring their technology cannot be abused for mass surveillance, it is surely telling that the two tech giants felt they could openly dictate terms to elected governments by setting limits on the information they make available to the authorities on what is, after all, a population health emergency.[15]

---

[14]Yuval Noah Harari, "The world after coronavirus," *Financial Times,* March 20, 2020, https://www.ft.com/content/19d90308-6858-11ea-a3c9-1fe6fedcca75
[15]Alex Hern, "NHS in standoff with Apple and Google over coronavirus tracing," *The Guardian*, April 16, 2020, https://www.theguardian.com/technology/2020/apr/16/nhs-in-standoff-with-apple-and-google-over-coronavirus-tracing

In other areas, as disparate as education, personal health, and a free and viable press, Big Tech's influence on society is more difficult to see but encroaches ever further onto what most would consider government terrain. While the tech giants' investment in education and health has been broadly welcomed—being able to use Google's AI capabilities in diagnostics is particularly helpful—let's not fool ourselves that there aren't costs too around privacy and freedom of choice.

Take Google's involvement in America's—and increasingly the world's—public education system. Today, Google's G Suite for Education is used by 80 million educators and students globally, while the company's low-cost Chromebooks are used by 30 million, and Google Classroom has over 40 million users worldwide,[16] meaning that the tech giant has an outsized influence on a critical public provision and in effect "owns" the data of tens of millions of kids. "Google has established itself as a fact in schools," Hal Friedlander, former chief information officer at New York City Department of Education, and now co-founder or the Technology for Education consortium, told the *New York Times*.[17] In embracing the full gamut of Google apps, children are acquiring the Google habit in their formative years.

Google and other giants have been making deep inroads into the most intimate parts of our lives too: our health. In November 2019, the *Wall Street Journal* landed a hot scoop when it revealed that Google was harvesting personal health data from one of America's largest healthcare systems, involving the information from millions of people across 21 states.[18] Code-named Project Nightingale, the initiative as described by the *Journal* is "the biggest effort yet by a Silicon Valley giant to gain a toehold in the health-care industry," noting that Amazon, Apple, and Microsoft were also "aggressively pushing into healthcare." Nightingale had begun under the radar in 2018 with St. Louis–based Ascension—a Catholic hospital chain consisting of 2,600 hospitals, doctors' surgeries, and other facilities. "The data involved in the initiative encompasses lab results, doctor diagnoses, and hospitalization records, among other categories, and amounts to a complete health history, including patient names and dates of birth," reported the *Journal*. While permissible under federal law, the situation raised ethical questions because neither patients nor doctors had reportedly been notified at the time the story was published.

---

[16]John Vamvakitis, "Around the world and back with Google for Education," Google, The Keyword, January 22, 2019, https://www.blog.google/outreach-initiatives/education/around-the-world-and-back/

[17]Natasha Singer, "Education disrupted: How Google Took Over the Classroom," *New York Times,* May 13, 2017, https://www.nytimes.com/2017/05/13/technology/google-education-chromebooks-schools.html

[18]Rob Copeland, "Google's 'Project Nightingale' Gathers Personal Health Data on Millions of Americans," *Wall Street Journal,* November 11, 2019, https://www.wsj.com/articles/google-s-secret-project-nightingale-gathers-personal-health-data-on-millions-of-americans-11573496790

Google responded with a "nothing-to-see-here" blog post,[19] stating that its "partnership with Ascension" was simply "a business arrangement to help a provider with the latest technology, similar to the work [it does] with dozens of other healthcare providers." The post went on to emphasize, "These organizations, like Ascension, use Google to securely manage their patient data, under strict privacy and security standards. They are the stewards of the data, and we provide services on their behalf." Ascension's data, Google insisted, "cannot and will not be combined with any Google consumer data."

Given Google's somewhat sketchy track record on data privacy—including the recent revelation that Alphabet-owned YouTube had agreed to pay a record $170 million in fines for allegedly collecting kids' personal information without parental consent[20]—it's unlikely that the tech giant's assurances will cut much ice.

In the end, Huxley feared that what we love will ruin us—and this second future scenario is based on the evidence that suggests he was on to something. In a data economy that monetizes human addiction, we have become complicit in our own fate: lambs to the slaughter, if you will. We have willingly traded in our privacy for the cheap buzz and dopamine hits of social media, our time for binge-watching video served up by streaming services and video and mobile games (it's telling that people are now seeking help from therapists for addiction to services like Netflix)[21] while, for convenience's sake, we've delegated our consumption—-and even some of our decision-making on what to buy next—to the likes of Amazon and Alibaba.

In this scenario, ten years from now, if the tech giants are not restrained and their power as data-monopolies becomes further entrenched, governments will find themselves increasingly sidelined and impotent. Reduced to mere gatekeepers, politicians and civil servants will likely retreat behind algorithmic government, with laws shaped by data and machine learning, with all its inherent biases and imperfections, and public services gradually surrendered to private businesses. Indeed, we should expect just about every area of human existence, currently managed by government, to be dominated by Big Tech and its outriders: from the future of finance (just about everyone), to healthcare (Google), and from low-cost

---

[19]Tariq Shaukat, "Our partnership with Ascension," Inside Google Cloud, November 11, 2019, https://cloud.google.com/blog/topics/inside-google-cloud/our-partnership-with-ascension

[20]FTC press release, "Google and YouTube will pay record $170 million for alleged violations of Children's Privacy Law," September 4, 2019, https://www.ftc.gov/news-events/press-releases/2019/09/google-youtube-will-pay-record-170-million-alleged-violations

[21]Bill Gardner, "Three people treated for 'binge watching' addiction to TV in first cases of their kind in Britain," *The Telegraph,* January 6, 2020, https://www.telegraph.co.uk/news/2020/01/06/binge-watching-tv-addicts-treated-harley-street-therapists-first/

housing (Apple, Google) to education (Google, again) and autonomous vehicles (Tesla, Alphabet, Amazon, Apple, etc.).[22]

For a glimpse of the way Big Tech barons view these limitless horizons, look no further than Mark Zuckerberg's "Building Global Community," a wordy 2017 blog post[23] with Huxleyan implications, which argues that "progress now requires humanity coming together not just as cities or nations, but also as a global community"—powered by (who'd have guessed it!) Facebook. He goes on to imply that the platform doesn't just want to be part of an environment; it wants to be *the* environment: a virtual alternative to government. "I am reminded of my favorite saying about technology," he declared. "'We always overestimate what we can do in two years, and we underestimate what we can do in ten years.' We may not have the power to create the world we want immediately, but we can all start working on the long term today. In times like these, the most important thing we at Facebook can do is develop the social infrastructure to give people the power to build a global community that works for all of us."

Alphabet's Sidewalk Labs had similarly outsized ambitions. In June 2019, the smart city subsidiary unveiled a 1,524-page master plan to convert 12 acres of Toronto's valuable waterfront into a high-tech city-within-a-city. According to The Verge, the project "represents Alphabet's first, high-stakes effort to realize [Google co-founder and former Alphabet CEO] Larry Page's long-held dream to experiment with innovations like self-driving cars, public Wi-Fi, new health care delivery solutions, and other city planning advances that modern technology makes possible."[24]

However, the project also stirred up deep-rooted concerns about Big Tech overreach and data harvesting, sometimes branded "data-extractivism"—the collection and conversion of data about all inhabitants—including from high-profile tech figures. Jim Balsillie, cofounder of BlackBerry developer Research in Motion, branded it "a colonizing experiment in surveillance capitalism attempting to bulldoze important urban, civic and political issues."[25] Meanwhile Roger McNamee, venture capitalist, early Facebook investor-turned-critic, and author of *Zucked:*

---

[22]CB Insights, "40+ Corporations Working On Autonomous Vehicles," March 4, 2020, https://www.cbinsights.com/research/autonomous-driverless-vehicles-corporations-list/.
[23]Mark Zuckerberg, "Building Global Community," Facebook Notes, February 16, 2017, https://www.facebook.com/notes/mark-zuckerberg/building-global-community/10154544292806634/
[24]Andrew J. Hawkins, "Alphabet's Sidewalk Labs unveils its high-tech 'city-with-a-city' plan Toronto," The Verge, June 24, 2019, https://www.theverge.com/2019/6/24/18715486/alphabet-sidewalk-labs-toronto-high-tech-city-within-a-city-plan
[25]https://www.tvo.org/transcript/2541401/jim-balsillie-dragging-canada-into-the-21st-century

Waking up to the Facebook Catastrophe, wrote a letter to the Toronto City Council in which he similarly described the project as "the most highly-evolved version to date of what Harvard professor Shoshana Zuboff calls 'surveillance capitalism.'...[Google's] goal is to replace democracy with algorithmic decision-making, believing the latter to be more efficient." He concluded, "It is a dystopian vision which has no place in a democratic society."[26] In the event, their worst fears will not be realized, at least on this occasion. At the time of writing, Sidewalk Labs had just walked away from the project, citing the economic fallout from the pandemic, despite having blown a reported $50 million to get to this point.[27]

***

Both these alternate futures (tyrannical in different ways) are not simply plausible; they are all-but-certain should Big Tech's ambitions remain unchecked. Worse, what we are currently experiencing is a combination of both the Orwell and Huxley visions of the future. "The Huxley dystopia is powering the Orwell dystopia," said campaigner Aza Raskin during his interview with me. "The two are converging, like two walls closing in from both sides."

Yet it's in our societies' power to decide to change this situation. I believe that we can act so that the past decade will one day come to be seen as an aberration rather than the norm. There is no inexorability to the tech giants' continual expansion of their powerbase. Tech is no force of nature. Toxicity is not inevitable. Tech is a human creation after all. Yet, much like the climate emergency, the window of opportunity is narrowing fast.

---

[26]https://twitter.com/sdbcraig/status/1136048737657204741
[27]Joshua Oliver, "Google parent abandons plan for Toronto smart city," *Financial Times,* May 7, 2020, https://www.ft.com/content/097867fb-6915-41d2-acc2-27fa3297e3f4

Two

Fixing the Chaos Factory

So far in *Trampled by Unicorns* I have been delving into the myriad malign effects of Big Tech on users and the wider world, as well as investigating some of the complex reasons that lie behind the turmoil. In Part II, I will offer solutions for each stakeholder, from industry players such as founders and CEOs, to investors, boards, and the public markets, to government and regulators, the media and private individuals. But first a few caveats.

None of these solutions is a universal remedy, nor will any of them work on their own. Most of them require further development before they're properly implemented—with Big Tech, the devil is forever in the details.

Some of my suggestions are already being discussed. It is my hope that by the time you read this, some of what I advocate, particularly in those areas where momentum already exists (e.g., tackling tax minimization), will have been implemented or will at least be well under way. That would be good news because there is little time to waste. COVID-19, which hit the world just as I was putting the finishing touches on this book, will also likely have a major impact on the tech industry's future and modus operandi; indeed, it already has.

It is important to note also that there are some leaders, across all industry stakeholders, working actively to put humans back at the heart of tech, by making decisions that are painful in the short term, yet will pay dividends further down the line for citizens and shareholders alike. Many of the unicorns are trying to address some of the issues I've raised. As well as unveiling its AI principles, Google, for example, convened an AI ethics board, too, even if the initiative did end up disintegrating in acrimony within a week.[1] In addition, the search giant cancelled its censorship-friendly Chinese search engine, known as Project Dragonfly,[2] after pressure from within and outside the company, and it has even quietly tweaked its algorithms to counter the problem of misinformation in the aftermath of mass shootings and similar atrocities. Of the other giants, Apple introduced "grayscale mode" on its devices—which drains all color from the screen—in part to combat smartphone addiction. According to the Center for Humane Technology, grayscale, which was first introduced with iOS8 in 2014[3] and is also available on Android devices, removes positive reinforcements: "Colorful icons give our brains shiny rewards every time we unlock. . . . [Grayscale] helps many people check their phone less."[4] Meanwhile, Facebook has expanded the role of moderators and offered more transparency with initiatives such as its "Community Standards Enforcement Report," and at the time of writing was testing the effect of hiding Facebook Likes, as well as making reactions, view counts, and Likes visible only to the post's author, in an attempt to wean users off the sugar rush this affirmation can bring.[5]

Along with other tech giants like Apple, Alphabet, and Twitter, Facebook has banned notorious far-right conspiracy theorist Alex Jones and other extreme figures.[6] In addition, Twitter announced that it would ban all political advertising.[7] It also started adding fact-checking verification notices and a "manipulated media" label to some of Donald Trump's tweets.[8] Facebook, while still refusing to take systematic steps in fighting misinformation, took down some Trump campaign

---

[1]Kelsey Piper, "Exclusive: Google cancels AI ethics board in response to outcry," Vox, April 4, 2019, https://www.vox.com/future-perfect/2019/4/4/18295933/google-cancels-ai-ethics-board

[2]BBC News, "Google's Project Dragonfly 'terminated' in China," July 17, 2019, https://www.bbc.co.uk/news/technology-49015516

[3]Mick Symons, "How to enable grayscale for visual accessibility on your iPhone or iPad," iMore, September 17, 2014, https://www.imore.com/how-enable-grayscale-visual-accessibility-your-iphone-or-ipad

[4]https://humanetech.com/resources/take-control/

[5]Corinne Reichert, "Facebook has begun hiding likes," CNET, September 30, 2019, https://www.cnet.com/news/facebook-has-begun-hiding-likes/

[6]Katie Paul, "Facebook bans Alex Jones, other extremist figures," Reuters, May 3, 2019, https://www.reuters.com/article/us-facebook-extremists-usa/facebook-bans-alex-jones-other-extremist-figures-idUSKCN1S82D7

[7]BBC News, "Twitter to ban all political advertising," October 31, 2019, https://www.bbc.co.uk/news/world-us-canada-50243306

[8]BBC News, "Twitter labels Trump tweet 'manipulated media' for the first time," June 19, 2020, https://www.bbc.com/news/technology-53106029

ads featuring a symbol used by the Nazis[9] and a campaign video with COVID-19 misinformation.[10] And after a threat to boycott social media in the UK, following the racist abuse of Manchester United and France footballer Paul Pogba and many other black players on Twitter, representatives of the microblogging platform said it would meet with football stars, clubs, and other stakeholders to explain what it was doing to address the issue.[11] (To date this courtesy has unfortunately not been extended to other less visible—and less media-friendly—victims of Twitter hate and harassment.)

While I don't believe that government regulation is any kind of cure-all (not least because of the time I spent in Russia, India, and China, where I saw first-hand the impact an omnipresent state has on a country, its population, and businesses), without an overhaul of some of our outdated laws, many of the problems I've described in these pages will not be addressed. Yet much of the heavy lifting still needs to be done by the industry itself, which is why I have kicked off Part II by exploring what needs to change within tech's emerald cities.

Finally, it's also perhaps worth taking a moment to remind ourselves why all this matters so very much. I still passionately believe that properly restructured, refocused, and regulated, the tech giants can be a force for good, for human progress and empathy for years to come. From Amazon to Zoom, just imagine what the pandemic would have been like without tech's contributions to humanity. Rather than the exception, there's no reason that couldn't become the rule.

---

[9]Taylor Hatmaker, "Facebook removes Trump campaign ads featuring Nazi symbol," TechCrunch, June 18, 2020, https://techcrunch.com/2020/06/18/facebook-trump-campaign-nazi-imagery-red-triangle/
[10]Kurt Wagner, "Facebook pulls Trump video for Covid misinformation on kids," Bloomberg, August 5, 2020, https://www.bloomberg.com/news/articles/2020-08-05/facebook-pulls-trump-video-for-covid-misinformation-on kids
[11]Jamie Jackson, "Manchester United and Kick It Out to meet Twitter after racism incidents," *The Guardian,* August 21, 2019, https://www.theguardian.com/football/2019/aug/21/kick-it-out-twitter-racial-abuse

CHAPTER 9

We Should All Be Chief Empathy Officer

When I left the Boston Consulting Group over a decade ago, I genuinely believed that you could solve any problem with the right Gantt chart clearly defining roles, responsibilities, key performance indicators (KPIs), and deadlines. That if something wasn't working, I just needed to work a little harder. That empathy and emotions were weaknesses and people just needed to toughen up a bit.

It took the kind yet relentless feedback of people I admired and who cared about me to change my mind. Not to mention many hours of executive coaching, quite a few heartless decisions on my side that had negative repercussions that I couldn't understand, and for my dad to be discarded like trash by the company to which he had given 18 years of his life. Eventually I was convinced that empathy had to be a baseline requirement for the companies I was leading if they were to succeed, both commercially and ethically. Or, as Daniel Lubetzky, the CEO of the snack company Kind put it:[1] "For me, empathy is an existential question—it's about the survival of the human race. That is, it's imperative for us to overcome the challenges we face. Unless we can join forces and recognize each other's humanity, how can we do business together, let alone make progress on the increasingly complex and difficult problems in society?"

There are plenty of books about how to cultivate empathy on a personal level. I have a lot of them at home, and they've been tremendously helpful. This chapter, or this book for that matter, is not about that. It's about how you create a successful, empathetic, human-focused *company* that marries technology and humanity.

---

[1] Ashoka, "Meet the CEO Who Is Championing Kindness and Whose Company Runs On It," *Forbes,* February 17, 2016, https://www.forbes.com/sites/ashoka/2016/02/17/meet-the-ceo-who-is-championing-kindness-and-whose-company-runs-on-it

It starts with the mission, vision, and values tech companies claim. Tellingly, none of the mission statements of Facebook, Amazon, Apple, Microsoft, Google, Uber, Airbnb—or most tech companies I know for that matter, either public or private—explicitly uses the word *human* or *humanity*. Microsoft comes close with its use of *person* in its (somewhat bland) strapline "to empower every person and every organization on the planet to achieve more."[2] Tech companies rarely stop congratulating themselves for being hyper-mission-focused and goal-oriented. While admittedly it would be more symbolic than practical, it would be an important step for them to include in their missions a constant reminder that, ultimately, they aspire to work for the benefit of humanity.

The next step is to implement and live these values with empathy, which is harder than it sounds. Most tech companies I know tend to be pretty good at "living by their values." But a value can be implemented with or without empathy. The same process can be designed to be human-centric or not. You can move fast (a core value of the tech world) and trample everything in your path. This will have long-term implications, both human and financial, from the way your customers perceive you, to your ignorance of costly minor execution details, employee turnover, or the way governments decide to regulate and fine you. Or you can move fast but just a little less fast in the short term as you think through the impact on people and the best ways to limit negative consequences. Speed at all costs, as with growth at all costs, is a far more expensive strategy in the long run. One complaint I often hear is that "too much" empathy stops you from making tough decisions and results in a tendency to put the well-being of individuals above that of the business. Yes, there is absolutely such a thing as overuse of empathy that leads to decision paralysis or getting your priorities plain wrong. But I have yet to meet a tech company whose problem is too much empathy. Silo mentality, decision process complexity, lack of clear goals, the inability to say no to projects—I've seen these problems more times than I can count. A surfeit of empathy? Not yet.

I think the people who make that argument tend to confuse "affective empathy" with the cognitive variety I'm advocating. Affective empathy implies sharing, almost physically, the feelings of other people. It makes it harder to share direct feedback (you don't want to hurt people's feelings) and make tough calls (you want to make everybody feel good about a decision). Cognitive empathy, on the other hand, helps you understand how other people feel and think, and as a result helps you adapt your decisions and behavior accordingly; it thus enables better-informed decision-making. As a leader, you should still act in the best interest of your business, but by understanding how your decisions affect other people, both positively and negatively, you're better able to act with clarity and decisiveness, with fewer negative side effects.

---

[2]https://www.microsoft.com/en-us/about/values

WHAT DOES AN EMPATHETIC COMPANY LOOK LIKE?

From a distance, highly empathetic companies act much the same as any other business, albeit with a slightly different spin. They tend to make psychological safety a priority, embrace diversity of thought, and encourage employees to "be themselves" at work, which also includes being unafraid to disagree with others (although that doesn't mean being combative). Respectful yet intense questioning to understand the other perspective is the rule. People then embrace meetings because they are places to be heard, where real issues are aired and debated.

That openness means there is less office politics, fewer silos between teams, and fewer bristling egos. Companywide communications tend to be more transparent, while HR and managers at all levels are invested in the success of employees. As people engage more with one another and are emboldened to express their disagreements, as they get creative and take risks, cross-pollination of ideas becomes common and complicated problems benefit from multiple and sometimes unexpected sources of expertise.

The empathy-led company believes that its long-term commercial success is intimately linked to the environment around it, whether that's the immediate community in which it operates, the country that provides infrastructure without which the business couldn't function, or ultimately the planet. It tends to be purpose-led and develop thorough sustainability programs and long-term plans. As a result, employees are highly engaged, and often excited to come to work. Involuntary turnover is almost nonexistent.

While no company is perfect, a few companies have been actively engaged on this corporate empathy path. Under Satya Nadella's leadership, Microsoft notably promotes empathy as a key source of business innovation and growth for employees, leading to a more productive and successful company. Another is SalesForce, where CEO Marc Benioff has been vocal about the responsibility of companies: "To my fellow business leaders and billionaires, I say that we can no longer wash our hands of our responsibility for what people do with our products. Yes, profits are important, but so is society. . . . It's time for a new capitalism—a more fair, equal and sustainable capitalism that actually works for everyone and where businesses, including tech companies, don't just take from society but truly give back and have a positive impact."[3] Those companies are big names, and there are numerous other startups with lower profiles but that are equally active.

What I find disconcerting is the quasi-absolute certitude I hear from most tech leaders I speak with that their companies are empathetic, leading them to roll their eyes when I raise many of these issues. And yet in each case, their employees have

---

[3] Marc Benioff, "We Need a New Capitalism," *New York Times,* October 14, 2019, https://www.nytimes.com/2019/10/14/opinion/benioff-salesforce-capitalism.html

a less rose-tinted view of the empathy level at their place of work. Businessolver, a benefit administration technology company that publishes an annual "State of Workplace Empathy" study,[4] explains that 92 percent of CEOs believe their organizations are empathetic, yet only a year earlier the same study had found that 92 percent of employees believed that empathy remained undervalued. And while 71 percent of men viewed organizations as a whole as empathetic, only 33 percent of women did.[5]

This gap between CEO's and employees' assessments of the empathy levels at the same companies is consistently so significant that it pushed me to work with a team of psychometric and organisational psychology experts to create my own measurement of corporate empathy as a foundation for more fact—based discussions. If you're interested, it is now available for free on my website (www.maellegavet.com).

So how then do you build an empathetic, human-focused company? While the answer to this question is quite complex and multifaceted, a lot of progress can be accomplished by focusing on two elements that matter most: people and decision-making processes.

1. PEOPLE

While every person in a company has an opportunity to increase the level of corporate empathy, three groups are particularly impactful: CEOs, HR teams (or People and Culture, as they are often called in tech), and employees as a whole.

"It All Starts and Ends with the CEO"

The tech world, probably more than any other industry, has developed deep veneration, bordering on cultlike worship, for founders and CEOs, often seen as visionary prophets guiding humanity toward a future that few can see. As such I shouldn't have been surprised when, talking to a famous VC about how to improve the culture of a well-known tech startup I was considering joining as COO that displayed a worrying lack of empathy toward their employees and the world around them, he told me, "It all starts and ends with the CEO. Whatever he does is the cultural norm."

Those words confirmed what I already knew: there was little I was going to be able to achieve if the CEO wasn't going to become an empathy champion (which led me to deciding not to join that company because I didn't believe that he would actually be able to change, despite his claims to the contrary).

---

[4]State of Workplace Empathy 2019, Businessolver, https://blog.businessolver.com/the-2019-state-of-workplace-empathy-study-the-competitive-edge-leaders-are-missing
[5]State of Workplace Empathy 2018, Businessolver, https://info.businessolver.com/hubfs/empathy-2018/businessolver-empathy-executive-summary.pdf

Since then I've thought a lot about what can be done to help CEOs become more empathetic other than the usual advice to "Listen more"—pointless as they invariably have so little time and so many people to listen to, and most of them are "momentum junkies" anyway. (What's more, most of them are as successful as they are because at some point they decided to ignore what people were telling them about all the reasons why their business would fail and just do what they believed needed to be done.)

It all starts with CEOs believing that they actually need to be more empathetic. Without this conviction, trying to make their companies more empathetic is a fruitless exercise in navel gazing. Beyond the usual list of bumper sticker mantras ("Be a better listener," "Be vulnerable," "Be more transparent," etc.) and leading by example, I believe that there are six actionable, high-impact things that CEOs can quickly put into action:

- Hire an executive coach focused on helping them develop their empathy skill. "I'm not a people person" is no longer an acceptable excuse. Get over it: you're the CEO.
- Make it a personal goal to hire and promote a critical mass of empathetic people, starting with their immediate teams.
- Ensure that performance is measured both on achieved results and on behavior. CEOs should ensure that top achievers who don't exhibit empathy despite repeated feedback and coaching are ultimately let go.
- Build empathy into core processes (see examples later in this chapter).
- Stop delegating empathy to other people, generally the COO or head of HR, and be on the frontline of difficult debates about trade-offs that the company inevitably needs to make and how they affect employees, customers, communities, and other stakeholders. Empathy starts with not just listening, but actually hearing other people's opinions and responding to them. One of the best ways to do that is for CEOs to answer all tough "people questions" during all hands meetings rather than assign them to somebody else in the leadership team.
- Launch an annual employee survey about the CEO's performance, including questions measuring his or her empathy and make the results public.

"The Toilet Paper Isn't Soft Enough": Employees Have a Responsibility Too

Many tech employees should take a long, hard look in the mirror too. Here's why:

First, most outsiders would be shocked by the sorts of topics I've heard raised at all-hands meetings I have attended as a senior executive or heard about from close colleagues and friends. Over the years I have heard questions and complaints—much like the senior engineer griping that the free gourmet food was making him fat—about snack supplies running low, how there needed to be a wider variety of free meals on offer, why the office was too small (I always wonder whether these individuals had ever spent time in non-tech company offices, such as call centers), whether they could bring their dog to meetings, and once even a plea for softer toilet paper. Each time a thought flashed through my mind: "Really? You look at the world around you and *this* is what you care about?"

I've also seen tech employees behave as if their venture-fueled company was awash with cash, and then claim to be shocked when the "mind-blowing parties" end, the money runs dry, and their employer needs to shed staff. Sure, that hedonistic devil-may-care culture seeps down from the top, but when you work for a loss-making startup, buoyed up by someone else's money, maybe you should at least pause to consider how financially sustainable your employer actually is.

I am not claiming that this attitude of entitlement exists among all employees—far from it. I include it simply to offer a flavor of what I encountered and remind readers that tech workers, particularly those at the most celebrated of the giants, often live a gilded, privileged life and shouldn't forget it. Moreover, founders didn't create the crisis in tech on their own. Instead, they were enabled not just by their boards and investors, but by their leadership teams, the people reporting to those executives, as well as those further down the chain of command. The products and services and their disastrous consequences I've described in the first half of this book were the work of many hands, hearts, and minds.

Indeed, we need more engineers and other employees standing up and raising concerns. Surely you cannot plead ignorance just because you aren't senior management, when you are designing and building tech tools that are ultimately taking advantage of human weaknesses and prioritizing financial reward while sowing chaos in their wake.

This is to say that employees shouldn't simply consider taking a stand on points of principle—for a healthy industry to flourish, it is incumbent upon them to actually do so and ideally do so early on, before major issues emerge. Nor should they tolerate unacceptable behavior, or be treated like subversives and agitators when what they are really doing is blowing the whistle. Some are already doing so.

In June 2018, *Gizmodo* landed a sizzling-hot scoop.[6] Anonymous sources at Google had tipped off a senior reporter at the science and technology blog that the Valley giant would not be renewing its contract with the U.S. Defense Department's Project Maven, once the existing deal had expired. Launched in 2017, Maven was described as a "fast-moving effort... to accelerate the department's integration of Big Data, artificial intelligence and machine learning into DoD programs."[7]

---

[6]Kate Conger, "Google Plans Not to Renew Its Contract for Project Maven, a Controversial Pentagon Drone AI Imaging Program," Gizmodo, June 1, 2018, https://gizmodo.com/google-plans-not-to-renew-its-contract-for-project-mave-1826488620
[7]Cheryl Pellerin, "Project Maven Industry Day Pursues Artificial Intelligence for DoD Challenges," DoD News, October 27, 2017, https://www.defense.gov/Explore/News/Article/Article/1356172/project-maven-industry-day-pursues-artificial-intelligence-for-dod-challenges/

Specifically, Google was providing AI tools to help analysts sift through the large volume of drone footage the DoD assembles daily.

The campaign group Tech Workers' Coalition, a diverse group of social justice warriors within the tech industry, hailed the decision in a somewhat breathless Medium post.[8] "During the last few months, we have seen unprecedented levels of unrest within the tech industry from fellow disgruntled workers who are opposed to technologies that their own companies are developing." The post went on to also cite Microsoft and Salesforce workers protesting against contracts with ICE and border patrol, and Amazon workers organizing against the development of (mostly facial recognition) tech for domestic policing and surveillance.

The question of the utilization of private technologies by governmental organizations is complex. I share the views of many Big Tech employees who don't want technology they helped build to be used to round up illegal immigrants, spy on fellow citizens, or kill people on the other side of the world. I also believe that a healthy collaboration between the private and public spheres, particularly in work for the military, is a critical part of ensuring a country's strength and safety. If the U.S. or European governments can't leverage American or European firms' technology, what are they expected to do? Give up as China accelerates? Use tax dollars to try to replicate their own? It is, in my opinion, naive to believe that the world would be a better place if the U.S. and Europe didn't benefit from cutting-edge innovation developed by companies on their own soil.

Independent of where you stand on this difficult question though, the fact remains that employee activism is a key driver of change inside Big Tech and critical to increase corporate empathy toward the human impact of technology's deployment. Employees need to require as much transparency as possible from their employer, make their voices heard around what they consider acceptable and not in terms of the use of the technologies they build, and then follow their conscience.

Unfortunately, the companies don't always like it. Kathryn Spiers, a security engineer at Google, certainly did that. She was one of five Google workers fired in the space of a few weeks for "intentional and often repeated violations of [our] longstanding data security policies."[9] "We spoke up when we saw Google making unethical business decisions that create a workplace that is harmful to us and our colleagues," wrote Laurence Berland, a senior site reliability engineer and 11-year

---

[8]RK Upadhya, "Tech workers against imperialism," Tech Workers Coalition, November 22, 2018, https://medium.com/tech-workers-coalition/tech-workers-against-imperialism-2d8024e461a7

[9]Julia Carrie Wong, "Fifth Google worker-activist fired in a month says company is targeting the vulnerable," *The Guardian*, December 17, 2019, https://www.theguardian.com/us-news/2019/dec/17/fifth-google-worker-activist-fired-in-a-month-says-company-is-targeting-the-vulnerable

Google veteran, Paul Duke, a software engineer with eight years on the clock, and Rebecca Rivers and Sophie Waldman, also software engineers with four years and almost two years at Google, respectively.[10]

They went on to list issues such as demanding Google improve its treatment of temporary, vendor, and contract workers, support unionizing colleagues, and challenge the protection of executives who sexually assault employees,[11] opposing its retaliation against employees[12] who have complained about or protested against mistreatment and discrimination, as well as strategic decisions like Google's work with Customs and Border Protection.[13]

"So we spoke up, and how did they respond? Google didn't respond by honoring its values, or abiding by the law. It responded like a large corporation more interested in revenue growth than in ensuring worker rights and ethical conduct. Last week, Google fired us for engaging in protected labor organizing."

Whatever the specifics of that particular case, Big Tech employees need to continue to make their voices heard. They are making some progresses with the causes they champion. On top of the examples previously mentioned, Google, eBay, Airbnb, and Facebook have also agreed to cease applying forced arbitration in cases of sexual misconduct.[14] More needs to be done.

"I Desperately Wanted Not to Have to Interact with HR Ever Again"

Finally, while HR can't be held solely accountable for ensuring that a company is as people-driven as it is performance-driven, that department has a critical role to play. The inconvenient truth, unfortunately, is that HR has broadly failed many employees and contributed to empathy taking a backseat in tech corporate culture.

When it comes to showcasing the failure of HR to hold managers, and indeed a wider culture to account, few have made bigger waves than Susan Fowler. In one of tech's milestone #MeToo moments, Fowler, then an engineer, blogged about Uber's cultural problems in February 2017 to devastating effect. In her post entitled

---

[10]https://medium.com/@GoogleWalkout/google-fired-us-for-organizing-were-fighting-back-d0daa8113aed

[11]https://medium.com/@GoogleWalkout/google-employees-and-contractors-participate-in-global-walkout-for-real-change-389c65517843

[12]https://medium.com/@GoogleWalkout/retaliation-at-google-3df5674bc725

[13]https://medium.com/@no.gcp.for.cbp/google-must-stand-against-human-rights-abuses-nogcpforcbp-88c60e1fc35e

[14]Kerri Anne Renzulli, "Workers at Google, Facebook, eBay and Airbnb can now sue over sexual harassment—here's what that means for employees," CNBC, November 19, 2018, https://www.cnbc.com/2018/11/19/google-facebook-airbnb-employees-can-now-sue-over-sexual-harassment.html

"Reflecting On One Very, Very Strange Year at Uber,[15] Fowler described, among other, things being sexually pestered by her line manager:

> *On my first official day rotating on the team, my new manager sent me a string of messages over company chat. He was in an open relationship, he said, and his girlfriend was having an easy time finding new partners but he wasn't. He was trying to stay out of trouble at work, he said, but he couldn't help getting in trouble, because he was looking for women to have sex with. It was clear that he was trying to get me to have sex with him, and it was so clearly out of line that I immediately took screenshots of these chat messages and reported him to HR.*

After describing how HR handled her situation, she wrote, "I desperately wanted to not have to interact with HR ever again"

Fowler is now an editor at the *New York Times* and author of a memoir, *Whistle-blower: My Journey to Silicon Valley and Fight for Justice at Uber*. Her post ultimately led to Uber boss Travis Kalanick's departure in June 2017 and a management overhaul. Fowler also lifted the lid on a widespread corporate practice known as forced arbitration, which enables businesses to shepherd employee complaints into secretive hearings, while gagging victims with nondisclosure agreements (NDAs) and effectively shielding offenders.[16] Complaints about Uber's permissive culture of gender discrimination and sexual harassment made in 2017 led to the intervention of the U.S. Equal Employment Opportunity Commission (EEOC), who began gathering evidence through interviews with Uber staffers. Just before Christmas 2019, the EEOC announced that Uber had entered into "a nationwide agreement to strengthen its business culture against sexual harassment and retaliation" and the company had agreed to set up a $4.4 million fund to compensate anyone whom the EEOC determines experienced sexual harassment and/or related retaliation from January 2014 onward.[17]

The settlement ended "an extensive investigation in which the EEOC found reasonable cause to believe that Uber permitted a culture of sexual harassment and

---

[15]Susan Fowler, "Reflecting On One Very, Very Strange Year at Uber," February 19, 2017, https://www.susanjfowler.com/blog/2017/2/19/reflecting-on-one-very-strange-year-at-uber

[16]Sam Levin, "Susan Fowler's plan after Uber? Tear down the system that protects harassers," *The Guardian,* April 11, 2018, https://www.theguardian.com/technology/2018/apr/11/susan-fowler-uber-interview-forced-arbitration-law

[17]EEOC, press release, "Uber to Pay $4.4 Million to Resolve EEOC Sexual Harassment and Retaliation Charge," December 18, 2019, https://www.eeoc.gov/newsroom/uber-pay-44-million-resolve-eeoc-sexual-harassment-and-retaliation-charge

retaliation against individuals who complained about such harassment." In addition, the firm was obliged to agree "to create a system for identifying employees who have been the subject of more than one harassment complaint and for identifying managers who fail to respond to concerns of sexual harassment in a timely manner."

Clearly this story is of a tumultuous period at a particular tech company, and it would be misleading to extrapolate across the industry. However, alongside many other similar stories circulating in the tech world, it helped shape the perception among tech workers that HR's ultimate job is to protect the company and its leadership, rather than ordinary employees. With that in mind, there are a few things that tech HR departments need to urgently implement to ensure more empathetic environments for staff:

- Create a safe, effective, and anonymous way of reporting inappropriate behavior (and worse) and ensure that all claims are treated equally and properly investigated. If required, use a third party to set up an employee complaint hotline for an extra layer of anonymity.
- Refuse to include forced arbitration agreements clauses in employees' contracts.
- Ensure full and continuous disclosure of diversity numbers, as well as what is being done to address this. (Incidentally Microsoft has led the way here with its EEO-1 Survey, which publicly shares detailed information about workers by their occupation, gender, and ethnicity.)[18]
- Make an empathy KPI a critical component of performance reviews. This might be the way staff engage and support coworkers and customers, or devote time to nonprofits/CSR projects.
- Insist that behavior be as important as results in the performance review of every employee.
- Implement systematic and widespread empathy training.

2. DECISION-MAKING PROCESSES

While there are many decisions made that affect a company, few are more impactful when it comes to empathy in tech companies than the ones related to product development and people.

Product Decisions

I remember the first time I used the word "empathy" in a room full of engineers, explaining that in my experience (very limited at the time), the best engineers had

---

[18]https://justcapital.com/companies/microsoft-corporation

mastered empathy as a skill. From the way they looked at me, I thought I had used the wrong word. (I was CEO of OZON at the time, and all the meetings were in Russian.) Turns out I was using the right Russian word, but that wasn't a concept that engineers considered remotely relevant. As I was walking to my office, a senior engineer I had a good relationship with came up to me and said, "You may want to avoid lecturing them on empathy being a core engineering skill. It makes you look like you really don't understand what engineering is about." Luckily, things have changed since those days. And yet there's still much to do. As former Facebook Chief Security Officer Alex Stamos famously told a large crowd of security and software professionals at the Blackhat conference in 2017, "We have a real inability to put ourselves in the shoes of the people we're trying to protect."

Indeed, the majority of large tech companies I know are far from purposefully, systematically, and successfully implementing a more empathetic approach for their product, design, and engineering teams, and then measuring progress against both human and financial targets. This process begins with helping these teams understand how cognitive empathy is pertinent to software-building, and can help them build better products, while also dealing with the thorny problem of legacy code, built without biases that result in some software ignoring a large number of their users.

I've come to believe there's a great deal to be said for sending engineering, design, and product teams out of the office to burst the "campus bubble" in which most tech giants operate. All varieties of engineer should spend a fixed number of days (it might be one day a month) meeting actual users and customers, and not behind the safety of a screen remotely observing a focus group, but face-to-face to understand what people actually do with their product or service, how they use them, where true pain points are, and so on. To date, most companies only have their user experience (UX) researcher and product managers do this. Engineers rarely spend meaningful time in person with real-life customers.

Finding time to take engineers away from their screens and into the field, when under relentless pressure of deadlines, is hard. But "proximity promotes empathy" is a principle I enthusiastically endorse, as it can lead to a seismic shift in perception. But more than that, imagine a senior Facebook engineer (or indeed Andrew Bosworth, Jack Dorsey, or Susan Wojcicki) being sent to Myanmar to meet genocide victims, to understand firsthand, undiluted, how their product has been abused or used to disseminate hate or propaganda or to justify killing. Or imagine a Twitter executive sitting, once a week for a year, across a table from women who've been harassed online with rape and death threats, or threatened because of their ethnic background. This executive would likely return home with a very different understanding of what to focus on, and strain every sinew (or so you'd hope) to design more empathetic tech and fix these issues rather than utter yet more warm words. And this would need to happen regularly to have a genuine impact—otherwise there's a risk of companies saying, "Don't worry, we checked that box two years ago."

Similarly, Big Tech firms must do far more to encourage their employees to engage with the community on their own doorstep. James Higa, who ran special operations for Steve Jobs at Apple, thinks one way around the luxurious isolation provided by Big Tech is for these companies to give their teams tasks to perform in their local community. He offers the example of assigning to an engineering team the mission of building an LED lighting system for a neighborhood youth basketball team, to enable them to play at night. Out in the real world, problems would be solved, connections would be forged, and empathy would likely flourish. Engineering talent could even be promoted based on leadership performance on projects of this sort.

Furthermore, it's critical to ensure that empathy is embedded in the product development process itself. One possible step would be to have an empathy committee, composed not just of product and engineering and business people, but also of sociologists, ethicists, philosophers—in short, people who are focused on thinking at human scale. This group would review the concept and the code of major products and features, thinking through the scenarios and pitfalls. On a day-to-day basis, a lighter approach would be to have a few dedicated engineers who would be responsible for challenging product and engineering teams throughout the development process to take into account the larger impact of their code on the world. I acknowledge that both measures would be cumbersome, but I believe that they are the best way to change attitudes.

In a similar vein—and a cause I have long championed—the tech giants should be more aggressive in recruiting people with humanities backgrounds, people as familiar with Voltaire and Thomas Paine as with Java and Python, and create special career pathways for them in product and engineering. With the rise of computational design—which harnesses computing power, machine learning, and data and applies them to the design process—over time, people with non-programing backgrounds will increasingly become product designers and engineers. This offers a huge opportunity to bring in more diverse candidates with a wide variety of experience, which will not only result in smarter teams, according to research by McKinsey,[19] but ones with greater emotional intelligence who are more innovative too.[20]

In one of my previous roles, where we had a relatively small engineering team of about 50, we started recruiting non-engineers who wanted to move into product and engineering. They were hired initially to work in quality assurance (QA) and from there, after a couple of years, they would make the transition into engineering. Whereas the overwhelming majority of engineers are still young white males,

---

[19]David Rock, "Why Diverse Teams Are Smarter," *Harvard Business Review,* November 4, 2016, https://hbr.org/2016/11/why-diverse-teams-are-smarter

[20]Rocio Lorenzo, "How Diverse Leadership Teams Boost Innovation," Boston Consulting Group, January 23, 2018, https://www.bcg.com/publications/2018/how-diverse-leadership-teams-boost-innovation.aspx

two of my first non-engineering hires happened to be women of color. This isn't an overnight process, but the end result will be more diversity of thought and varieties of background and experience at tech companies.

People Decisions

Hiring: Most companies will hire based on a resume and a few rounds of interviews. Sometimes they will add a technical exercise. The most advanced will conduct in-depth reference checks that will focus not just on results, but also on interpersonal skills or even some kind of challenge assignment, so that they can see how a candidate interacts with their possible future colleagues.

Large tech firms usually have a well-structured framework with which to assess candidates based on their values and the results they want to see them driving. However, very few test explicitly for empathy.[21] What might "testing for empathy" look like? It would involve asking questions that, for example, probe a candidate's ability to view a given problem, task, or situation from multiple perspectives. Or explore a candidate's experience in resolving conflicts in a fair and sensitive manner for everyone involved. Two of my favorites are asking a candidate to describe a time when they had a positive impact on someone, as a way to understand their ability to see when other people need help and actually do something about it, and systematically including in the review process report how "the people who do not matter in the interview process" were treated by the candidate.

Feedback: Again, most companies will follow a fairly similar approach—annual or biannual performance reviews leading to decisions around compensation and promotion. They may also mention continuous feedback. Very few will implement that in reality. Because, let's face it, giving good feedback is hard and time-consuming. Especially in a large organization, training all managers to be able to give empathetic feedback once a year, let alone throughout the year and to all employees, amounts to a Herculean task.

Like many senior managers, I have implemented and advocated regular formal performance reviews and "stack ranking" processes (during which employees' performances are measured along a bell curve, also referred to as "calibration process," where 10 to 20 percent of employees are rated as high performers, 60 to 70 percent as average performers, and 10 to 20 percent as low/nonperformers). They are pretty useful tools, though they are often misused and they definitely should not replace continuous feedback. Over the years, I've come to the opinion that stack rankings should be viewed as a performance indicator rather than a

---

[21]Not to be confused with an "empathy interview," a technique used to better understand the behavior, stories, journeys, and processes of a candidate, or with conducting the interview process with empathy to ensure that candidates have a positive experience and build relationships from the very beginning.

strict target to be implemented. If half of your employees are low performers not meeting expectations, then you need to urgently review your expectations and/or the profiles you're hiring. Likewise, if half of them are top performers exceeding expectations, you probably have the wrong expectations.

But performance reviews and stack rankings should not be used exclusively as tools to sideline and fire people. For me, assuming the recruiting process is effective, they allow a company first and foremost to identify the 10, 20, or 30 percent of employees who need extra support, either because they're still in the learning phase, they're in the wrong position, they're going through difficult personal times, or they have the wrong manager. The problem is that this is not how most companies operate. For all the conversations about the "right to fail," if you have one bad performance review in a high-performing tech company, you will likely end up being exited within the year. This leads to people becoming more short-term focused and pushing features/products without really debating whether their "side effects" are acceptable, beyond usability issues.

Separation: How you treat people when they become "surplus to requirements" is a pretty good indicator of your empathy level. And I'm not only talking about the exit package, but the way you communicate it to the employee in question, and to the rest of the company, and the way you help the employee to process what's happening and how to get back on their own two feet, and how much you believe that the company failed them as much as they failed the company. (There are, of course, extreme cases where people are ill-intentioned, have broken fundamental values of the company, or caused irreparable damage. There should be a zero-tolerance policy regarding things like sexual harassment, racism, bullying, stealing, etc.)

I have conducted more than my fair share of "separation conversations" because over time I've learned how to conduct these meetings in an empathetic way, to the point that I'm actually still in touch with quite a large number of people whom I have exited over the years. As a result, I have been asked to handle these conversations rather a lot. To be clear: I don't enjoy them, I'd rather avoid them if I could, and I have extremely mixed feelings about being praised for my "firing skills." Having said that, I believe that there is a good way and a bad way to fire people and from what I've seen, the tech industry mainly does it the wrong way, which includes:

- Limited feedback beforehand or more often, nonactionable feedback.
- No real explanation. General counsels have played a huge role in explaining all the bad things that could happen if the employee was given too much information that they could then use to attack the company. Legal departments need to find a way to protect companies against major risks without hiding the truth or hurting individual employees.
- No human conversation, no empathy. Again, general counsels have cautioned generations of managers and HR leaders against saying things like, "I'm so sorry

for what is happening to you," or "We, as a company, should have done a better job."
- No opportunity to say goodbye properly.

Here's a better way to do it (and while I understand that what I'm about to suggest potentially exposes the company to higher legal risks, my personal experience is that the vast majority of employees will actually be less likely to sue you if you treat them with empathy and transparency):

- Provide a clear and transparent explanation. (And if you don't have one that you feel you can share with the employee, and you wouldn't be ashamed if it was to become public, then you really need to think again about whether firing is justified. And, if it isn't, go back and think again.)
- Set a meeting that is not time-restricted; some people need ten minutes to process the news; others will need an hour.
- Offer genuine human care for their well-being, which can include discussions about the best next position for them, whether they should take some time off, potential people you could recommend them to, outplacement, and so on. Don't promise things that you can't deliver or won't do, but try to think about how you can really help a fellow human being in what is, for most, a very difficult time.
- Discuss how to best say goodbye to colleagues and hand over projects.
- Rehearse. Finding the right words can be difficult. Answering emotional questions too. You likely prepare for all important meetings. Do the same for what is a very important meeting for a member of your team.

3. BUSINESS MODEL AND ECONOMICS

Beyond people and decision-making processes, and at a time when we have a better grasp of the impact of Big Tech on humanity, these companies need to face the difficult question of the long-term viability and ethics of their business models and economics.

In quite a few cases, the only way to make technology serve humans and wider society, rather than the other way around, is likely to involve disrupting existing sources of revenues and altering key aspects of their business models. A few examples in which companies should confront the hard trade-offs between short-term financial impact, long-term sustainability, and moral responsibility:

- Preserving anonymity and providing a platform to humanity to communicate versus preventing falsehoods, bullying, or hate (Twitter, Facebook, YouTube)
- Offering consumers anything they want (or think they need) at lower prices, versus cracking down on bogus or potentially dangerous products or situations (Amazon, Airbnb)

- Promoting individual versus societal welfare (all of them)
- Supporting legitimate security efforts of democratic governments versus enabling surveillance, profiling, and government overreach (Google, Microsoft, Apple)
- Extending their products and services to China versus not jettisoning democratic values (all of them)

For Big Tech, these and many other similar decisions are currently made based on what will yield maximum shareholder value, with limited to no supervision, and more importantly without having to pay for any of the consequences. It's easier to praise anonymity and free speech when you are not liable for fraud, or undermining democracy, or even genocides that can result. It's more lucrative to believe that data gathering is for the greater good of consumers and businesses when there is no serious punishment for data leakage. It's simpler to focus on consumer choice when your merchants will be the ones responsible for any lives that might be endangered. So while I believe that the right thing to do would be for the leaders and employees of these companies to proactively choose the path of empathy and humanity, I have little doubt that external "help" will be required. I'll explore this in the next chapters.

***

Before I do that though, I want to reemphasize that empathy is a skill that can be measured and developed. Tech people—from executives to engineering, legal, HR, and all the other employees—have a responsibility to build empathy into their own company and products, all the way to the core of their business models. Everything we do at work is ultimately human. Every line of code we release has a human impact sooner or later. If we are going to do business with human beings, we have to do it in a human way. The payoff will come in human terms first, through better relationships, better conversations, better feelings. But gradually it will start to pay off in business terms, too: better reputations, better attraction and retention, more engagement, better problem-solving, more creativity, and more productivity. Empathy pays you back.

CHAPTER 10

A Multiplayer Game: Corporate Governance in Tech

I wrote in the previous chapter about what CEOs and their teams can do. But there are other influential players who can push for changes of this sort and drive higher ethical standards: investors, boards, and even the public markets, who unfortunately so far have pretty consistently failed to hold Big Tech's rogue's gallery to account. As long as founder-CEOs "played the game" by delivering hyper-growth, lavish returns, and soaring valuations, a lot of them have turned a blind eye to their transgressions. That needs to change. In my experience, investors, boards, and other stakeholders are usually under no illusions about characters like Uber cofounder Travis Kalanick, of whom I once heard an early investor say, "I know he's an asshole, but he's *my* asshole."

Ultimately, of course, this boils down to better corporate governance, and what follows is my take on what the key stakeholders—from VC investors and boards to the public markets and what I call "glue agents" (investment bankers and proxy advisors)—can do to build a tech industry in which startups are more empathetic to their staffs, their users, and the wider world.

1. INVESTORS

Most due diligence processes to invest in private tech startups focus on the same important elements: the quality of the team, the size of the addressable market, the top line growth to be expected through the lenses of product-market fit and current momentum, valuation, and so on. This unfortunately leaves very little time and space for checking on the ability for the company to be humanity-focused and empathy-driven. For example, more and more investors are asking questions about the diversity of the leadership team. What if, rather than just looking at a snapshot of the current situation at the executive level, they asked instead for a three-year diversity roadmap to demonstrate how the business plans will increase the percentage of women and minorities every year at every level of the company—and then made the execution of this plan a regular item at future board meetings? Or what if, next to the traditional opportunity/threat analysis for the company, founders provided the same analysis of opportunity/threats to their employees and contractors, customers, and wider society, and for each threat, produced a detailed contingency plan?

When it comes to established tech companies, what if on top of the audited accounts, investors routinely asked for an independent audit of how independent contractors and suppliers are being treated? Or what if they said using NDAs to muzzle victims of bullying or sexual harassment was a red line for them—and they would never invest where there was evidence of either?

Or what if they very publicly used "empathy-focused" criteria to inform investment decisions? After all, revenues, growth rates, and market cap are no longer the only benchmarks companies are measured against. JUST Capital, for example, ranks the most "just" publicly traded companies in the U.S. based on the issues Americans care about most, including fair pay, ethical leadership, benefits and work/life balance, equal opportunity, and environmental impact.[1] Indeed, some of the best-known tech giants occupy the top of the rankings, with Microsoft, NVIDIA, Apple, Intel, and SalesForce hogging the top five positions at the time of writing.[2]

Similarly, when it comes to impact investing, there are now a plethora of socially responsible Exchange Traded Funds (ETFs). A gender diversity Social ETF, for example, measures the ratio of women to men at America's top 1,000 firms and is listed on the New York Stock Exchange as SHE,[3] while another Social ETF, for LGBTQ rights, was listed as EQLT, but closed last year.[4] An NAACP Minority Empowerment ETF selects companies based with strong racial and ethnic diversity policies.[5]

2. BOARDS AND SHAREHOLDERS

In an industry where referrals are so important and everybody is connected to everyone else, too often VC board members of tech startups, in particular, want to be "friends" with an entrepreneur, and fret about losing future deals due to reputational damage if they are perceived to be too critical of founder behavior. As a result, they sometimes tolerate unethical and unacceptable conduct for profit and prestige.

---

[1]https://justcapital.com/issues/
[2]https://justcapital.com/rankings/
[3]https://www.etf.com/SHE#overview
[4]https://www.etf.com/sections/daily-etf-watch/lgbt-friendly-etf-close
[5]https://impactetfs.org/naacp-etf/

Expectations are nevertheless changing, in particular toward public tech companies. Large U.S. and UK pension funds recently supported an effort to have worker representation on the board at Alphabet,[6] in the wake of increased employee activism. In a similar vein, activist Amazon shareholders recently pushed back against the cloud and retail giant's controversial Rekognition facial recognition technology, introducing two (admittedly nonbinding) proposals, one of which would have prohibited sales to government agencies, for a vote. While official company policy ultimately prevailed,[7] it was perhaps a sign of things to come: from within, or externally, Big Tech is on notice and will have to justify its actions.

Tech-giant boards should also start insisting that CEOs or top-tier decision-makers appear when asked to give evidence to congressional or parliamentary committees (or equivalent). Clearly executives cannot spend their lives crisscrossing the globe on planes at the whim of every small to medium-size country's policy makers, but when a product or service has a disastrous impact on a large number of people, senior people from that company have an ethical duty to account for themselves. Whenever the UK's Digital Select Committee, for example, invited Mark Zuckerberg or senior Facebook executives to give evidence, it was invariably fobbed off to "in-country policy spokespeople" instead, says former committee chairman Damian Collins, MP. "[Those people's] jobs [are] to talk about Facebook and not to decide how it's run, and they only know what they're told. We've constantly run up against problems when we ask people things they don't know about and we have to follow up in writing to get the answers that we need, or some new evidence comes out which suggests that what we were told in the hearing wasn't true," he says.

"It's a challenge and not just for us. I convened the initial international grand committee meeting to bring [together] 25 parliamentarians from nine different countries and they all have the same experience: getting answers out of them is difficult, getting people together for hearings, certainly relevant people with information about particular products and who are the decision-makers in the business is very difficult. And I know from talking to people in Congress, the Americans have the same experience too." Boards and shareholders must no longer tolerate this state of affairs. Big Tech has a moral imperative to explain its decisions and their consequences to the public's elected officials when called upon to do so.

Boards, generally, have a critical role to play in corporate governance, especially in an industry that is still too often in thrall to ego-crazed founders. To be fair to board members, there is only so much you can truly know about a business that you

---

[6]Owen Walker, "Alphabet faces call by pension groups for workers to join board," *Financial Times,* May 24, 2019, https://www.ft.com/content/60339bd4-7e24-11e9-81d2-f785092ab560
[7]Natasha Singer, "Amazon Faces Investor Pressure Over Facial Recognition," *New York Times,* May 20, 2019, https://www.nytimes.com/2019/05/20/technology/amazon-facial-recognition .html

don't—and shouldn't—run on a day-to-day basis. Yet I continue to be astonished by the number of tech companies that don't have independent directors until very late in the day, as well as the continuing lack of diversity on most of these boards: in 2019 just 22 percent of board members of tech public companies are women (as opposed to the marginally better, though still lamentable, 26 percent for S&P 500 firms).[8] It is telling that I couldn't find readily available statistics about the representation of people of color on boards of tech companies.

Beyond gender and racial diversity, boards would benefit from having more varied profiles to question orthodoxies and challenge assumptions. Moral philosophers, social scientists, psychologists, and others can shake up an organization, and at a stroke make its thinking more diverse and better equipped to identify and develop features/products/business models that don't prey on human weakness and compulsions. VC and entrepreneur Saul Klein is an avowed fan of this approach and frequently cites in talks an op-ed written by the philosopher and author Alain de Botton back in 2014, "The case for putting philosophers into company boardrooms."[9] "de Botton's argument was, someone on the board needs to ask the question: Why do we exist?" says Klein. "I would argue that not only do you need philosophers, but you also need ethicists. Once businesses have a reason for existing beyond 'here's a product that works and it can make us money,' then you need to say: What are our ethics and how do we hold ourselves accountable to those ethics?"

Additionally, boards need to look beyond growth and its enablers. It's not just about the path to profitability. They should get more aggressive in pushing tactics and strategies that can help bring empathy to the core of their companies, such as a more stringent approach to fighting misinformation or more accountability around how gig workers are being treated. On top of their focus on regulatory and compliance duties (particularly critical in an era when companies stay private for longer), boards need to allocate time to engage more deeply on "soft" topics like company culture, diversity, treatment of third-party partners, etc. . . .

A major factor in the industry's seeming inability to change and tackle some of its long-running sores is the prestige and compensation associated with being on the board of a leading tech firm. So-called independent directors are often chosen by powerful founders/CEO because they can be counted on not to challenge them. VC board members, meanwhile, are likely unwilling to step aside from keeping watch over their investments. Thus, very few board members are willing to walk away from major tech firms on a point of principle unless there is a significant conflict of interest. Greater openness to holding unicorn leadership to account through

---

[8]2019 U.S. Technology Spencer Stuart Board Index, https://www.spencerstuart.com/research-and-insight/-/media/2019/techbi-2019/us-tech-board-index-2019.pdf

[9]Alain de Botton, "The case for putting philosophers into company boardrooms," *Financial Times,* January 1, 2014, https://www.ft.com/content/a688be46-714d-11e3-8f92-00144feabdc0

being prepared to walk away would be another lever with which to improve standards.

I'd also urge more tech companies to implement an annual independent performance review of their board. While "92% of boards [of public tech companies] perform some form of evaluation annually," per Spencer Stuart, only "57% evaluate the full board and committees."[10] Of course, this is a mere snapshot of opinion, but of the 15 senior tech executives in my network whom I surveyed, working at a private unicorn, only three said their company holds them in one way or another. That should change.

3. STOCK EXCHANGES

Stock exchanges, along with the Securities and Exchange Commission, have been critical in strengthening corporate governance, not just of public companies but also of private ones as they begin preparations for a potential IPO—or at least keep the door open to one. As a result, I believe that they have greater abilities to help put tech companies on the right path and fight entrenchment mechanisms and nonvoting shareholder capitalism (most big tech companies have created ownership systems that make it near impossible to remove the founder and/or make key strategic decisions without their approval) than they're being given credit for.

There are a few things boards and the SEC could do to improve corporate governance in tech:

1. Implement strict guidelines (or at least disclosure) around data privacy and the deployment of user data—for example, by making it easy for customers to access all of the data gathered about them and for them to ask for that data to be deleted. Alternatively, customers could be asked for their explicit consent for the type of data they are prepared to share and which providers have access to it. The standard response to the latter is that it would be too complicated to implement. I don't deny it would be complex, but I only wish as much time was spent on solving this problem as there is on increasing frequency of usage.
2. Make it mandatory to have a majority of independent directors on the board, even if the company is considered a "controlled company" (i.e., where more than 50 percent of the voting rights are held by an individual, group, or another company after IPO).
3. Be stricter around multiple class shares or supermajority requirements for key corporate decisions.

---

[10] 2019 U.S. Technology Spencer Stuart Board Index, https://www.spencerstuart.com/research-and-insight/-/media/2019/techbi-2019/us-tech-board-index-2019.pdf

4. Introduce the compulsory separation of the CEO and chairman roles. Without this, it's hard for the board to properly supervise and restrain a CEO, who may be at risk of going rogue. (There could be a caveat where this is compulsory only if the CEO is also a significant shareholder.)
5. And probably the most controversial and least likely to happen: limit CEOs' tenure in the same way that there is a limit on board member tenure in Europe, where the European Commission has said that an appropriate maximum tenure for a director is three terms, or 12 years.[11]

4. INVESTMENT BANKERS AND PROXY ADVISORS

This chapter wouldn't be complete without a mention of the people who act as "glue agents" in tech investment: investment bankers and proxy advisors, who in many cases help link leadership teams with new investors (both when they're private or when they're getting ready to go public), as well as supporting them when they do go public and managing existing investors. They can absolutely play a role too.

Goldman Sachs, Wall Street's biggest underwriter of IPOs in the U.S., announced that they will no longer take a company public in the U.S. and Europe if it lacks at least one diverse board member, with a particular focus on women.[12] The same goes for proxy advisors, who have been shown to be able to sway votes, though this regularly raises concerns about conflicts of interest and undue influence.[13] If these firms were to share the opinion that the long-term success of a company is linked to its ability to have a diverse workforce and products that help humanity, they would have a critical role in convincing investors to vote accordingly. Proxy advisory firms Glass Lewis and ISS generally recommend voting against the nominating committee chair of a board that has no female members.

Ideally, they should go further and resist the siren song of pure financial interest, by refusing to work with companies that are obviously bad corporate citizens. Let's not be naive here though—this is easier said than done when you are a public institution yourself, with shareholders expecting attractive growth and ROI. Yet WeWork, once again, is a cautionary tale in this context. Although the company's

---

[11]Steven Haas, "A closer look at the emerging debate over board tenure," NACD BoardTalk, March 24, 2015, https://blog.nacdonline.org/posts/a-closer-look-at-the-emerging-debate-over-board-tenure

[12]Elizabeth Dilts Marshall, "Goldman Sachs to companies: Hire at least one woman director if you want to go public," Reuters, January 23, 2020, https://uk.reuters.com/article/us-goldman-sachs-ipo-diversity/goldman-sachs-to-companies-hire-at-least-one-woman-director-if-you-want-to-go-public-idUKKBN1ZM2MK

[13]Timothy M. Doyle, "The conflicted role of proxy advisors," Harvard Law School, May 22, 2018, https://corpgov.law.harvard.edu/2018/05/22/the-conflicted-role-of-proxy-advisors/

implosion was primarily a failure of clinical business judgment, lack of corporate oversight was at least a contributory factor. So the question then becomes: "If this had been a financially sound business, should they have taken the deal, given everything else that was known about the culture of the business?" Glue agents could have played a role as whistle-blowers here.

5. INDUSTRY BODIES

Another good way to ensure higher ethical standards is to ramp up sector-specific codes of practice. There's only so much an industry regulator—even the industry-sourced, overhauled, rapid-reaction regulator I believe is required—can do in a global, multifaceted, and constantly evolving industry like tech. That's why it's time for all of the major tech firms, ideally collaborating with rivals, to publish their own ethical blueprints for industries that are often breaking new ground.

There's an incentive here too; steps like these can also be a business differentiator. A great example of this is the European micro-mobility company VOI Technology. The startup launched a voluntary code of conduct for e-scooter companies, which has already been adopted in its native Stockholm.[14] Or indeed the way evolution and experimentation from within to raise ethical standards brought about Instagram's new anti-bullying tool, which uses AI to determine when text resembles posts that are most frequently flagged as inappropriate by users.[15] If a person types, say, "You are so ugly and stupid," the words "Are you sure you want to post this? Learn more" pop up. While the user can still post the comment anyway, Instagram claims tests "have found that it encourages some people to undo their comment and share something less hurtful once they have had a chance to reflect."

Ethics committees or ethics boards are set to be another invaluable internal resource. Yes, they have a mixed record so far—Google's hastily disbanded ethics board proved a public relations disaster—however, that doesn't mean that they aren't of critical importance. Indeed, as Bloomberg reported, at the time of its ethics board debacle, Google already had a similar panel with an identical name, the Advanced Technology Review Council, "that does hold real power to shape Google's approach to its ethical quandaries," beyond immediate commercial interest.[16]

---

[14] Amy Lewin, "From Voi to Circ, we compare Europe's scooter startups," Sifted, July 15, 2019, https://sifted.eu/articles/scooter-startups-comparison-voi-flash-bird-lime-dott-wind-tier/
[15] Dave Lee, "Instagram now asks bullies: 'Are you sure?,'" BBC News, July 8, 2019, https://www.bbc.co.uk/news/technology-48916828
[16] Joshua Brunstein and Mark Bergen, "The Google AI Ethics Board with Actual Power Is Still Around," Bloomberg, April 6, 2019, https://www.bloomberg.com/news/articles/2019-04-06/the-google-ai-ethics-board-with-actual-power-is-still-around

As the deployment of AI continues to accelerate, throwing up all manner of ethical conundrums, their role in building trust with all stakeholders will only grow. Marc Benioff, chairman and co-CEO of Salesforce, stole a march in this sphere by appointing Paula Goldman as the company's first Chief Ethical and Humane Use Officer back in December 2018.[17] The company says the new role "merges law, policy, and ethics," adding, "We understand that we have a broader responsibility to society, and aspire to create technology that not only drives the success of our customers, but also drives positive social change and benefits humanity."[18]

I'm also intrigued by the idea from Helen Fry, associate mathematics professor at University College London, that mathematicians, computer engineers, and scientists should take a Hippocratic oath to protect users from new technologies being developed in labs and by tech firms. "We need a Hippocratic oath in the same way it exists for medicine," she told the The Guardian.[19] "In medicine, you learn about ethics from day one. In mathematics [and computer science], it's a bolt-on at best."

---

[17]Salesforce press release, "Paula Goldman Joins Salesforce as VP, Chief Ethical and Humane Use Officer," December 10, 2018, https://www.salesforce.com/company/news-press/stories/2018/12/121018-i/
[18]Trailhead Salesforce learning module, "Understand the Ethical Use of Technology," https://trailhead.salesforce.com/en/content/learn/modules/responsible-creation-of-artificial-intelligence/understand-the-ethical-use-of-technology
[19]Ian Sample, "Maths and tech specialists need Hippocratic oath, says academic," *The Guardian,* August 16, 2019, https://www.theguardian.com/science/2019/aug/16/mathematicians-need-doctor-style-hippocratic-oath-says-academic-hannah-fry

CHAPTER 11

Breaking Up Big Tech?

The sheer scale and breadth of the tech giants' reach stretches far beyond the confines of their respective industries into almost every corner of life. When we talk about the power of Google or Facebook, say, we're not only talking about their extraordinary influence over advertising; nor when we discuss Amazon or Apple do we think of them as monoliths of retail or devices. These are givens. What should really concern us is their power over our private information, our health and education data, our politics, our news, our culture, and so much more besides. Arguing whether the effective duopoly of the advertising market created by Facebook and Google is healthy is important, of course. I'd like to be shown an industry where monopoly or extreme concentration of economic power has actually brought innovation and extraordinary customer service in the long term. Telecoms? Airlines? Healthcare? Media? Oil and gas? Banking? But it also distracts us from the debate we really should be having: how as a society we choose to handle the fact that both these tech giants (and a few others) are effectively now more powerful than democratically elected governments, have the ability to shape and shift people's opinions and behaviors, and have accumulated more spending power than a medium-sized national economy—Facebook had $55 billion in cash at the end of 2019[1] and has a $605 billion market cap as I write, while Alphabet was sitting on $117 billion[2] and became the fourth tech giant, alongside Apple, Amazon, and Microsoft, to join the trillion-dollar club at the start of 2020.[3] That question is an existential one both for capitalism and for democracy itself.

---

[1] https://investor.fb.com/investor-news/press-release-details/2020/Facebook-Reports-Fourth-Quarter-and-Full-Year-2019-Results/default.aspx

[2] Richard Waters, "Google parent Alphabet overtakes Apple to become new king of cash," *Financial Times,* July 31, 2019, https://www.ft.com/content/332dd974-b349-11e9-8cb2-799a3a8cf37b

[3] Amrith Ramkumar, "Alphabet Becomes Fourth U.S. Company to Reach $1 Trillion Market Value," *Wall Street Journal,* January 16, 2020, https://www.wsj.com/articles/alphabet-becomes-fourth-u-s-company-to-ever-reach-1-trillion-market-value-11579208802

And even if you're convinced that Jeff, Mark, Tim, Jack, and Sundar are all well-intentioned individuals who endeavor to use the size of their companies for humanity's greater good, can you be sure that their successors will do the same? Can you guarantee that these companies will not one day soon take on a life of their own and ruthlessly pursue their own interests at the expense of the wider society? Despite the fact that history has shown repeatedly that the failure to limit extreme industrial concentration, and to put in place economic policies that serve the population at large, leads to extremisms of all kind (think about fascist Germany[4] and Japan or the American Social Darwinism advocated by Rockefeller and Morgan), do you feel confident that history will not repeat itself?

BIG TECH'S ANTICOMPETITIVE BEHAVIOR

Alphabet, Google's holding company established in a surprise shake-up in 2015, is only one glaring example. Recent research by CB Insights[5] highlighted how the colossus—which of course includes billion-plus-user products like Google Maps, Gmail, YouTube, Chrome, and Android—was leveraging its sheer scale, and its dominance in search and advertising, to develop its next billion-dollar businesses. The report singled out the ten sectors the tech giant is specifically targeting: consumer electronics, healthcare, next-gen computing, transportation, energy, smart cities, travel, gaming, media, and banking. It's also finding synergies between these industries.

Sure, many of its new (and not so new) ventures will transpire to be money-devouring flameouts, but that's the point of them. Innovation is a high-stakes game. Instead, our concern should focus on the fact—given the near-monopolistic scale and power of Google's traditional business, and the potential of at least some of its non-core businesses to become market-defining companies—that this is no run-of-the-mill old-school multinational, but rather an entirely new breed of behemoth. And it should be treated as such. Just ask Richard Stables. The British CEO of the French-born European shopping search and comparison site Kelkoo Group, which also includes Ciao and LeGuide, has repeatedly made the case—both in Brussels (with Executive Vice President Margrethe Vestager of the European Commission), where the EU has already fined the company over

---

[4]Daniel A. Crane, "Antitrust and Democracy: A Case Study from German Fascism," April 17, 2018, https://repository.law.umich.edu/cgi/viewcontent.cgi?article=1266&context=law_econ_current

[5]"Alphabet's next billion-dollar business: 10 industries to watch," CB Insights, https://www.cbinsights.com/research/report/industries-disruption-alphabet/

$9 billion for antitrust violations,[6] and in Washington, at the U.S. Department of Justice (DoJ)—that Google's dominance allegedly not only distorts the e-commerce market and inhibits competition, but it also fails consumers. With DoJ officials already looking into Google's activities[7] as part of a wider review of anticompetitive behavior by the tech giants,[8] Stables has urged officials on both sides of the Atlantic to respond more robustly to Google's behavior, which he alleges threatens not only the future of other comparison sites, but businesses in other sectors too.

Of the tech giant he says bluntly, "I think that they've got no moral compass. They are just trying to dominate every single market they can and try and take as much data as they possibly can and they have abused the market in shopping, they've done the same in advertising and they've done the same with Android, according to the [European] commission," he says, referring to the way Google has stifled competition by pushing its own services to Android users.[9] "We think there are lots of other verticals that they've done the same with, but they just haven't been investigated on those."

In 2017 Google was fined €2.42 billion ($2.8 billion) by the EU for manipulating search results in favor of its own products.[10] The spotlight was then on the tech giant's Google Shopping service, which enables users to compare products and prices, and source deals from online retailers and manufacturers as well as platforms like Amazon and eBay. The commission found that Google had "systematically given prominent placement to its own comparison shopping service" and "demoted rival comparison shopping services in its search results." The ruling stated, "Google's practices amount to an abuse of Google's dominant position in general internet search by stifling competition in comparison shopping markets. Market dominance is, as such, not illegal under EU antitrust rules. However,

---

[6]James Vincent, "Google hit with €1.5 billion antitrust fine by EU," The Verge, March 20, 2019, https://www.theverge.com/2019/3/20/18270891/google-eu-antitrust-fine-adsense-advertising

[7]Brian Fung, "Google hit by DOJ demand for antitrust records," CNN Business, September 6, 2019, https://edition.cnn.com/2019/09/06/tech/justice-department-antitrust-google/index.html

[8]Brian Fung, "Justice Department launching broad antitrust review of Big Tech," CNN Business, July 23, 2019, https://edition.cnn.com/2019/07/23/tech/justice-department-big-tech-antitrust/index.html

[9]Tony Romm, "Europe hits Google with record $5 billion antitrust fine over bundling of its apps on Android," *Washington Post,* July 18, 2018, https://www.washingtonpost.com/technology/2018/07/18/europe-penalizes-google-with-record-billion-antitrust-fine-way-it-bundles-its-apps-android-smartphones-tablets/

[10]European Commission press release, "Antitrust: Commission fines Google €4.2 billion for abusing dominance as search engine by giving illegal advantage to own comparison shopping service," June 27, 2017, https://ec.europa.eu/commission/presscorner/detail/en/IP_17_1784

dominant companies have a special responsibility not to abuse their powerful market position by restricting competition."

Stables is adamant that the remedies introduced by Google to give rival services greater prominence simply haven't worked and that the company continues to leverage its dominant position. "Now have they built some really fantastic tools and done some amazing things? Absolutely. You cannot knock that. But they have got so much power . . . and that power has gone to their heads. . . . What I'm hearing on both sides of the Atlantic now is a clear move by politicians, establishment, the press that suddenly Big Tech is actually pretty bad and they're right. I mean if you look at the amount of attention and e-commerce that's controlled between the GAFA [companies] and then you can consider the amount of what I would call soft power these companies have, I would say that probably Google's got more power than France. I mean they could move elections. They change behaviors. It has enormous power across the globe."

Google is far from alone, of course. Whether it's Google's and Facebook's stranglehold on digital advertising spend; Facebook's devouring of the perceived threats of Instagram and WhatsApp; or Google joining Apple, Amazon, and Microsoft in the trillion-dollar club; Big Tech's resources, revenues, and reach are unparalleled.

"Being big in a digital platform data-driven economy is a completely different thing to being big in a non-digital economy," notes Margrethe Vestager, who says a tipping-point moment has been reached. "And since the technological revolution is everywhere—it's in business lives, it's in government, it's in democracy, it's in our personal lives—and because we see this now, the tides are turning."

THE ANTI-ANTITRUST COCKTAIL

There were "a number of reasons, working together" that enabled the tech giants to get away with this for so long, unchecked, according to Vestager. "One, of course, is excellent marketing." She goes on to list some of the stock phrases that mesmerized many, from officials to much of the media, into a false sense of security: "We started this idea in a garage." "We've built an amazing company." "We're serving a public good."

"Second, the dynamics of a digital business and the digital economy are different to a bricks-and-mortar physical manufacturing business. [And in the early days] it's not that easy to see what is going on, it's not easy to grasp it." She expands: "Part of the reason this is new, is exactly the platform [model, which] has this double side that on the one hand it looks very familiar—because advertising is advertising—on the other hand, the fact that it is data and network-driven makes it so much more powerful than what we saw in previous decades. . . . So the question of speed, here, is of the essence, which is why the response will also have to be fast because these are issues that move very, very fast."

But there is a third reason that led us to such a feeble response to this staggering concentration of wealth and power in the hands of a few companies. As brilliantly argued by Tim Wu in his book *The Curse of Bigness*, the focus on the economic impact and more specifically the impact on consumer price is not how antitrust was originally designed by U.S. lawmakers and supported by American voters. Writing about the original U.S. antitrust law—the Sherman Act, the way it was further developed by Louis Brandeis, Associate Justice of the U.S. Supreme Court, and then implemented by President Roosevelt in their respective fights to limit the power of large corporations, Wu says, "Antitrust was . . . a check on private power, by preventing the growth of monopoly corporations into something that might transcend the power of elected government to control." He then goes on to explain that the law was weakened to the point of becoming useless by the theory developed by the Chicago School (a group of leading scholars and economists in the 1970s and 1980s largely associated with the University of Chicago) that "the Congress of 1890 exclusively intended the antitrust law to deal with one very narrow type of harm: higher prices to consumers. . . . Promising greater certainty and scientific rigor, it has delivered neither, and more importantly discarded far too much of the role that law was intended to play in a democracy, namely constraining the accumulation of unchecked private power and preserving economic liberty."

REINVIGORATING ANTITRUST

As Executive Vice President Vestager has shown in Europe, it is ultimately governments that must take the lead. For it is only they who have the heft to make Big Tech accountable and wrangle them—incentivize, yes, but also force them where necessary—into playing a meaningful and constructive role within the corporate landscape and wider society, but also to break them up when necessary. As a nonexpert in this field, I am not about to review in detail the required changes to antitrust laws on both sides of the Atlantic. Nor am I suggesting that antitrust laws need to be completely rewritten from scratch or that prohibiting all mergers or breaking up Big Tech are the only ways to solve all the problems I mentioned in the first half of this book. However, following is a list of measures that, if implemented, would in my view take us a long way down the path to making Big Tech less threatening to society, more accountable, and ultimately more likely to develop a culture of empathy that seeks to serve humanity as much as their own narrow self-interest.

Aligning on Antitrust Goals

It should start with reviewing the goal of antitrust legislation and what constitutes anticompetitive behavior. I may be biased, but on the whole I prefer the European approach to determining anticompetitive behavior to the U.S. stance, largely because it's broader in scope. In both instances antitrust policy aims to create a level playing field for companies and consumers and penalize those who engage in anticompetitive behavior. However, the U.S. approach requires there to be evidence that the actions of a company considered a monopoly have had an anticompetitive impact on consumers, whereas in Europe companies ruled to have monopoly power are limited in the type of actions they can engage in that are presumed to have an anticompetitive effect.[11]

When applied to Big Tech, the European approach is in my opinion more effective and relevant: rather than "economic absolutism" focused on the pure and established cost that consumers have to pay—especially when many tech "goods" are free—it tries to take into account the global effect on society and the opportunity cost of having one less innovative company.

Revising Merger Approval Process

Once the goal is clarified, governments should revise the actual process of merger review. To start—and, again, as argued by Tim Wu—the process should allow for transparency. "It is hard for the public or the press to care without any opportunity to know what is going on.... Industry comments on a major merger should be filed publicly, not in secret, and any interested member of the public should be encouraged to file comments.... In major mergers, the agency, if it plans on a consent agreement, should put out its proposed remedy for meaningful public comment."

As for redefining approval criteria for mergers, there are a few key steps that would make merger review more applicable to Big Tech. First, designate large digital companies as having strategic market status and thus automatically subject to review. In the U.S., with some exceptions, mergers above a value of $94 million must be submitted for review,[12] but this is not sufficient. Just because the value of an acquisition is small, it might still sufficiently strengthen a dominant player seeking to take out a potential competitor.

Another problem is market definition. Traditionally, if, say, a trucking company acquires a pet food manufacturer, anticompetitive effects are nonexistent. This is not so for the new digital platforms, whose network effects and overall power are strengthened by swallowing companies—even small ones—in many seemingly separate businesses. Facebook's acquisition of the WhatsApp messaging application in 2014[13] is a classic example. On the surface, Facebook is not a messaging company,

---

[11] Juan Delgado, "EU Vs. U.S.—Whom to Trust on Antitrust," The Globalist, October 10, 2007, https://www.theglobalist.com/eu-vs-u-s-trust-antitrust/

[12] U.S. Federal Trade Commission, "Merger Review," https://www.ftc.gov/news-events/media-resources/mergers-and-competition/merger-review

[13] Adrian Covert, "Facebook buys WhatsApp for $19 billion," CNN Business, February 19, 2014, https://money.cnn.com/2014/02/19/technology/social/facebook-whatsapp/index.html

and could claim it was in a different market. You might say that conglomerates such as General Electric often collect disparate businesses, but the primary effect simply strengthens their financials. Mark Zuckerberg was willing to pay $19 billion for a little-known (at least in the U.S.), rapidly growing messaging app because he understood that it would help secure Facebook's worldwide hegemony as the primary way people communicate online. He can monetize this in several ways, but it also means tremendous power and influence. What was originally looked upon as an insane purchase price is now seen as a tremendous bargain. In judging mergers, U.S. antitrust policy needs to be adjusted to account for these kinds of platform effects. (The WhatsApp acquisition received only cursory review, and approval, from the Federal Trade Commission.)

I like the way author and technologist Ben Thompson attacks this problem by defining anticompetitive behavior in the internet space: "Any company that derives dominant market power from the size of its user base should not be allowed to acquire a company that has a significant and growing user base."[14] In the social media realm, judging anticompetitiveness based on price impact is a fool's errand, because the cost to the user is free. This is in large measure because the product (e.g., the content) is largely provided by those users. And the more scale, the more data and advertising. Indeed, the only tweak I would make is to change the "significant *and* growing" to "significant *or* growing," because "or" encapsulates why Mark Zuckerberg acquired Instagram and the aforementioned WhatsApp, which were both growing at a jaw-dropping rate when Facebook waved the checkbook: these startups represented the next phase of user growth for the tech giant. Finally, we should shift the burden of proof that a merger will preserve competition, benefit consumers, and increase innovation to the company rather than ask the government to prove that it won't.

And just because it's hard to predict exactly whether a particular deal is going to turn out to be anticompetitive a decade down the line, or whether Big Tech will abide by their promises (e.g., Facebook told the European Commission that it was technically impossible for Facebook and WhatsApp to share their user data; then, lo and behold, a few months later, WhatsApp started sharing data with Facebook), every merger approved should systematically contain ex-ante rules, where regulators would bake into the M&A validation process certain triggers and/or thresholds that would result in the deal being reversed if they were to be met or crossed. If that had been included in the Facebook-WhatsApp merger, rather than it ultimately resulting in a fine of €110 million ($123 million), which was less than 1 percent of the

---

[14]Ben Thompson, "First, Do No Harm," Stratechery, February 12, 2020, https://stratechery .com/2020/first-do-no-harm/

deal value, Facebook would have been forced to reverse the merger (or stop sharing user data).[15]

Levying Punishing Fines

European legislators and watchdogs were quicker off the mark regarding fines, which has enabled the European Commission to be a trailblazer, with Vestager leading the charge against the U.S. tech giants on the continent. (Let me also point out that rather than being anti-American—a charge often leveled at Europe on this side of the Atlantic—the EU has fined a wide range of European companies in industries other than tech. For example, European truck manufacturers were fined $2.9 billion for price collusion.[16] It just so happens that the U.S. is the dominant player in tech; if the tech giants were European, I'm certain they would be treated the same way.)

As I have already written, Vestager's department has fined Google, alone, a total of $9.4 billion (roughly €8.2 billion) since 2017. Amazon, meanwhile, is currently under investigation[17] for alleged antitrust breaches by the European Commission over its use of independent merchants' data, which according to one estimate could see it fined 10 percent of its annual revenue of $233 billion in 2018.[18] And Facebook also faces a separate investigation from the commission, alongside Google, into "the way data is gathered, processed, used and monetized, including for advertising purposes."[19]

The commission even has Apple in its sights. In June 2020 it announced it was opening two investigations. The first was to "assess whether Apple's rules for app

---

[15]European Commission, "Mergers: Commission fines Facebook €110 million for providing misleading information about WhatsApp takeover," May 18, 2017, https://ec.europa.eu/commission/presscorner/detail/en/IP_17_1369

[16]Sean Farrel, "Truckmakers fined by Brussels for price collusion," *The Guardian,* July 19, 2016, https://www.theguardian.com/business/2016/jul/19/truck-makers-fined-by-brussels-for-price-collusion

[17]European Commission press release, "Antitrust: Commission opens investigation into possible anti-competitive conduct of Amazon," July 17, 2019, https://ec.europa.eu/commission/presscorner/detail/en/IP_19_4291

[18]Mary Hanbury, "The EU just launched a big antitrust probe into Amazon, and it could lead to a fine of up to $23 billion," Business Insider, July 17, 2019, https://www.businessinsider.com/amazon-eu-launches-antitrust-investigation-2019-7

[19]Emily Nicolle, "EU Commission to open investigation into data usage by Google and Facebook," City AM, December 2, 2019, https://www.cityam.com/eu-commission-opens-investigation-into-data-usage-by-google-and-facebook/

developers on the distribution of apps via the App Store violate EU competition rules."[20] The probe would look into whether there were parallels with Google over its fine for unfairly disadvantaging rivals on its platform and whether, as Vestager said in a statement, "Apple obtained a 'gatekeeper' role when it comes to the distribution of apps and content to users of Apple's popular devices." She added, "We need to ensure that Apple's rules do not distort competition in markets where Apple is competing with other app developers, for example with its music streaming service Apple Music or with Apple Books." The second one will review Apple's payment system, Apple Pay, and in particular the restriction the tech giant put in place for competitors to use the iPhone's NFC capabilities (enabling tap-and-go features).[21]

Given their cash reserves and revenues, it's obvious that even large fines are little more than a nuisance to the tech giants—fleabites that irritate rather than bring about behavioral change, a cost of doing business that doesn't require for them to fundamentally rethink their business practices. Indeed, *The Economist* has calculated that the fines and penalties imposed amount to less than 1 percent of the Big Five's combined market value.[22] Moreover, their share price barely flickered at the time, confirming that investors saw these fines as nonevents. But that's not the point of them, says Vestager. "The fines [alone] will not do the trick. The fines are a punishment for past behavior." She has also introduced "interim measures," which act like cease-and-desist orders and effectively tell offenders, "Stop what you're doing!"

However, the area she says the commission will work much more on is what she terms "market repair." "Because if you have won the market by illegal means, it is still very difficult for anyone else to get a foothold. And now, of course, we're pushing for this, and we have the legal basis in our decisions," she explains. "It will be interesting to see how the Android preference menu of search and browser options...will work, if competitors to Google search will have a real chance with consumers," she says, referring to her decision that Google must offer a choice

---

[20]European Commission, "Antitrust: Commission opens investigation into Apple practices regarding Apple Pay," June 16, 2020, https://ec.europa.eu/commission/presscorner/detail/en/ip_20_1075
[21]European Commission, "Antitrust: Commission opens investigations into Apple's App Store rules," June 16, 2020, https://ec.europa.eu/commission/presscorner/detail/en/ip_20_1073
[22]The Economist, "How to make sense of the latest tech surge," February 20, 2020, https://www.economist.com/leaders/2020/02/20/how-to-make-sense-of-the-latest-tech-surge

of search apps and browsers on Android devices. "But that is indeed a work in progress."

Breaking Up Companies

Next after blocking potentially harmful mergers and levying hefty fines for anticompetitive behavior comes the ultimate sanction: breaking up companies. Way back in the opening salvos of the race to become the Democrats' nominee for president, one of the early frontrunners, Senator Elizabeth Warren, brought the issue of breaking up Big Tech to national attention[23] (even if the topic was to fall off the radar, like almost everything else, due to the pandemic). In a long read, which still largely stands the test of time, entitled "Here's how we can break up Big Tech," published on Medium[24] back in March 2019, Warren essentially argued that splitting up the tech giants will clear the way for competition and "new, groundbreaking companies to grow and thrive—which pushes everyone in the marketplace to offer better products and services."

Warren argued that she would restore competition by introducing two measures. First, she would appoint regulators committed to reversing illegal and anticompetitive tech mergers. As examples of mergers she would undo, she cites Amazon's acquisitions of Whole Foods and Zappos; Google's snapping up of Waze, Nest, and DoubleClick; and, unsurprisingly, Facebook buying WhatsApp and Instagram. Her second proposal is somewhat more complicated, aimed at stopping the tech giants from creating their own products or services to compete against those who are using the platforms for their businesses.

Senator Warren had some significant support. A couple of months after she published her Medium post, Facebook co-founder Chris Hughes wrote a lengthy and wave-making op-ed in the *New York Times*,[25] in which he argued that the moment has arrived for Facebook to be broken up. Hughes, once a close friend of Zuckerberg's—he describes the platform's CEO as "a good and kind person"—wrote that Facebook should be split into multiple companies and that the FTC, working alongside the DoJ, should enforce antitrust laws by unstitching the acquisitions of both Instagram and WhatsApp and introduce a moratorium on future acquisitions. "The F.T.C. should have blocked these mergers, but it's not too late to act," he said. "There is precedent for correcting bad decisions—as recently as 2009, Whole Foods

---

[23]Kiran Stacey, "Which antitrust investigations should Big Tech worry about?," *Financial Times,* October 28, 2019, https://www.ft.com/content/abcc5070-f68f-11e9-a79c-bc9acae3b654
[24]Elizabeth Warren, "Here's how we can break up Big Tech," Medium, March 8, 2019, https://medium.com/@teamwarren/heres-how-we-can-break-up-big-tech-9ad9e0da324c
[25]Chris Hughes, "It's Time to Break Up Facebook," *New York Times,* May 9, 2019, https://www.nytimes.com/2019/05/09/opinion/sunday/chris-hughes-facebook-zuckerberg.html

settled antitrust complains by selling off the Wild Oats brand and stores that it had bought a few years earlier."

The breakup could work by allowing Facebook a brief period in which to spin off Instagram and WhatsApp, where each would become separate and probably listed companies. "Facebook shareholders would initially hold stock in the new companies, although Mark and other executives would probably be required to divest their management shares," he suggested. "Until recently, WhatsApp and Instagram were administered as independent platforms inside the parent company, so that should make the process easier. But time is of the essence: Facebook is working quickly to integrate the three, which would make it harder for the F.T.C. to split them up."

ZUCKERBERG'S PUSHBACK (AND WHERE HE'S WRONG)

It will shock precisely no one that Zuckerberg himself has been strident in his opposition to breaking up Big Tech. In conversation with Nicholas Thompson, editor-in-chief of *Wired*, he offered three reasons for retaining the status quo:[26]

1. He argued that breaking up platforms into smaller companies won't make them compete on the things we're all worried about, such as safety and privacy. They'll still prioritize growth above all else—and if platforms are smaller, they'll have fewer resources to invest in large numbers of moderators and similar schemes.
2. Breaking up U.S. giants will hand the initiative to China, because certain types of technology—such as AI—require huge data sets, which only the giants have (by contrast the Chinese government is helping its homegrown giants).
3. Facebook's acquisitions of Instagram and WhatsApp were successful and neither of those companies would have flourished in the way they have without Facebook's resources behind them.

When it comes to the first reason (i.e., that breaking up companies won't solve some of the problems created by Big Tech), I agree with him about safety and security being unlikely to improve. But with the absorption of user data from these acquired companies, privacy is another matter. And as mentioned at the beginning of this chapter, antitrust is required to bring Big Tech down to a size where we can then start exercising some control over them so that they don't control us (more to come about this later on in this chapter and in the next chapter).

---

[26]Nicholas Thompson, "Tim Wu Explains Why He Thinks Facebook Should Be Broken Up," *Wired*, July 5, 2019, https://www.wired.com/story/tim-wu-explains-why-facebook-broken-up/

Meanwhile, the line of argument that breaking up the giants will be to play into China's hands and offer the East competitive advantage is fallacious. No Chinese company, no matter how big—even the mammoths like Tencent, Baidu, and Alibaba—has been able so far to come even close to displacing Western tech companies in the West. To date, only TikTok is a potential rival outside of China (although it's far too early to tell), while most of us continue to use the GAFA companies without a second thought. TikTok is successful because "winning" isn't only about the volume of data you're gathering, but how you innovate and the product or service you build. When TikTok began snapping at the heels of Western social media, it wasn't because it had access to more data. It was because it created a great product. Big Tech has more than enough data to compete (although at this writing TikTok was in talks to be acquired or combined with one of the American Big Tech firms).[27]

Moreover, the hypocrisy in the China argument is evident when you consider that these companies are desperate to operate in the giant Chinese market and are actively working with the government to do so. Microsoft, in conjunction with state-owned tech entities, has built "Windows 10 China Government Edition," which will include China's encryption system, government-controlled updates, and remote equipment monitoring. Google, eager to break into China, recently said it would bow to the government's censorship demands over search results, only to reverse itself after an employee revolt. In 2017, Apple removed the *New York Times* news app from its Chinese App Store because it violated "local regulations," while back in 2014 LinkedIn agreed to China's censorship demands when it launched a Chinese version of the platform.[28] Even more recently, in June 2020, Zoom, a U.S. videoconferencing company, shut down the account of Zhou Fengsuo, a Chinese dissident based in California (it was later restored) and terminated sessions commemorating the Tiananmen Square events at the request of the Chinese government.[29] Other examples abound that makes one wonder how many more requests from the Chinese government Big Tech has complied with that just haven't been made public yet, despite potentially affecting non-Chinese citizens.

Similarly, I wholeheartedly agree once again with Tim Wu that "national champion"–style arguments, that governments are duty-bound to protect their

---

[27]Georgia Wells, Cara Lombardo, "Twitter, TikTok have held preliminary talks about possible combination," *Wall Street Journal*, August 8, 2020, https://www.wsj.com/articles/twitter-tiktok-have-held-preliminary-talks-about-possible-combination-11596925449

[28]Julia Horowitz, "The compromises that companies make to do business in China," CNN, May 9, 2018, https://money.cnn.com/2018/05/09/news/economy/foreign-companies-china-taiwan-compromise/index.html

[29]Zoom, "Improving Our Policies as We Continue to Enable Global Collaboration," June 11, 2020, https://blog.zoom.us/improving-our-policies-as-we-continue-to-enable-global-collaboration/

biggest companies, don't hold water either. In an enlightening interview with the *American Conservative*,[30] Wu said:

> When we're talking about international competitiveness, there's an argument that suggests we shouldn't interfere too much with Facebook or Google because they are our champions in facing Chinese competition, and if we hurt our companies at home then how are they going to take on their Chinese rivals? I'm not a believer in national champion-style industrial policy. I don't think that it has a good track record. In the 1970s and 1980s, people saw Japan as a rising threat. You might have said we should leave AT&T and IBM alone because we need them to fight off our Japanese rivals. But I think it was good to break up AT&T, good to challenge IBM, and that the American tech and computer industries, even though they went through a lot of turmoil during that period, ultimately emerged incredibly stronger from the antitrust actions and breakups. That coupled with the action against Microsoft helped us ensure a generation of American supremacy in tech. Frankly, the fact that Japan never took on their monopolists ended up hurting them.

To be clear, I think China's tech expansion is dangerous for the democratic values we defend in the West, and I do not want to live in a world dominated by the autocratic regime of China. There should be even stricter conditions for Chinese companies to acquire U.S. or European companies, and more broadly on getting access to intellectual property developed by the West, which is sometimes a condition for entry into the Chinese market.

As for Zuckerberg's third argument (Instagram and WhatsApp wouldn't have been able to flourish without Facebook), it may be true when looking at the past (Facebook's resources definitely helped), but it doesn't have to define the future. It is likely that Instagram and WhatsApp would indeed struggle a bit more without Facebook's infrastructure and resulting synergies, but that's part of the purpose of breaking up a monopoly and reigniting competition! Besides, as two of the top 10 most popular apps on the planet,[31] Instagram and WhatsApp are undoubtedly in a position to build out infrastructure and forge a path on their own.

I have heard other arguments against a stricter antitrust approach, the most prominent being that antitrust destroys value by eliminating economies of scale and dampens innovation. History demonstrates the contrary: from the breaking up of Standard Oil in 1911 that generated some of the most valuable companies on the

---

[30]Daniel Kishi, "Against Bigness? Begin By Breaking Up Big Tech," *American Conservative*, November 28, 2018, https://www.theamericanconservative.com/articles/against-bigness-begin-by-breaking-up-big-tech/

[31]Amandeep Singh, "Top 10 Most Popular Applications in 2020," Net Solutions, May 30, 2019, https://www.netsolutions.com/insights/top-10-most-popular-apps-2018/

planet (Chevron, Exxon, Mobil) to AT&T in the early 1980s, mentioned by Tim Wu earlier, which helped ignite competition in the telecom industry, which some believe helped the internet emerge, and—though it has been fiercely debated—to Microsoft, the last big antitrust case in the U.S.

Back in late 1998, the U.S. government and 20 states accused Microsoft of abusing its dominance in the PC market by integrating its Internet Explorer web browser so tightly into its operating system (which at that time had 90 percent market share) that competing browsers could not gain traction with users. This was especially important because it was becoming clear that many computer applications—think search, for example—were migrating to, or relying on, the browser as the gateway to the burgeoning internet. The DOJ didn't break up the company—although many of the states wanted the browser to be spun off as a separate business—but rather forced the company to make its operating system more accommodating to competing browsers and to give them more prominence so users could choose them and be sure they would work properly. European regulators eventually went further, forcing Microsoft to sell versions of its operating system with and without its own browser.

The decision paved the way for alternative browsers such as Firefox and Google's Chrome to emerge (Microsoft's tactics had all but killed Netscape by that point). And it enabled developers of numerous applications to enjoy interoperability across different operating systems and browsers. This, in turn, forced Microsoft to compete in those areas, such as search. It had mixed success, but eventually, Microsoft flourished anew without its monopoly position and is again among the top five most valuable companies in the world.

Just to be clear: it is absolutely the case that, in a Big Tech–dominated world, innovation still happens. When Apple produced the iPhone in 2007, it pushed Google to roll out Android, which now has market share of about 86 percent.[32] Facebook and Google are fighting tooth and nail over the advertising market. Cloud computing wouldn't be where it is right now without the competition between Amazon, Google, and Microsoft. Yet this argument doesn't take into account how much innovation has been lost.

Particularly in the U.S., the Big Tech firms have been largely accepted as "natural monopolies," their dominance supposedly achieved through marketplace preference and network effects, rather than illegal means (and the July 2020 congressional hearing with Facebook, Microsoft, Apple and Amazon, while historical, is unlikely to change anything about this).[33] This obscures the reality of these firms using their

---

[32] IDC, "Smartphone Market Share," April 02, 2020, https://www.idc.com/promo/smartphone-market-share/os

[33] Rachel Lerman, Reed Albergotti, Elizabeth Dwoskin, Heather Kelly, "Big Tech is worth even more the day after congressional grilling," *Washington Post*, July 30, 2020, https://www.washingtonpost.com/technology/2020/07/30/amazon-apple-facebook-google-earnings/

giant war chests to buy potentially threatening startups simply to take their patents and shut them down. Or of venture capitalists denying funding to startups for fear that it would be too easy for their technologies to be replicated and crushed by the scale of the big firms. Or even—to paraphrase technologist Jeff Hammerbacher—of all those brilliant innovative minds that were lost to thinking about "how to make people click ads."

ANTITRUST IS NOT A UNIVERSAL TOOL

We have to be careful not to consider that breaking up companies and limiting their growth, whether organic or through mergers, is a one-size-fits-all solution to the cornucopia of Big Tech–related problems. With the FTC demanding information from the big five U.S. tech giants regarding their acquisitions of smaller startups, as part of a review into potentially anticompetitive behavior, it's worth stating that universally banning—or heavily restricting—acquisitions by large tech companies altogether makes little sense. As the analyst Ben Thompson argues,[34] if we were to go down that road it would mean a world where "new technology would be diffused far more slowly (as the new startup scales), if at all (if the startup goes out of business). . . . The amount of investment in risky technologies without obvious avenues to go-to-market would decrease, simply because it would be far less likely that investors would earn a return even if the technology worked. The risk of working for a startup would increase significantly, both because the startup would be less likely to succeed and also because the failure scenario is unemployment."

As *The Economist* emphasized in a 2019 article entitled "Breaking up is hard to do: Dismembering Big Tech," "break-ups alone will not suffice to tame big tech."[35] The piece went on to reference Harold Feld at the think tank Public Knowledge, who noted the intriguing-named "starfish problem": "Some starfish have incredible powers of regeneration: tear them up and the pieces quickly grow into complete new creatures. Similarly, one part of a tech giant could become dominant again because of network effects. Break-ups, he argues, need to be complemented by regulation that weakens this effect, for instance with requirements that a user of one instant-messaging service can exchange texts with another." The same is true of simply blocking M&A.

***

No company should be more powerful than a country or government, which is why I do believe components of Big Tech will need to be hived off. And this isn't

---

[34]Ben Thompson, "First, Do No Harm," Stratechery, February 12, 2020, https://stratechery .com/2020/first-do-no-harm/
[35]"Breaking up is hard to do: Dismembering Big Tech," *The Economist,* October 24, 2019, https://www.economist.com/business/2019/10/24/dismembering-big-tech

about innovation or the tech arms race with China. Rather, no company should be in a position to make unilateral, uncontrolled decisions about things that affect hundreds of millions, let alone billions, of people. However, breaking up Big Tech won't achieve the desired outcome in every case and is only one element of a multipronged approach to galvanizing competition for the greater good, alongside punitive fines and drawing up legislation to force some companies to make their data available to third parties.

Like EU Executive Vice President Vestager, I believe that the tech giants' stardust-sprinkled marketing has distracted the authorities, and they need to put antitrust back at the top of their agenda. But it's also plain that a fundamental failure to understand how these platforms work also played its part. Lawmakers and regulators "get" traditional media and telecoms—they use it every day; they don't need their kids to explain it to them. Much of tech baffles at least some of them. Who can forget the way Mark Zuckerberg paused incredulously when the silver-haired (and since retired) U.S. Senator Orrin Hatch of Utah asked him how Facebook could sustain a business model in which users don't pay? "Senator, we run ads," said the social media mogul, unable to suppress a smirk.[36] Or the toe-curling time Google's Sundar Pichai was obliged to remind a U.S. Congressman that Google doesn't make the iPhone.[37] The reality is that Big Tech has used the ignorance or naivete of policy makers to avoid scrutiny, let alone regulation. This also feeds the libertarian/tech narrative that government is laughably incompetent. It is indeed a massive failure of government officials that they are not more knowledgeable, and they need to remedy that quickly, and not be intimidated, or back down from holding the platforms to account, leveling the competitive playing field and forcing higher standards.

---

[36] https://www.youtube.com/watch?v=n2H8wx1aBiQ
[37] Adi Robertson, "Google's CEO had to remind Congress that Google doesn't make iPhones," The Verge, December 11, 2018, https://www.theverge.com/2018/12/11/18136377/google-sundar-pichai-steve-king-hearing-granddaughter-iphone-android-notification

CHAPTER 12

Tax, Privacy, and Other Running Sores

When it comes to regulating tech companies, intent matters far less than the outcome. There are no prizes for talking a good game when it comes to reform. Results are all that matter. The vast majority of founders didn't set out to create the harmful effects we've ended up with today. The same goes for most employees. It doesn't change the fact that they should be held accountable for the results of their actions.

We must also cut governments and regulatory bodies a little slack. Never before have companies reached such scale so fast, and overseeing an ever-shifting sector, an industry that is steadily reinventing every aspect of our lives, is a daunting task that takes time to get right. Consider this for a moment: the first petrol-powered car was invented in 1885. In the U.S., the first law making the installation of seat belts compulsory for manufacturers was passed in 1968. The first law making them required for drivers in 49 states took nearly another 30 years. It's still not compulsory for over-18s in New Hampshire. I'm often perplexed by people who seem to expect perfection from legislators and complain, for example, about GDPR (General Data Protection Regulation, Europe's data protection and privacy regime), and yet allow genuine leeway to tech giants as they chart their course through trial and error. It's absurd to expect the public sector to get it right the first time. The pace at which tech is evolving means that it should be perfectly acceptable to allow officials and lawmakers the time and space to iterate, and we should instead push for them to develop the agility required to respond when confronted with new evidence.

Today, to the extent that tech is regulated at all, it is a hodgepodge. Individual countries in Europe, and individual states in the U.S., have sometimes taken different approaches, especially around privacy and industry self-regulation. This state of affairs is antiquated, confusing, and bad for both the industry and consumers. As with other industries that have a profound impact on society—such as banking, healthcare, insurance, and automotive—we need federal or super-regulators, with real teeth and clearly defined rules of engagement. A change of this sort would offer companies stability and clarity, foster further innovation, promote healthy competition, but also hold large tech corporations accountable for the impact that they have.

I am not suggesting there is no role for states or individual countries in tech oversight; sometimes more creative approaches come from them. But in the digital realm, many of these issues are central to civic life without regard to borders.

Having said that, not everything needs to be regulated. As argued by Lisa Quest and Anthony Charrie in *MIT Sloan Management Review*,[1] regulation should focus on three overarching objectives and be proportionate to the level of risk:

- Safety: protecting individuals and societies, such as governments mandating air bags, or the use of the seat belts, but not the size or form of cars
- Competition: ensuring that there is healthy competition and a real chance for innovation to flourish, principles that are at the core of the capitalist model upon which today's Western world is based
- Privacy: establishing understandable and consistent parameters for data privacy and monetization

Beyond the core issue of antitrust we explored in Chapter 11, I would focus on five urgent and important initiatives: implementing fair and equitable taxation, modernizing labor laws, protecting privacy, fighting for the preservation of facts and civil discourse, and setting standards for AI/facial recognition.

IMPLEMENTING FAIR AND EQUITABLE TAXATION

Solving Big Tech's tax problem is critically important because it helps solve a host of other problems, reasserts the principles of fairness and transparency in taxation, and if implemented across all corporations helps reestablish governments' power to fight inequality. And as for the criticism I frequently hear voiced in the U.S., that ensuring that tech giants pay their fair share of tax would disincentivize innovation and send them scuttling to the Far East—or even more fancifully, that they give back through philanthropy—I say nonsense.

As the Dutch historian Rutger Bregman noted in a talk in Davos in 2019, in 1950 in the U.S., under (Republican) President Eisenhower, the top marginal tax rate was 91 percent—and yet industry flourished.[2] There's no reason to believe a higher tax rate would inhibit innovation (without it having to be 91 percent!). As for philanthropy, frankly, I'd like to see the big-name founders' fondness for ego-massaging

---

[1] Lisa Quest, Anthony Charrie, "The right way to regulate the tech industry," *MIT Sloan Management Review,* September 19, 2019, https://sloanreview.mit.edu/article/the-right-way-to-regulate-the-tech-industry/
[2] https://www.youtube.com/watch?v=r5LtFnmPruU

"vanity projects" called out for what it is: a way of deflecting attention away from missteps and the real-world problems their companies might have caused, as well as under- (or non-) payment of taxes. As a French-born U.S. resident, I find myself repeatedly being told how wealthy Americans are so much more generous than their European counterparts. "Look at all the museums, schools, hospital wings, university endowments, and so on, these people are financing" is usually how the argument starts. My riposte is pretty simple: In Europe, adequate corporate and individual taxes pay for all that. Why on earth would I want Jeff Bezos, Bill Gates, or Mark Zuckerberg to decide which students get free books, which disease gets cured first, or which city gets a new museum? I'm not saying European governments are perfect, far from it. But when I look at what they have achieved over the last 100 years, their quality of life, the cradle-to-grave care their citizens get, they've done a much better job than Americans often give them credit for.

I appreciate that it sounds a little naive to expect better behavior from Big Tech than from giants of other sectors when it comes to tax avoidance. After all, all of them are beholden to shareholders, many of whom would view minimizing tax liabilities as a given, and, strictly speaking, they are behaving legally when it comes to taxation. Yet I believe that paying their (genuinely) fair share of taxes would actually be a smart business move on behalf of the tech unicorns. And it would mean they are at least partially living up to the grandiose visions they lay claim to by giving back to the societies that enabled them to thrive in the first place. They could, for example, make a big, bold statement by ceasing to use tax havens, or they could try to pay taxes in each of their territories more proportionally to the profits they generate there. Even if their motives were opportunistic, I believe it would not only earn them plaudits, but it would be good for business too, by winning over customers and talent, and enabling more fruitful partnerships with governments. Taking such steps couldn't be timelier. They can certainly afford it. In Europe, for example, which is waging a war on tax minimization generally, this problem has become highly contentious and shot up the news agenda, leading the tech giants to draw considerable popular ire. This is increasingly true in the U.S. today too, particularly in an election year.

I don't expect many of the large tech brands to actually do what I just suggested, which begs the question: what needs to happen instead?

Toward the end of 2019, the OECD announced proposals to build a new and "stable" international tax environment to prevent corporations from moving their profits around the world to minimize their tax liability.[3] "In a digital age, the allocation of taxing rights can no longer be exclusively circumscribed by reference to physical presence," it announced. "The current rules dating back to the 1920s are

---

[3]OECD Public Consultation Document, "Secretariat Proposal for a 'Unified Approach' under Pillar One," October 9–November 12, 2019, http://www.oecd.org/tax/beps/public-consultation-document-secretariat-proposal-unified-approach-pillar-one.pdf

no longer sufficient to ensure a fair allocation of taxing rights in an increasingly globalized world."

Two critical elements are expected to come from the work that the OECD is conducting. First is a redesign of rules so that businesses are taxed based on where the value is created, as opposed to where they have a physical presence, and to define what to tax in tech businesses that are driven by intangible assets such as data and knowledge. One of the most challenging problems is an accounting maneuver that allows the companies to account for transactions among subsidiaries or offices around the world in ways that take advantage of places where taxes are lowest. As explained in chapter 3, while the legal structures involved are quite complex and constantly evolving, they are widely used by Big Tech. They have, for example, created numerous shell companies in tax havens around the world, whose only purpose is to hold intellectual property (IP) rights and charge other companies of the same group for their use of this IP. The royalties collected by the shell company yield little to no tax income and the profits registered in countries with higher taxes are decreased proportionally. Until as recently as December 2019, when it announced that it would no longer use the "Double Irish, Dutch sandwich" tax loophole, the Dutch Google subsidiary would shift revenue from royalties earned outside of the U.S. to Google Ireland Holdings, an affiliate incorporated in Bermuda, where it paid no income tax. In 2018 alone Google moved $24.5 billion through its Dutch holding to Bermuda.[4]

Second is the introduction of a global minimum corporate tax rate.[5] This would allow countries to tax foreign subsidiaries' profits at a minimum level, regardless of whatever cross-border transfers might allow companies to shift their tax liabilities to lower-tax jurisdictions.[6]

The EU, and the federal government in the U.S., have been slow to tackle the tax problem for tech, leading to individual efforts. The French government, for example, approved in July 2019 a 3 percent levy on large tech companies' total local sales (after tense discussions between the U.S. and French governments, it was agreed that the tax would not be applied if the OECD reached a deal by the end of 2020).[7] That is the right idea in my view, but doing it piecemeal is not. This is why the work of the OECD to try to develop a consensus-based, longer-term solution to tech taxation is

---

[4]Toby Sterling, "Google to end 'Double Irish, Dutch sandwich' tax scheme," Reuters, December 31, 2019, https://www.reuters.com/article/us-google-taxes-netherlands/google-to-end-double-irish-dutch-tax-scheme-filing-idUSKBN1YZ10Z
[5]OECD, "Global Anti-Base Erosion Proposal ('GloBE') - Pillar Two," 2019, https://www.oecd.org/tax/beps/public-consultation-document-global-anti-base-erosion-proposal-pillar-two.pdf.pdf
[6]Chris Giles, "OECD proposes global minimum corporate tax rate," *Financial Times,* November 8, 2019, https://www.ft.com/content/f17a406e-021a-11ea-b7bc-f3fa4e77dd47
[7]BBC, "France agrees to delay new tax on tech giants," January 21, 2020, https://www.bbc.com/news/business-51192369

both important and urgent. The plan was due to be delivered to the G20 in 2020. Unfortunately, at the time of the writing, the U.S. has called for a suspension of the talks and threatened European nations with tariffs if they implement targeted taxes on tech companies. Europe vowed to pursue its digital tax plans.[8]

Independently of these international talks, the EU has taken a number of steps toward the fairer taxation of global tech companies within its borders. But more needs to happen. Specifically:

- Move forward with the March 2018 Common Consolidated Corporate Tax Base[9] proposal, which would establish a single set of rules to calculate companies' taxable profits in the EU.
- Crack down heavily on any EU member that acts as a tax haven to allow Big Tech (and multinationals in other sectors) to shuffle profits from one location to another to slash their corporation tax bills. These include low corporate tax jurisdictions like Ireland, Luxembourg, and Malta, which have sought to attract tech jobs by offering excessive tax breaks. This, too, is starting to happen. Google, for instance, whose European HQ is in Dublin, has agreed to pay $1 billion in tax and fines to the French authorities,[10] after a four-year investigation in the country. And this could set a legal precedent for other tech giants' French operations. Meanwhile, Netflix was accused of channeling hundreds of millions of dollars of profit made in the UK into the Netherlands,[11] a tax haven. Make no mistake, the smaller countries are not going to take this lying down; a proposed new European rule that would have obliged multinationals to reveal how much profit they make in each of the EU's 27 member states, thus exposing their tax avoidance, was blocked by 12 EU countries, including (surprise, surprise!) Ireland, Luxembourg, Malta, and Cyprus.[12] My recommendation? Inform countries that engage in the practice of slashing

---

[8]Sam Schechner, "After U.S. Declares Impasse on Digital Taxes, Europe Continues Push," *Wall Street Journal,* June 18, 2020, https://www.wsj.com/articles/after-u-s-declares-impasse-on-digital-taxes-europe-continues-push-11592481834

[9]https://ec.europa.eu/taxation_customs/business/company-tax/common-consolidated-corporate-tax-base-ccctb_cn

[10]Simon Carraud, "Google to pay $1 billion in France to settle fiscal fraud probe," Reuters, September 12, 2019, https://www.reuters.com/article/us-france-tech-google-tax/google-to-pay-1-billion-in-france-to-settle-fiscal-fraud-probe-idUSKCN1VX1SM

[11]Mark Sweney, "Netflix accused of funnelling UK profits through Netherlands," *The Guardian,* January 14, 2020, https://www.theguardian.com/media/2020/jan/14/netflix-accused-of-funnelling-uk-profits-through-netherlands

[12]Rupert Neate, "12 EU states reject move to expose companies' tax avoidance," *The Guardian,* November 28, 2019, https://www.theguardian.com/business/2019/nov/28/12-eu-states-reject-move-to-expose-companies-tax-avoidance#img-1

corporate tax rates to the bone that they risk stiff fines and ultimately being booted out of the union (while admittedly highly unlikely, given the increased need to raise revenues it is no longer unthinkable). Additionally, the EU must implement its proposal to force multinationals to reveal their profits earned in each member state.

■ Ramp up the collection of fines and interest payments on unpaid corporate taxes, while systematically going after the most consistently egregious offenders. Apple, for example, has reportedly agreed to settle a $570-million-plus tax bill in France,[13] but was still challenging the EU's order to repay $14.5 billion in back taxes to the Irish authorities at the time of writing.[14] Ireland's open door to Apple came at a cost: $14.9 billion in lost corporation tax is a hefty price tag, for a nation whose total public expenditure on its citizens will amount to about $90 billion in 2020.[15]

To those critics in the U.S. who say that Europe is biased against American tech companies, Margrethe Vestager replied that between 2000 and 2016, out of the 150 tax rulings made by the European Commission, only 2 percent involved U.S. companies.[16]

Following the EU's determination to fix its taxation policy[17]—and given the increased urgency caused by a combination of the pandemic and multiple countries around the world actively reviewing their approach to tech-industry taxation—it's high time for the U.S. to become significantly more active on its own territory, too. A few U.S. states, including New York, West Virginia, Nebraska, and Maryland, have started working on bills to tax tech companies on income generated from digital advertising and services.[18] Huge tax breaks and other inducements to persuade companies to relocate are increasingly coming under fire. While these state proposals

---

[13]"Apple agrees to pay back-taxes to French authorities," Reuters, February 5, 2019, https://www.reuters.com/article/us-apple-france/apple-agrees-to-pay-back-taxes-to-french-authorities-idUSKCN1PU0VS

[14]Stephanie Bodoni, Aoife White, "Apple wins fight over $14.9 billion tax bill in blow to EU," Bloomberg, July 15, 2020, https://www.bloomberg.com/news/articles/2020-07-15/apple-wins-eu-court-fight-over-14-9-billion-tax-bill

[15]https://whereyourmoneygoes.gov.ie/en/

[16]"EU tax move on Apple not anti-US bias: Vestager," Science X, September 19, 2016, https://phys.org/news/2016-09-eu-tax-apple-anti-us-bias.html

[17]"'Making Tax Work for All': Speech by Commissioner Paolo Gentiloni on the Commission's priorities for EU taxation policy," May 3, 2020, https://www.epc.eu/en/Publications/taxation-fair-taxation-think-tank-Brussels-European-Policy-Centre~2fd03c

[18]Ashley Gold, "States Advance Efforts to Tax Digital Revenue," The Information, March 11, 2020, https://www.theinformation.com/articles/states-advance-efforts-to-tax-digital-revenue

face significant headwinds before becoming law, they indicate a growing desire and need—in the U.S. as well as Europe—to see Big Tech pay their fair share.

I recognize that the U.S. federal government cannot dictate local tax policies, but it should make the case that this is a race to the bottom. At the very least, the U.S. has to remain engaged in international talks and stop adopting the defensive position that such moves are informed by a desire by the rest of the world to penalize U.S. companies. The current system is unsustainable and governments around the world have made it clear that they will no longer kowtow to the tech leviathans. Lost revenues will be clawed back. Playing fields will be leveled. And the U.S. needs to be fully engaged in building the new consensus.

MODERNIZING EMPLOYMENT AND LABOR PROTECTIONS

It has been clear for some time that existing labor laws are obsolete in this new digital era. And, if anything, the COVID-19 pandemic has made this even more painfully obvious: the gig economy has left millions of workers and their families utterly exposed in their lack of social protections and benefits such as a minimum wage, hazard pay, and sick leave. While tech employees were sent home for their own protection, warehouse employees were required to work in conditions that put them (and their households) at risk, highlighting the double standards that Big Tech applies to its workforce. As Tim Bray, a senior engineer and VP at Amazon, summarized on his blog when he resigned in May 2020 to protest against the firing of activists raising concerns about the lack of information and protective equipment in Amazon's warehouses:

> *Amazon is exceptionally well-managed and has demonstrated great skill at spotting opportunities and building repeatable processes for exploiting them. It has a corresponding lack of vision about the human costs of the relentless growth and accumulation of wealth and power. If we don't like certain things Amazon is doing, we need to put legal guardrails in place to stop those things. We don't need to invent anything new; a combination of antitrust and living-wage and worker-empowerment legislation, rigorously enforced, offers a clear path forward.*[19]

While the role of employee-led actions remain critical to making Big Tech take the necessary steps to protect workers—as demonstrated by employee activism in France that led to Amazon substantially improving safety conditions for workers

---

[19]Tim Bray, "Bye, Amazon," ongoing by Tim Bray, May 4, 2020, https://www.tbray.org/ongoing/When/202x/2020/04/29/Leaving-Amazon

during the COVID-19 crisis[20]—some specific legislative changes are required when it comes to the gig economy:

- Classification differences between employees and independent contractors needs to be fundamentally reviewed. A gig worker whose gig is their full-time job and only source of revenue has more in common with a full-time employee than with another gig worker who only works a few hours a week and specifically doesn't want a fixed minimum number of hours. (Companies don't like to talk about the former when they defend their business models.) Revising these classifications would allow for practical solutions to provide benefits and protections for full-time gig workers, while allowing flexibility and autonomy for people who just want to supplement their income.
- All workers should benefit from the exact same protections, no matter their status, regarding discrimination, harassment, rights to organize, whistleblower rights, and so on.
- No gig should be paid at less than the local minimum hourly wage, whether the person is an independent contractor or an employee. Flexibility shouldn't be an excuse for exploitation.
- A "portable reputation" program should be created to allow workers to carry their ratings from one platform to another.
- In the U.S., specifically, benefits such as healthcare and unemployment insurance should be available to gig workers, depending on the number of hours worked. Special financial instruments for retirement savings, akin to 401(k)s, should be created for gig workers and be portable, so if they move to a different platform it goes with them. This could open up incentives for the companies who might want to offer some sort of matching or other benefit, for recruitment and retention.

Actions on these fronts are starting to be taken all around the world. California passed Assembly Bill 5 in January 2020, which forces the reclassification of most gig workers as employees. A few months later, the state sued Uber and Lyft for defying the new law and refusing to reclassify the workers.[21] Meanwhile, collective bargaining agreements are being signed in the UK[22] and Germany to give gig

---

[20]Cole Stangler, "How French Workers Took on Amazon in the Middle of a Pandemic and Won," *New York Times,* April 29, 2020, https://www.nytimes.com/2020/04/29/opinion/amazon-france-coronavirus.html

[21]Dave Lee, "California sues Uber and Lyft over gig economy law," *Financial Times,* May 5, 2020, https://www.ft.com/content/f0d13081-619d-4938-a048-a07f85ba98c1

[22]Sarah O'Connor, "Gig economy agreements promise a brighter future for trade unions," *Financial Times,* February 26, 2019, https://www.ft.com/content/25271b48-38eb-11e9-b856-5404d3811663

workers the opportunity to choose between minimum hours and benefits or total flexibility without benefits.

PROTECTING PRIVACY AND RETHINKING DATA OWNERSHIP

The next urgent task for governments and regulators to confront is the preservation of privacy, which has been so remorselessly trampled during the decade in which Big Tech has run amok. Consumers face a double-barreled threat: breaches by hackers, and misuse and abuse of their personal data by the companies themselves.

Facebook—a serial offender in both areas—suffered three privacy breaches in 2019 alone, the most disastrous of which saw the records of over 540 million of the platform's users exposed on Amazon's cloud servers.[23] From eBay (145 million hacked),[24] to Uber (57 million hacked, and the company attempted to cover its tracks),[25] to Yahoo (1 billion accounts breached),[26] Big Tech's record on protecting user data is so sketchy that unless the numbers involved are stratospheric, breaches may not even make the news.

Perhaps more on the minds of consumers, however, is what these companies do with our data. According to a 2019 YouGov survey for Amnesty International,[27] which polled nearly 10,000 people in nine countries—Brazil, Denmark, Egypt, France, Germany, India, Norway, South Africa and the U.S. —73 percent want their governments to do more to regulate Big Tech, with almost as many (71 percent) "worried about how tech companies collect and use their personal data." Of those worried about their personal data, 62 percent are most concerned with the violation of their right to privacy. "The poll results are stark and consistent—a clear majority of people are worried about the power Big Tech has over their lives," said Director

---

[23] Jason Silverstein, "Hundreds of millions of Facebook user records were exposed on Amazon cloud server," CBS News, April 4, 2019, https://www.cbsnews.com/news/millions-facebook-user-records-exposed-amazon-cloud-server/

[24] Jim Finkle, "Hackers raid eBay in historic breach, access 145 million records," Reuters, May 22, 2014, https://uk.reuters.com/article/uk-ebay-password/hackers-raid-ebay-in-historic-breach-access-145-million-records-idUKKBN0E10ZL20140522

[25] Andy Greenberg, "Hack Brief: Uber Paid Off Hackers to Hide a 57-Million User Data Breach," *Wired,* November 21, 2017, https://www.wired.com/story/uber-paid-off-hackers-to-hide-a-57-million-user-data-breach/

[26] Nick Wells, "How Yahoo's 1 billion account breach stacks up with the biggest hacks ever," CNBC, December 15, 2016, https://www.cnbc.com/2016/12/15/how-yahoos-1-billion-account-breach-stacks-up-with-biggest-hacks-ever.html

[27] Amnesty International press release, "New poll reveals 7 in 10 people want governments to regulate Big Tech over personal data fears," December 4, 2019, https://www.amnesty.org/en/latest/news/2019/12/big-tech-privacy-poll-shows-people-worried/

of Amnesty Tech's Tanya O'Carroll. "The results are a damning indictment of how Big Tech companies harvest and use our personal data. People want to see an end to tech companies trampling over our right to privacy."

There are several things governments can do to fix this in the short term. First is to end what's known as "ambient surveillance," meaning you are being tracked around the web or in the physical world, the latter of which can happen just by having your mobile phone with you. Many apps have location services on by default, forcing users to opt out of some or all of them.

This has happened almost by stealth, and a characteristic of this new normal is that we cannot entirely opt out of it, any more than we might opt out of, say, automobile culture, Maciej Ceglowski, founder of Pinboard, told the U.S. Senate Committee on Banking in May 2019:[28]

> *However sincere our commitment to walking, the world around us would still be a world built for cars. We would still have to contend with roads, traffic jams, air pollution, and run the risk of being hit by a bus. Similarly, while it is possible in principle to throw one's laptop into the sea and renounce all technology, it is no longer possible to opt out of a surveillance society. When we talk about privacy in this... more basic sense, the giant tech companies are not guardians of privacy, but its gravediggers...*
>
> *Tech companies will correctly point out that their customers have willingly traded their private data for an almost miraculous collection of useful services, services that have unquestionably made their lives better, and that the business model that allows them to offer these services for free creates far more value than harm for their customers.*
>
> *Consumers will just as rightly point out that they never consented to be the subjects in an uncontrolled social experiment, that the companies engaged in reshaping our world have consistently refused to honestly discuss their business models or data collection practices, and that in a democratic society, profound social change requires consensus and accountability.*

Governments and regulators are starting to fight ambient surveillance by default that has been a cornerstone of the internet. EU's GDPR is the most famous piece of legislation in that area. Among many other data protections, it requires explicit informed consent from a user for a company to capture and process their data. GDPR is far from perfect; there are already signs of opt-in fatigue for consumers, it's very costly for small businesses, it may make it hard for free services to survive (although that may force some business to rethink their business model and offer a true paid alternative), and it potentially makes it harder to track some cybercrime. Its biggest problem though is that so far it doesn't seem to have changed

---

[28] https://www.banking.senate.gov/imo/media/doc/Ceglowski%20Testimony%205-7-19.pdf

anything regarding the data monopoly of Big Tech and their business model—not that GDPR alone was ever going to achieve that. And while there is legitimate criticism and need to further improve it, GDPR has served as a catalyst for a global wave of data protection regulations in India, Brazil, Japan, and other countries.[29] Some U.S. states have also followed up, most famously California, which adopted the California Consumer Privacy Act in January 2020.[30]

Tech giants like Apple, Microsoft and Cisco have become advocates for America to follow suit with a (perhaps less onerous) U.S. version of the European legislation.[31] Yes there's self-interest in their calls—what's troublesome and binds your hands when you're a startup insulates you from competition when you're an effective monopoly—but they can also read the writing on the wall. Federal statutory data protection is coming, and better the devil you know, as GDPR-like rules look set to emerge, with reform, as the industry gold standard globally.

GDPR has also, indirectly, spawned quite a few other initiatives. One of the most interesting is from the UK's Information Commissioner's Office, an independent body established to uphold data protection and information rights law, of a digital industry code of practice for protecting children. With children reckoned to make up about 20 percent of those online, "Age appropriate design: a code of practice for online services"[32] lays out the 15 standards expected from designers, developers, and providers of online products, including apps, connected toys and games, social media platforms, educational sites, and streaming services. Among its requirements, the code requires digital services to set "a built-in baseline of data protection whenever they download a new app, game or visit a website," including high privacy settings by default. The code still has to go before the UK Parliament for approval, and even then a 12-month "transition period" will follow. But with similar initiatives under active consideration in the U.S., Europe, and globally by the OECD, teething problems notwithstanding, this too appears to be a good template to follow.

GDPR is a good starting point, but a lot more needs to be done in order to strengthen users' privacy. While by no means exhaustive, this list is what I would focus on:

---

[29]Jonathan Greig, "How more countries plan to pass stringent privacy laws in 2019," TechRepublic, June 25, 2019, https://www.techrepublic.com/article/how-more-countries-plan-to-pass-stringent-privacy-laws-in-2019/

[30]Dimitri Sirota, "California's new data privacy law brings U.S. closer to GDPR," TechCrunch, November 14, 2019, https://techcrunch.com/2019/11/14/californias-new-data-privacy-law-brings-u-s-closer-to-gdpr/

[31]Alana Foster, "Tech giants urge US to adopt GDPR laws," IBC, February 5, 2019, https://www.ibc.org/regulation/tech-giants-urge-us-to-adopt-gdpr-laws/3570.article

[32]https://ico.org.uk/for-organisations/guide-to-data-protection/key-data-protection-themes/age-appropriate-design-a-code-of-practice-for-online-services/

- Tracking and data collection: Under GDPR, most websites ask for users to confirm that they're allowing their data to be processed (which is the default setting) and users have to specifically opt out for each type of data they don't want to be processed. To advance affirmative consent of users around data collection, the default setting should be reversed: no data collected and users can opt in. The Do Not Track setting in all browsers should be activated by default. The management of all these settings should be easy and intuitive for the average user.
- Data access and correction: The right to download your own data and to correct it exists in GDPR. Access needs to be in real time (rather than a month) and data should be in an understandable format rather than raw.
- Data ownership and portability: Companies should be required to delete all user data they have stored upon request by users, with exceptions only for what is legally required. Meanwhile, users should be able to quickly and easily transfer their data to other platforms.
- Storage and communication: In June 2020, Google made auto-delete of location history and web and app activity after 18 months and YouTube data after 36 months the default setting for new users.[33] I would make auto-delete of all behavioral data after 6 months compulsory for all users of all tech companies, data brokerages included. Encryption and pseudonymization of stored data should be made mandatory.
- Correlation and profiling: The Cambridge Analytica scandal shined the light on the ability to identify and target users by harvesting and compiling technically anonymous data. Data brokers around the world have made a business of collecting and augmenting data sold without users' knowledge. In 2018 the state of Vermont introduced the first and only law regulating data brokers, requiring them to register and implementing security and disclosure standards.[34] This needs to be further strengthened and emulated by other states and countries around the world.
- Certification and accreditation: GDPR introduced the concept of certification but the actual details of this certification remain to be disclosed. In the same way that we created standards around concepts like "organic," which ended up being useful information for consumers but also marketing tools for companies, we need standards around "privacy-friendly" companies.

---

[33]Sundar Pichai, "Keeping your private information private," Keyword, June 24, 2020, https://www.blog.google/technology/safety-security/keeping-private-information-private/

[34]Devin Coldewey, "Vermont passes first law to crack down on data brokers," TechCrunch, May 27, 2018, https://techcrunch.com/2018/05/27/vermont-passes-first-first-law-to-crackdown-on-data-brokers/

- Enforcement: No regulation is effective without proper enforcement. Data protection agencies' budgets need to be reviewed so that they can go after companies breaching privacy laws.

Finally, I oppose the oft-suggested idea of requiring the platform companies to pay us for the use of our data on some regular or metered basis. Not only would the amount of money individuals would get be small (Facebook earns less than $35 per user and per year, which is nevertheless more than Snap, Pinterest, or Twitter),[35] but at that point people would lose all control over how the platforms used it. Instead, as explained above, we should ensure that a minimum set of protective measures are in place for all users and then have companies offer an additional option completely tracking free for payment.

One last thing: to be more socially useful, platform companies should be required to share some of their (anonymized) data with policy makers, law enforcement, and research institutions. This does not mean "open data." Legal frameworks would need to be put in place to protect civil liberties. They should contain several fundamental data sharing principles, as French Parliamentarian Paula Forteza and MP advisor Marianne Billard have argued.[36] These would include proportionality, the principle of "do no harm," and full respect for the EU's GDPR. It should also include guidelines on which type of data can be shared, how to recognize the public interest, and when data can be shared for free or how to set prices, they wrote. To achieve this, my compatriots advocate that governments define public interest projects, and they are only able to access data that meets those criteria.

With such safeguards in place, I see no reason why it shouldn't be mandatory, say, for ride-hailing apps or e-scooter/micro-mobility companies or video surveillance systems to share certain specified data sets with the cities in which they operate, as well as central government, to enable smarter, better-informed decision making. This would help local authorities fine-tune public transport provision, highlight accident hot spots, assist with traffic management, and even improve policing (providing, once again, civil liberties implications were properly thought through). A similar arrangement with the likes of Airbnb and food delivery services could help shape housing policy and urban planning. Transparency about income generated on these platforms would enable the authorities to properly tax all independent contractors, reinvest the sums raised in city infrastructure, and

---

[35] Salvador Rodriguez, "Why Facebook generates much more money per user than its rivals," CNBC, November 1, 2019, https://www.cnbc.com/2019/11/01/facebook-towers-over-rivals-in-the-critical-metric-of-revenue-per-user.html
[36] Paula Forteza and Marianne Billard, "Why data from companies should be a common good," Apolitical, October 1, 2019, https://apolitical.co/en/solution_article/why-companies-should-share-their-data-with-government

more effectively regulate activities. Tech giants, willing to share data in this way, would be participating in a public good.

FIGHTING FOR THE PRESERVATION OF FACTS AND CIVIL DISCOURSE

In October 2019, Facebook announced how it was working to consign the fake news business and its avaricious yarn-spinners to history—or at least stem the flow of lies. In a blog post by, among others, VP of Integrity Guy Rosen, the company said it had "a responsibility to stop abuse and election interference on our platform. That's why we've made significant investments since 2016 to better identify new threats, close vulnerabilities and reduce the spread of viral misinformation and fake accounts."[37] It went on to announce several new measures: "fighting foreign interference" by "combating inauthentic behavior," and "protecting the accounts of candidates, elected officials, their teams and others through Facebook Protect"; "increasing transparency" by "making Pages more transparent, including showing the confirmed owner of a Page," "labeling state-controlled media on their Page and in our Ad Library" and "making it easier to understand political ads, including a new US presidential candidate spend tracker"; "reducing misinformation" by preventing the spread of viral misinformation, "fighting voter suppression and interference, including banning paid ads that suggest voting is useless or advise people not to vote," and "helping people better understand the information they see online, including an initial of investment of $2 million to support media literacy projects."

In a memo published in January 2020 on his internal Facebook page and leaked,[38] Andrew Bosworth, now leading Facebook's virtual and augmented reality division, conceded to colleagues that the "scrutiny" the platform was now under "[was] warranted given our position in society as the most prominent new medium" and that most of the criticisms leveled at Facebook "have been valid." He went on: "So was Facebook responsible for Donald Trump getting elected? I think the answer is yes, but not for the reasons anyone thinks. He didn't get elected because of Russia or misinformation or Cambridge Analytica. He got elected because he ran the single best digital ad campaign I've ever seen from any advertiser. Period."

Half a dozen paragraphs later, he said: "If we limit what information people have access to and what they can say then we have no democracy at all." In fact,

---

[37] Facebook News, "Helping to Protect the 2020 US Elections," October 21, 2019, https://about.fb.com/news/2019/10/update-on-election-integrity-efforts/

[38] "Lord of the Rings, 2020 and Stuffed Oreos: Read the Andrew Bosworth Memo," *New York Times,* January 7, 2020, https://www.nytimes.com/2020/01/07/technology/facebook-andrew-bosworth-memo.html

companies (including Facebook) can and do make decisions all the time about what conduct and content they allow on their sites. The fact that Facebook believes that democracy rises and falls based on what happens on its platform is testimony to how it views its power as the center of digital communication and why self-regulation is not sufficient.

Bosworth argued that even if the current policies, which are staying in place, lead to the president's reelection, it was still the right decision to allow politicians and their campaigns to use Facebook to microtarget portions of the electorate and not to fact-check what they say. Fast-forward a few months. Unlike Twitter, which banned political ads,[39] and Google, which restricted their ability to target audiences in the run-up to 2020, Facebook hasn't.[40] Under public pressure, employee unrest, and growing advertiser boycott, Mark Zuckerberg announced (as I was finishing writing this book) that Facebook would ban posts attempting to suppress voting, prohibit hateful content in ads, and indicate when a post "may violate [their] policies" (Twitter chose instead to clearly mark misinformation with a "Get the facts" label). He added, "Even if a politician or government official says it, if we determine that content may lead to violence or deprive people of their right to vote, we will take that content down."[41]

For many, myself included, it feels too little too late. As Samantha Power, former U.S. ambassador to the UN, wrote on Twitter, this announcement "comes the same week it is revealed that #Facebook has succumbed to pressure from fossil fuel industry and decided not to subject climate disinformation to fact checking, treating climate SCIENCE as opinion."[42] Facebook, which owns Instagram and WhatsApp, is inarguably the most persuasive media force of our age, and knows it. Together with Google, YouTube, and Twitter, it has the heft and scale to influence and even tilt an election in the world's most powerful democracy. It's done it before; it's conceded as much. Along with antitrust concerns and the systematic dismantling of privacy, fake news and disinformation— and Facebook's look-no-hands, laissez-faire approach (pretty much replicated by YouTube and Twitter)—are some of the most pressing Big Tech–derived issues we as a society face.

The time has long since passed for decisive government intervention. For far too long the major platforms have exercised power while minimizing responsibility, flunked test after test of responsible citizenship, and undermined facts and accuracy.

---

[39]Jason Abbruzzese and Ben Collins, "Twitter to stop accepting political ads," NBC, October 30, 2019, https://www.nbcnews.com/tech/tech-news/twitter-stop-accepting-political-ads-n1074171

[40]Mike Isaac, "Why Everyone Is Angry at Facebook Over Its Political Ads Policy," *New York Times*, November 22, 2019, https://www.nytimes.com/2019/11/22/technology/campaigns-pressure-facebook-political-ads.html

[41]https://www.facebook.com/zuck/posts/10112048980882521

[42]https://twitter.com/SamanthaJPower/status/1276706947329392640

The war on fake news is a litmus test. While the U.S. government has some-times gone after Facebook over its calamitous privacy breaches, it has pulled its punches so far with regard to disinformation. Other countries have had no such qualms. The admittedly authoritarian Singaporean government passed the Protection from Online Falsehoods and Manipulation Act in May 2019,[43] which gives the authorities sweeping powers to oversee and police online platforms. While critics worry that it could serve to stifle free speech in the island city-state,[44] the government says it will not be used to target opinion and private chats, but specifically "falsehoods, bots, trolls and fake accounts," Law Minister K. Shanmugam told parliament.[45] The authorities can now order internet companies to remove what they deem to be "false statements against the public interest," and those found guilty of doing this would face a heavy fine and/or jail. The use of fake accounts or bots to spread fake news is also prohibited. Those who are found guilty of the latter could be fined up to S$1m ($733,000) and face a jail term of up to ten years.

From some important vantage points the legislation was viewed as a sledgehammer-to-crack-a-nut approach to tackling fake news; the Committee to Protect Journalists condemned the act's "broad and arbitrary powers to demand corrections, remove content, and block webpages," arguing that it "could be used to stifle reporting and the dissemination of news," and "called for the punitive measure's immediate repeal."[46]

France's National Assembly passed similar legislation in November 2018.[47] It places particular emphasis on election campaigns and efforts to influence election results, as well as a "transparency obligation" on digital platforms that must identify sponsored content by publishing the name of the author and the amount paid. It also empowers an interim judge to determine "fake news" and order its removal if it is "manifest," is "disseminated deliberately on a massive scale," and could "lead to a disturbance of the peace or compromise the outcome of an election."

The German Bundestag passed the NetzDG law (or Network Enforcement Act) in 2017,[48] which will fine social media platforms up to €50m ($56m) for failing to

[43] https://sso.agc.gov.sg/Acts-Supp/18-2019/Published/20190625?DocDate=20190625

[44] Ashley Westerman, "'Fake News' Law Goes into Effect in Singapore, Worrying Free Speech Advocates," NPR, October 2, 2019, https://www.npr.org/2019/10/02/766399689/fake-news-law-goes-into-effect-in-singapore-worrying-free-speech-advocates

[45] Tessa Wong, "Singapore fake news law polices chats and online platforms," BBC News, Singapore, May 9, 2019, https://www.bbc.co.uk/news/world-asia-48196985

[46] Committee to Protect Journalists, "Singapore passes 'fake news' legislation that threatens press," May 9, 2019, https://cpj.org/2019/05/singapore-passes-fake-news-legislation-that-threat.php

[47] https://www.gouvernement.fr/en/against-information-manipulation

[48] https://germanlawarchive.iuscomp.org/?p=1245 and BBC News, "Germany starts enforcing hate speech law," January 1, 2018, https://www.bbc.co.uk/news/technology-42510868

remove within 24 hours "manifestly unlawful" posts, including hate speech, fake news, and defamatory content. However, the new law drew the ire of Human Rights Watch, who argued that the "flawed" act could lead to "unaccountable, overboard censorship" and "sets a dangerous precedent for other governments looking to restrict speech online by forcing companies to censor on the government's behalf."[49] The Malaysian and, ironically, the Russian governments have also passed legislation to curb fake news.[50] Yes, it's hard to stifle laughter at the latter.

Despite the flurry of legislative activity overseas to tackle a blight that U.S. companies have enabled, America's lawmakers continue to be reluctant to disrupt the status quo. Supporters like to point to U.S. Supreme Court interpretations of the First Amendment that have repeatedly held that false speech enjoys full protection. As the (unnamed) "discussion leader" in a 2017 Yale University workshop discussion, Fighting Fake News,[51] put it: "'fake news' would generally fall into the category of public discourse and receive substantial First Amendment protection, regardless of its accuracy."

What this argument fails to acknowledge is that private enterprises are free to make their own rules. Americans have the freedom to walk barefoot, but shopkeepers can require that shoes be worn inside their stores. Similarly, just because a periodical chooses not to publish certain content does not violate free-speech protections.

So it is patently absurd that while the news media, which have been pushed to the brink by Big Tech, can be held accountable in the courts for certain content, these far more powerful and infinitely better-resourced organizations can operate with near impunity. The authorities must call time on the "We're a platform not a publisher" defense that has enabled them to sidestep responsibility for any hate-filled, dangerous, and/or libelous content they host, even when this content actually breaks the law. For the removal of doubt, remember that far from being "neutral" conduits, Facebook, Google/YouTube, Twitter, and a few others, are in reality media companies in all but name, thanks to the proprietary algorithmic recommendations that decide what to show users and that are the digital equivalent of human editorial decision-making. If invariably cash-strapped media companies have to face the music for rogue, inflammatory, harmful, fake, or illegal content, then social media platforms need to be held to fairly similar standards (including facing meaningful fines, litigation, and being forced to publish prominent retractions).

[49]Human Rights Watch, News, "Germany: Flawed Social Media Law," February 14, 2018, https://www.hrw.org/news/2018/02/14/germany-flawed-social-media-law

[50]"Factbox: '"Fake News' laws around the world," Reuters, April 2, 2019, https://uk.reuters.com/article/uk-singapore-politics-fakenews-factbox/factbox-fake-news-laws-around-the-world-idUKKCN1RE0XH

[51]https://law.yale.edu/sites/default/files/area/center/isp/documents/fighting_fake_news_-_workshop_report.pdf

It is ironic that venture capitalist Peter Thiel, one of Facebook's earliest investors and who is libertarian in the extreme, bankrolled a lawsuit that successfully bankrupted Gawker media for content that was used to "exploit the internet without moral limits," including an article that outed Thiel as gay.[52] Had the content been published only on Facebook, the lawsuit would not have been possible.

Facebook and YouTube in particular tend to push the narrative that at heart they are platforms that promote something we in democracies supposedly cherish, namely free speech, ergo any regulation imposed upon them would be a threat to the same. Let's be honest: right now they are advertising platforms governed by the need to attract as many eyeballs to their content as they can and keep them there for as long as possible. Rather than free speech, they're driven by bottom line. But let's say, for the sake of argument, that free speech is their raison d'être, then as well as enjoying its protections, as do publishers, press, and broadcast media, they must shoulder accompanying responsibilities too, such as putting in place a much more stringent vetting system of content and ads they carry. Any legislation should also make them responsible for the propagation of fake news and disinformation. While it's completely unrealistic to hold them accountable for every single piece of content they carry, they could certainly be held responsible for any piece of content that is illegal or shared more than a certain number of times. The exact number should be low enough to make it very time consuming for scammers to push out their content in large quantities.

In the United States, enabling this regulatory shift would mean amending Section 230 of the Communications Decency Act (1996),[53] which—as I detailed in Part 1—states that "no provider or user of an interactive computer service shall be treated as the publisher or speaker of any information provided by another information content provider."

Big Tech will always fight hard to preserve Section 230, and there is no formidable groundswell to eliminate it. Which is why perhaps we should choose a different approach that would see scale legally bound together with responsibility. Says digital activist Aza Raskin:

> Let's say we change CDA 230 to include amplification liability, so that platforms were liable for any content which their algorithms promoted. Freedom of speech is not the freedom of reach. Users [could still] upload whatever they want, protecting freedom of speech, but freedom of reach is not guaranteed.

---

[52] Alan Yuhas, "Peter Thiel justifies suit bankrupting Gawker, claiming to defend journalism," *The Guardian,* August 15, 2016, https://www.theguardian.com/technology/2016/aug/15/peter-thiel-gawker-bankruptcy-lawsuit-hulk-hogan-sextape.
[53] Electronic Frontier Foundation, "CDA 230: The most important law protecting internet speech," https://www.eff.org/issues/cda230

If you as a digital curator promote hate speech or incitement to violence or anti-vaccine videos, or conspiracies, then you are liable. Remember, before the 2016 election, Alex Jones's videos were promoted by YouTube 15 billion times and 70 percent of all YouTube video watches (over 1 billion hours a day) come from the recommendation engines.

That's the true role of regulation: it's about making the things that are good for a society and humans cheaper, and the things that have lots of negative externalities more expensive.

There is another solution that seems to be gaining traction and would go beyond the issues enumerated above: banning, or significantly limiting, microtargeting. As the internet became a more sophisticated ecosystem, personalization and ultraprecision in advertising targeting became possible.

This is a tricky issue that must be handled carefully. Too often banning microtargeting is confused with killing recommendation engines, such as the "if you bought this you might like that" process pioneered by Amazon, to which I have no objection. By contrast, microtargeting allows a business or political entity to advertise or aim items only at a universe of people most likely to want or to be able to purchase a product or service, or to read certain content. This saves the advertiser money while giving it access to the most dominant communication platform, spares others from seeing ads that are irrelevant to them, and allows a platform like Facebook—despite its massive scale—to earn revenue from even a local baker. A win-win-win, right? Not so fast.

Effective microtargeting is enabled by mining your data and any content you post, like, or share, what you engage with (an ad, a game, or a poll), and any links you follow. Through these digital activities, Facebook learns about your preferences, your dislikes, personal habits, and even your movements. And by layering on sophisticated algorithms (and sometimes by buying information from third-party data brokers), it can create a sophisticated profile of you that includes everything from where you shop in the physical world, to political and religious leanings, to who and what kinds of people you are friends with. The company then allows advertisers—or anyone who wants to pay to place content—to target those characteristics as well, further refining (or expanding) the universe of people who will see an ad. This is the core of Facebook's business model, and it is critical to Amazon, Google, and Twitter as well.

To be clear, these platforms are not sharing these dossiers about you with advertisers. All the advertiser is supposed to know is that there are X number of people on the platform who fit the characteristics of the people the advertiser or content provider wants to reach. But there are problems nonetheless.

Microtargeting has become so finely tuned that, for example, it was possible at one time for advertisers to ask to target people interested in "white genocide conspiracy theory."[54] In another case, ProPublica found that "Jew hater" was a category. Figure 12.1 shows what the targeting page on Facebook looked like when that publication's staff sought to test the system by placing an ad.[55]

Until Facebook made some changes, the system also allowed you to exclude particular groups from the target audience, such as minorities, which could be discriminatory in, say, real estate advertising.

Facebook has removed these options and apologized when caught, but the abuses continue because the system creates silos in which only the people targeted see the offending content. Thus, they are unlikely to flag it, which is a boon to the purveyors of fake news and disinformation.

A second problem is that your data can in fact leak out indirectly. Let's say an advertiser wants to sell survivalist gear, and wants to target folks who camp and hike, are not fat, are men, and own guns. You click on the ad and buy a tent. Now the advertiser knows who you are (from the transaction), and since you came to them via Facebook, they know you meet the other criteria as well. That is a lot more than they would know if you had gone to the retailer directly.

We need to crack down on this. At the very least, microtargeting should be limited to broad geographic and demographic categories. At most, it should be banned. Make it impossible once again to target someone based on their sexual preference, political affiliation, whether that person is dieting, or the last 20 websites or physical locations he or she visited, and suddenly that data becomes less valuable and with it the temptation to collect it, steal it, and abuse it disappears.

This would likely force a lot of companies to explore other business models, including some kind of freemium service or simply other types of less intrusive advertising. Following the implementation of GDPR, the *New York Times* stopped all behavioral advertising and focused on contextual and geographical targeting. "The fact that we are no longer offering behavioral targeting options in Europe does not seem to be in the way of what advertisers want to do with us," said Jean-Christophe Demarta, SVP for global advertising at *New York Times International*.[56] "The desirability of a brand may be stronger than the targeting capabilities. We have not been impacted from a revenue standpoint, and, on the contrary, our digital advertising business continues to grow nicely."

---

[54]Sam Biddle, "Facebook Allowed Advertisers to Target Users Interested in 'White Genocide'—Even in Wake of Pittsburgh Massacre," The Intercept, November 2, 2018, https://theintercept.com/2018/11/02/facebook-ads-white-supremacy-pittsburgh-shooting/

[55]Julia Angwin, Madeleine Varner, and Ariana Tobin, "Facebook enabled advertisers to reach 'Jew Haters,'" ProPublica, September 14, 2017, https://www.propublica.org/article/facebook-enabled-advertisers-to-reach-jew-haters

[56]Jessica Davis, "After GDPR, The New York Times cut off ad exchanges in Europe—and kept growing ad revenue," Digiday, January 16, 2019, https://digiday.com/media/gumgumtest-new-york-times-gdpr-cut-off-ad-exchanges-europe-ad-revenue/

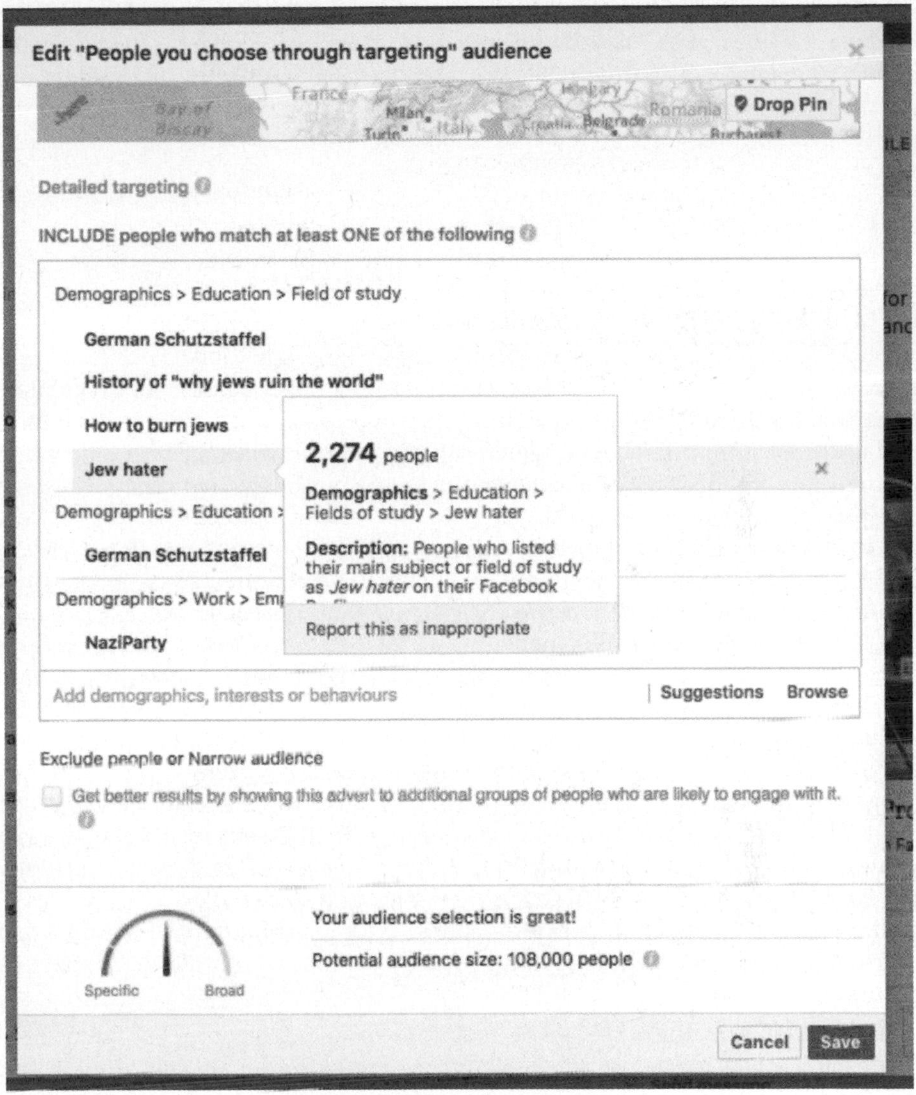

FIGURE 12.1 Facebook targeting page.
Source: ProPublica.

And to those who claim that this would likely threaten the platforms' business model completely: Yes! It would indeed very likely make it harder for them to make money. But how is it that we're comfortable making companies that pollute our physical environment pay for the damage and cleanup, but not these companies who are responsible for another kind of pollution, which—in its way—is equally destructive?

SETTING STANDARDS FOR ALGORITHMS, ARTIFICIAL INTELLIGENCE, AND FACIAL RECOGNITION

For the most part, this chapter has focused on how policy makers and regulators must tackle tech problems that have been festering for some time. It is just as important for these authorities to try to get ahead of problems, working with industry to ensure that consequences of new technologies are considered before they become entrenched and degrade civic life.

Corporate executives—especially in tech—will always respond to this idea with a bromide of their own, that governments are forever looking for solutions in search of problems. But not only does tech have a decade-long record of misdeeds and mistakes, there are emerging technologies that we know will be transformative and that will likely have dramatic impact on civil society. Indeed, they are already here, and we need to address them urgently.

I am speaking of algorithms, artificial intelligence, and one of its primary offshoots, facial recognition. Algorithms are basically a set of instructions given to a computer to process data, perform calculations, automate reasoning, and make decisions. Ever wonder how Google determines the order of search results? How Spotify proposes a new playlist? How a car GPS recommends the best way to avoid traffic? That's an algorithm (or more than one). Algorithms determine all manner of decisions in our day-to-day lives, yet although they have been around for a while, there is virtually no transparency in how they work, and they often reflect the biases of their programmers.

But if you think that's bad, take a look at artificial intelligence. For many, AI is a concept from the movies, in which machines created by humans start thinking for themselves, turn on their creators, and wreak havoc. The immediate future is not that dystopian, but there are plenty of danger signs.

A good way to think about AI is that it is programmed to learn and get smarter as time goes on, enabling it to "think" like a human and sometimes make decisions on its own, taking in data from external sources, without human intervention. Digital assistants such as Alexa and Siri are rudimentary examples, as are many smart home technologies that over time learn and act on your preferences for things like indoor temperature settings and energy management.

But think about self-driving cars. Or so-called "slaughterbots," self-aware robots that also go by the more cuddly name of lethal autonomous weapons systems. These and other AI implementations make decisions, sometimes with terrible outcomes. Autonomous vehicles have crashed. An experimental chat bot developed by Microsoft, programmed to learn conversation, was let loose on Twitter, and within 24 hours became a racist jerk.[57] A Google photo project mistook black people for gorillas.

The future of this technology is so potentially fraught with danger, uncertainty, and ethical conundrums that even leading science and technology luminaries such as Bill Gates, Elon Musk, and Steve Wozniak have warned of its dangers: "One can imagine such technology outsmarting financial markets, out-inventing human researchers, out-manipulating human leaders, and developing weapons we cannot even understand," Stephen Hawking wrote in an op ed in 2014.[58] "Whereas the short term impact of AI depends on who controls it, the long-term impact depends on whether it can be controlled at all."

What is needed for tech generally is for governments to establish new, rapid-reaction super-regulators, ideally comprising tech specialists and industry veterans, with the tools and expertise to move as quickly as the companies themselves. This putative body, skilled in a way elected officials and civil servants cannot reasonably be expected to be, would have a clearly defined mandate to investigate matters that require tech expertise.

This new industry regulator should be able to conduct "algorithm audits," a process that would see tech firms open up their black boxes to the disinfectant of daylight for evaluation; this would encourage both competition and better ethical conduct. The idea was first pushed by the Obama White House back in 2016 to ensure more fairness,[59] and the European Commission is currently carrying out in-depth analysis of algorithmic transparency,[60] which it describes as "an important safeguard for accountability and fairness in decision-making." Understanding how

---

[57] James Vincent, "Twitter taught Microsoft's AI chatbot to be a racist asshole in less than a day," The Verge, March 24, 2016, https://www.theverge.com/2016/3/24/11297050/tay-microsoft-chatbot-racist

[58] Stephen Hawking, Stuart Russell, Max Tegmark, and Frank Wilcezk, "Transcendence looks at the implications of artificial intelligence—but are we taking AI seriously enough?" *Independent,* May 1, 2014, https://www.independent.co.uk/news/science/stephen-hawking-transcendence-looks-at-the-implications-of-artificial-intelligence-but-are-we-taking-9313474.html

[59] Obama Whitehouse, "Big Data: A Report on Algorithm Systems, Opportunity, and Civil Rights," Executive Office of the President, May 2016, https://obamawhitehouse.archives.gov/sites/default/files/microsites/ostp/2016_0504_data_discrimination.pdf

[60] European Commission, "Algorithmic Awareness-Building," June 9, 2020, https://ec.europa.eu/digital-single-market/en/algorithmic-awareness-building

algorithms shape access to information in our personal and business lives is vital, and specialist audits, undertaken by subject-matter experts, could play a meaningful role in curbing Big Tech's worst impulses.

The super regulator should also create and police a code of practice for AI applications. For inspiration it should look no further than the equally ethically fraught realm of genetic engineering. As the technology futurist and author of *Hacking Darwin* Jamie Metzl put it in an interview with *The Economist*:[61] "Genetic technologies touch the source code of what it means to be human and must be regulated."

Precisely because of the certainty that AI will be abused, as with genetic engineering, every country will require its own regulatory framework in addition to certain guiding principles that align with internationally agreed standards. Yet AI has a far broader range of applications than genetic engineering, meaning that it will be impossible to have blanket laws that work in every case and that we may have to regulate sector by sector.

As for these guiding principles, I would begin by adapting Isaac Asimov's *Three Laws of Robotics*[62] and then add a few more rules:

- AI must not harm a human being, or indeed humanity generally, nor allow a human being to come to harm through inaction.
- AI must obey orders given by human beings, except where such orders would conflict with Asimov's First Law.
- AI shouldn't be trained on human data sets where the human source of that data hasn't given their explicit consent. Furthermore, those human sources should be able to opt out any time, and have all their data permanently deleted.
- Creators of AI (companies and individuals) must be held fully accountable for the effects of their technology. If the AI component of an autonomous vehicle, for example, makes a decision that ends up killing someone, the buck would stop with, say, Tesla, as the OEM—no ifs, buts, or lame excuses.
- People must be alerted immediately whenever they begin talking to, or otherwise interacting with, AI, where they might reasonably expect to be engaging with other humans. Today's status quo, in which, say, customer enquiries are handled by bots with human names, is the start of a slippery slope.
- Companies behind AI used to determine access to certain services, such as medical care, school admissions, loans, or mortgage applications—or for criminal justice purposes, such as sentencing—must make its source code openly available on request. A bit like Freedom of Information, this would ensure

---

[61] K.N.C, "How genetic engineering will reshape humanity," *The Economist,* April 25, 2019, https://www.economist.com/open-future/2019/04/25/how-genetic-engineering-will-reshape-humanity

[62] http://webhome.auburn.edu/~vestmon/robotics.html

transparency and protect against in-built biases. There will be exceptions, of course—how the IRS uses AI to identify fraudsters or financial services firms use it to spot fraudulent behavior are examples—but these should be kept to a bare minimum.

Meanwhile, to zoom in on one area where AI is increasingly applied, legislation needs to catch up with the huge leaps forward in facial recognition, perhaps the most sinister nascent application. San Francisco became the first U.S. city to ban the use of facial recognition by law enforcement altogether in May 2019,[63] with Aaron Peskin, the city supervisor who sponsored the bill, saying that the city's reputation for innovation meant that local legislators carried a special responsibility "to regulate the excesses of technology precisely because they are headquartered here."

Nevertheless, facial recognition is on the march, and not just under authoritarian regimes, where its use is hardly surprising, but by local, state, and federal law enforcement across much of America,[64] and by Scotland Yard on the streets of London,[65] where there have been eight major (and largely undisclosed) trials of the technology since 2016. On a single day in February 2020, the UK's biggest police force scanned more than 8,000 faces on London's (pre-coronavirus) retail mecca of Oxford Street. Seven of the eight alerts the technology triggered turned out to be false positives.[66]

Fears abound not just about the facial recognition's accuracy and the potential for miscarriages of justice, as dreadfully demonstrated by the "faulty facial recognition match [that] led to a Michigan man's arrest for a crime he didn't commit" reported by the *New York Times* in June 2020,[67] but about what private companies might do with it should they remain unfettered by regulations. Revelations in the *New York Times*[68] that Manhattan-based Clearview AI's facial recognition tech

[63]Kate Conger, "San Francisco Bans Facial Recognition," *New York Times,* May 14, 2019, https://www.nytimes.com/2019/05/14/us/facial-recognition-ban-san-francisco.html

[64]https://www.banfacialrecognition.com/map/

[65]Martin Robinson, "Hundreds of innocents face being grabbed in the street by police as Scotland Yard admits new facial recognition system gives false alerts one in every thousand faces," *Daily Mail,* January 24, 2020, https://www.dailymail.co.uk/news/article-7924733/Scotland-Yard-introduces-facial-recognition-cameras-hunt-watchlist-2-500-suspects.html

[66]Isobel Asher Hamilton, "British police scanned 8,600 people's faces in London without their consent, resulting in just 1 arrest and 7 false positives," Business Insider, March 4, 2020, https://www.businessinsider.com/met-police-scans-8600-faces-resulting-in-1-arrest-2020-3

[67]Kashmir Hill, "Wrongfully Accused by an Algorithm," *New York Times,* June 24, 2020, https://www.nytimes.com/2020/06/24/technology/facial-recognition-arrest.html

[68]Kashmir Hill, "The Secretive Company That Might End Privacy as We Know It," *New York Times,* January 18, 2020, https://www.nytimes.com/2020/01/18/technology/clearview-privacy-facial-recognition.html

had scraped more than 3 billion images from publicly available sites, including YouTube, Twitter, and Facebook, to assist around 600 law enforcement agencies across the country garnered widespread attention. That Clearview's tech was instrumental in solving a wide range of criminal activity, including murder and child sexual exploitation cases, will not assuage the fears of those who worry about the devastating privacy implications of this somewhat menacing technology, me among them. At the very least, the trade-off between enhanced security and safer streets on the one hand, and the attendant loss of privacy on the other, demands vigorous evidenced-based debate. This all boils down to the type of society people want to live in, and whether reducing the risk of crime merits the constant monitoring of citizens as they go about their lives. That's even before you dive into questions of where this data is stored, and who would have access to it and under which circumstances. And all of this is happening against a backdrop where crime across much of the developed world has fallen.

I often hear it said that "It's too late, the genie's out of the bottle" or "We cannot unlearn this technology." Unfortunately, I tend to agree, and while I would much rather see the use of facial recognition for law enforcement agencies purely and simply banned, I'm afraid it is indeed too late and cities like San Francisco will remain exceptions or even reverse their decision at some point in the future. I also expect commercial usage of the technology to keep increasing. The focus now needs to be on two fronts, each with multiple key topics:

- Civil liberties: definition of specific usage, information and opt-out options for consumers/citizens, due process and ability to appeal against algorithms, liability for the creator of the algorithm (not just the governmental or commercial entity using it)
- Accuracy of data used and recommendations made: discrimination resulting from inherent biases in data sets, and, as mentioned earlier regarding AI, accessibility of code and data to third-party audits

***

As governments explore the best ways to solve problems created by Big Tech without regulating them out of existence, the specialist super-regulator I've described could play a key role in preventing risks from materializing by joining forces with tech companies to identify and address newly emerging issues and responding accordingly with new rules—essential in a fluid industry like tech.

But it needs resources, and authority with teeth. As a first step, I wholeheartedly concur with another argument, made by Lisa Quest and Anthony Charrie in *MIT Sloan Management Review* that oversight needs to happen via digital access. "By replacing quarterly reports with technology platforms that permit regulators to pull information related to key risk indicators from companies' systems directly, regulators will be able to monitor companies more proficiently." This would require in-depth work, however, to ensure public disclosure when warranted.

Finally, where companies are in breach of regulations, sanctions must mean business. CEOs, boards, and senior leadership must no longer view disciplinary measures as a mild irritant to be tolerated, yet ultimately disregarded. Instead they must genuinely fear them and view serious breaches as potentially career-ending. Rather than just imposing fines and cease-and-desist orders, a revamped regulator should also have the power to bring criminal charges against named executives who blatantly ignore the impact of their decisions and fail to take appropriate preventive measures. That would mean that some of them might end up serving time. So be it. If those responsible for the subprime crisis of 2008, who put millions of people through years of turmoil, had faced the music, a precedent would have been set and perhaps society would be (marginally) less polarized today.

CHAPTER 13

Big Tech Broke the News Media: What's Next?

The perfect storm that the media industry has been trapped in for many years now, in which technology's impact was just one blow among many, is well-documented. As summarized by Robert Picard,[1] "mature and saturated markets, loss of audience not highly interested in news, the diminishing effectiveness of the mass media business model, the lingering effect of the economic crisis, and the impact of digital competitors have all taken a toll on news organizations. Compounding these factors are changes in technology and communication economics that are dismantling the traditional financial configurations that made Western media wealthy."

The result has been catastrophic for responsible coverage, particularly of local and regional news. According to Pew Research, "From 2008 to 2019, overall newsroom employment in the U.S. dropped by 23%, according to the new analysis."[2] Europe is not much better. Journalism that holds leaders accountable—a cornerstone of democracy—is in peril.

But what probably isn't quite so widely understood is how ravenously Big Tech has feasted on the news media's carcass. According to a study by the News Media Alliance,[3] a nonprofit trade association that represents more than 2,000

---

[1]Robert G. Picard, "Twilight or New Dawn of Journalism: Evidence from the changing news ecosystem," *Journalism Studies* 15:5 (2014), https://www.tandfonline.com/doi/abs/10.1080/1461670X.2014.895530

[2]Elizabeth Grieco, "U.S. newspapers have shed half of their newsroom employees since 2008," Pew Research Center, April 20, 2020, https://www.pewresearch.org/fact-tank/2020/04/20/u-s-newsroom-employment-has-dropped-by-a-quarter-since-2008/

[3]News Media Alliance press release, "New Study Finds Google Receives an Estimated $4.7 Billion in Revenue from News Publishers' Content," June 10, 2019, https://www.newsmediaalliance.org/release-new-study-google-revenue-from-news-publishers-content/

news organizations in the U.S. and globally, Google alone has profited to the tune of $4.7 billion—or "$4,700,000,000" as the *New York Times* coverage[4] of the report emphasized—from the work of news publishers in 2018 via Google search and Google News. "The amount of news in Google search results ranges from 16 to 40 percent, and the platform received an estimated $4.7 billion in revenue in 2018 from crawling and scraping publishers' content—without paying the publishers for that use," estimated the study, published in June 2019.[5] In some domains of life, Google's actions might be termed brazen or daylight robbery. David Chavern, News Media Alliance president and CEO, phrases it more descriptively: "Information wants to be free, but reporters need to get paid."

"SIGN A BIG CHECK, THEN GET OUT OF THE WAY"

It's long past time for the social media platforms to acknowledge their huge impact on the industry and their responsibility to connect readers/viewers with trustworthy journalism. High-quality content is also a key element of keeping users in their ecosystem as long as possible for Google and Facebook. Paying closer to the full syndication rates that other publishers and third parties cough up to license pieces of content, as well as a fairer cut of advertising revenues, will help critical content providers to continue to exist. If Google and Facebook continue to precipitate the disappearance of most for-profit journalism, their own platforms will ultimately have less value. As Mark Zuckerberg himself wrote, "A strong news industry is . . . critical to building an informed community. Giving people a voice is not enough without having people dedicated to uncovering new information and analyzing it. There is more we must do to support the news industry to make sure this vital social function is sustainable—from growing local news, to developing formats best suited to mobile devices, to improving the range of business models news organizations rely on."[6]

One way they could achieve this, as suggested by Steven Waldman in a *New York Times* op-ed,[7] is "establish a permanent endowment to fund local journalism."

[4]Marc Tracy, "Google Made $4.7 Billion from the News Industry in 2018, Study Says," *New York Times,* June 9, 2019, https://www.nytimes.com/2019/06/09/business/media/google-news-industry-antitrust.html
[5]http://www.newsmediaalliance.org/wp-content/uploads/2019/06/Google-Benefit-from-News-Content.pdf
[6]Mark Zuckerberg, "Building Global Community," Facebook Notes, February 16, 2017, https://www.facebook.com/notes/mark-zuckerberg/building-global-community/10103508221158471/
[7]Steven Waldman, "What Facebook Owes to Journalism," *New York Times,* February 21, 2017, https://www.nytimes.com/2017/02/21/opinion/what-facebook-owes-to-journalism.html

In much the same way that nineteenth-century robber baron Andrew Carnegie "built almost 3000 libraries," the tech giants could fund comprehensive public service journalism, on the understanding of course that the putative organization would have an independent board and gold-plated editorial independence. In effect Big Tech would sign a big check, then get out of the way.

Ethically compromised and facing regulatory probes, some of the worst offenders have half-heartedly attempted to resuscitate an industry they helped reduce to near rubble. In recent years, the platforms have waved a number of olive branches in the news industry's direction, including the Google News Initiative,[8] a $300 million three-year effort from the search giant "to help journalism thrive in the digital age," announced to great fanfare in 2018.[9] But critics have accused Google of self-interest and of attempting to garner soft coverage, with one in-depth report from the Google Transparency Project claiming that the giant was allegedly using its funding to track regulatory threats as well as "shifting funding from Europe to the U.S. amid a gathering backlash."[10]

Separately, Google announced a change to its algorithm that the company said would better enable it to surface original reporting in search results and ensure such articles stay visible for longer. "This means readers interested in the latest news can find the story that started it all, and publishers can benefit from having their original reporting more widely seen," blogged Richard Gingras, VP at Google News.[11] At the time of writing the platform had just announced for the first time that it would start paying some publishers for content in Australia, Brazil, and Germany.[12] For years, the platform categorically refused to pay publishers for their content. Despite an EU copyright directive that took effect in France in 2019, the first country to adopt it, Google had said it wouldn't be paying for licenses to show snippets of French news articles, ironically citing transparency as the reason. "We don't pay for links to be included in search results," Gingras told reporters in a conference call.[13] "Doing so

[8] https://newsinitiative.withgoogle.com/

[9] Shan Wang, "Google announces a $300M 'Google News Initiative'...," Nieman Lab, March 20, 2018, https://www.niemanlab.org/2018/03/google-announces-a-300m-google-news-initiative-though-this-isnt-about-giving-out-grants-directly-to-newsrooms-like-it-does-in-europe/

[10] Google Transparency Project, "Google's Media Takeover," October 2019, https://www.techtransparencyproject.org/sites/default/files/GTP-Media-Takeover.pdf

[11] Richard Gingras, "Elevating original reporting in Search," The Keyword, Google Blog, September 12, 2019, https://www.blog.google/products/search/original-reporting/

[12] Ryan Browne, "Google says it will pay some news publishers to license content, bowing to regulatory pressure," CNBC, June 25, 2020, https://www.cnbc.com/2020/06/25/google-will-pay-some-news-publishers-to-license-content.html

[13] Gaspard Sebag and Peter Chapman, "Google ordered to pay for news in French antitrust crackdown," April 9, 2020, Bloomberg, https://www.bloomberg.com/news/articles/2020-04-09/google-told-to-pay-up-in-french-crackdown-on-news-free-for-all

would not only skew the results we might provide but it would undermine the trust that users have in search and Google." A few weeks later, the search giant had been forced to acquiesce by the French competition authority.

Facebook, too, has funneled significant cash toward trying to fix the crisis in journalism, not least with its Facebook Journalism Project,[14] which "works with publishers around the world to strengthen the connection between journalists and the communities they serve" and "helps address the news industry's core business challenges." It also plans to spray a total of $300 million over three years into journalism projects, including nonprofits that specialize in local reporting.[15] More significantly, in the summer of 2019 it announced a move to pay publishers directly for their content. While there was again a degree of suspicion around the platform's motives, according to the *Wall Street Journal*,[16] "representatives from Facebook have told news executives they would be willing to pay as much as $3 million a year to license headlines and previews of articles for news outlets." The *WSJ* also reported that those news organizations pitched by Facebook included ABC News, the *Journal*'s own parent Dow Jones, the *Washington Post,* and Bloomberg.

While it's too soon to evaluate the impact of Google's and Facebook's latest news initiatives—and there have been letdowns in the past—we must be candid about the platforms' overall efforts to date. Whatever the tech giants' internal strategic objectives, their collective initiatives amount to little more than elaborately wrapped consolation prizes so far when set against a history of tens of billions of dollars in hemorrhaged advertising revenue globally.

There's another way in which some in Big Tech firms are magnanimously "saving" journalism; let's call it Elizabethan era–style patronage. This comes in two shapes: acquisition—of which Amazon CEO Jeff Bezos's personal purchase of the venerable, formerly loss-making *Washington Post* is the most high-profile example. Marc Benioff of Salesforce bought *Time*. Or they can set up journalism organizations such as eBay founder Pierre Omidyar's First Look Media,[17] which includes a for-profit entertainment division, Topic, as well as investigative site The Intercept, documentary unit Field of Vision, and the Press Freedom Defense Fund. The jury remains out on both of those ventures. Bezos's acquisition of the *Post* has largely been a success—he's spent tens of millions adding staffers (including significant numbers from a tech background), grown digital readership,

[14]https://www.facebook.com/journalismproject

[15]Mathew Ingram, "Facebook says it plans to put $300M into journalism projects," *Columbia Journalism Review,* January 15, 2019, https://www.cjr.org/the_new_gatekeepers/facebook-journalism-funding.php

[16]Benjamin Mullin, "Facebook Offers News Outlets Millions of Dollars a Year to License Content," *Wall Street Journal,* August 8, 2019, https://www.wsj.com/articles/facebook-offers-news-outlets-millions-of-dollars-a-year-to-license-content-11565294575

[17]https://firstlook.media/about

and according to the *Post*'s respected executive editor Martin Baron "doesn't inject himself at all into our [the *Post*'s] journalism."[18] But although the *Post* is reportedly profitable now,[19] whether the company has yet figured out the route to sustainable digital profitability will take time to prove out. Meanwhile, The Intercept has made cutbacks[20] and is reportedly still overwhelmingly dependent on its billionaire founder's deep-pocketed largesse.

FACEBOOK AND GOOGLE *ARE* NEW VERSIONS OF MEDIA COMPANIES

Unfortunately, paying its fair share for content, or providing other financial life-lines to media companies, is only half the battle to preserve a healthy and credible information ecosystem.

Facebook, Google/YouTube, Twitter, LinkedIn, and a handful of others are media platforms in all but name and need to be held to account for the content they publish, just as with TV channels and "print" publishers. *Wired* nailed it back in 2017,[21] when it urged Facebook to ask itself a number of questions—including "Are you the country's largest source of news?" "Do you sell ads against content?" and "Do you have a massive workforce of content moderators?"—all of which the platform would be obliged to answer in the affirmative. Crucially, they do not just serve users' content to their social group, but they actively shape what their users see through algorithmic and human editing.

So just as TV came after radio and print media, tech platforms/social media should simply constitute a new category: media platform companies. This reclassification, which recognizes that some differences with traditional media firms remain, is both urgent and critical, not only from a regulatory perspective and how we hold them accountable, but also to change the way these companies perceive themselves. If more employees at Facebook, Google/YouTube, and their peers understood that

---

[18]James Silver, "Martin Baron: 'We took Donald Trump seriously from the beginning," *The Guardian,* October 30, 2016, https://www.theguardian.com/media/2016/oct/30/martin-baron-we-took-donald-trump-seriously-from-the-beginning
[19]Sara Fischer, "Scoop: WaPo hits 2nd year of profitability, plans expansion," Axios, January 9, 2018, https://www.axios.com/washington-post-1515418495-9c9dc541-165f-4e99-b002-ad41416737ef.html
[20]Charles R. Davis, "The Intercept, a billionaire-funded public charity, cuts back," *Columbia Journalism Review,* March 15, 2019, https://www.cjr.org/business_of_news/layoffs-the-intercept.php
[21]Erin Griffith, "Memo to Facebook: How to tell if you're a media company," October 12, 2017, *Wired,* https://www.wired.com/story/memo-to-facebook-how-to-tell-if-youre-a-media-company/

they work for media firms, I believe it would encourage better decision making: you make very different calls when consider your primary role is to connect people, or catalog every piece of information available in the world, as opposed to when you believe that your job is to ensure people get accurate and relevant information, whether it's friends and family news, neighborhood, national, international news, or just 25 different ways to cook rice.

Similarly, we can't expect the news media to play their critical role in the democratic process, and hold the powerful to account, if the four or five best-resourced media companies in the world do no reporting and instead—thanks to legal protections as explained in Chapter 12—host all manner of fake news and offensive content without the responsibilities that come with being a publisher. It would be a bit like trying to understand and regulate retail and its impact on people's purchasing power and standards of living, while also being okay with Walmart saying that they're not a retailer but a logistics giant that moves goods around the world through an elaborate system of B2B warehouses, B2C warehouses, and a network of trucks, planes, and ships, and so couldn't participate on that basis.

Again, this is not about making them accountable for every single piece of content on their platform. Rather, it is about forcing them to solve two specific, yet solvable problems: illegal content and behavior, and deliberate disinformation.

To people who fear censorship, I would point out that if social media platforms behaved like responsible media, by fact-checking and refusing offensive material, it would strengthen the flow of credible information that is central to a healthy democracy. Furthermore, as private companies, social media businesses have the right to put in place rules for what content is allowed on their platform and they already have many. By focusing on freedom of reach rather than freedom of speech, we could preserve the ability of everyone to express their views while limiting misinformation.

Reclassification as media platform companies will also encourage the platforms to tweak their algorithms so that they surface trusted and reliable news sources first. Determining who those sources are, while contentious, could be achieved through a kite-mark system with titles endorsed by an expert panel to ensure certain criteria—including breadth of (mainstream) political opinion—are met. This will take a while to get right, will evolve over time, and will be quite controversial, but it cannot be any worse than the "black box" click-focused algorithm that they currently use. It will also help tackle the "fake news"/outrage problem.

NEWS ORGANIZATIONS NEED MORE THAN EVER TO KEEP BIG TECH ACCOUNTABLE

This book unfortunately will not be able to provide a blueprint on how to save media. Yet, and despite the economic pressure, it is critical that media continue to investigate Big Tech and report on their positive and negative impact on society. When it comes to writing about tech specifically, news media need to do better. While there's a fairly robust track record of critical reporting and investigations of tech, there are also countless examples of repeated failures to understand basic facts and difficult trade-offs facing tech companies and large amounts of ink and pixels wasted on vaporware. Too many specialist tech titles and industry correspondents are guilty of being too close to their subjects, treating big-name founders with the kind of reverence usually reserved for Hollywood stars, with access doled out allegedly in return for favorable coverage, while reporting on disruption as if it's a get-out-of-jail-free card and an end in itself. Particularly galling is the way certain titles dance to the venture capitalist tune by treating startup funding announcements and fund closes as "news" when in reality it very rarely is.

To ensure quality, independent journalism, there a few things that media companies should pursue:

- Paradoxically, more media mergers—mergers between the five or six top digital publishers, as advocated by Jonah Peretti, CEO of BuzzFeed. Or possibly between the largest legacy media companies. As Peretti explained in the *New York Times*[22] (actually when talking about a potential digital merger, but the logic could equally apply to a merger between legacy companies), "a larger entity could lobby for a higher percentage of the ad dollars Facebook and Google share with publishers whenever their content, videos in particular, runs on the platforms. In turn publishers can supply them with content that is safe for users and friendlier for advertisers."
- In the meantime, the Journalism Competition and Preservation Act (2019)[23] which is currently before U.S. lawmakers, would offer "temporary safe harbor for the publishers of online content to collectively negotiate with dominant online platforms regarding the terms on which their content may be distributed."
- Digital native publishers should stop raising venture capital investment. The VC model doesn't work in this context: it creates the wrong incentive, prioritizing short-term KPIs, which leads to quantity over quality. The same is true for private equity investment, which has scooped up many distressed media properties with no regard for the mission or role they play in society, and simply cut and cut some more to maintain any semblance of profitability, no matter that the product itself is nearly destroyed.

---

[22]Edmund Lee, "Founder's big idea to revive BuzzFeed's fortunes? A merger with rivals," *New York Times,* November 19, 2018, https://www.nytimes.com/2018/11/19/business/media/buzzfeed-jonah-peretti-mergers.html
[23]https://www.congress.gov/bill/116th-congress/house-bill/2054/

■ Media companies need to be smarter in their partnerships with Big Tech. Media publishers have been cowed into submission by Big Tech aggregators—they are forced to compete with every other publisher on these platforms and their content is commoditized as a result. On top of that, the revenue they earn from advertising is, to date, minimal (only the most niche of publications can possibly survive with the money they generate from Facebook, Google, and Apple, unless we're talking about grants), nor are they given access to user data.

As Rasmus Kleis Nielsen wrote, the digital revolution can make news "more accessible, more appealing, more contextual, more convenient, more immediate, more participatory, and more responsive."[24] But let's be blunt: without significant pushes both from legislators and Big Tech, the basic economics of journalism likely mean that while there will be more media per se, and certainly more noise, there will be fewer professional journalists to write and curate it. And that's something our democracies, and wider society, can ill afford.

---

[24] Rasmus Kleis Nielsen, "The Business of News," Chapter 4, *The SAGE Handbook of Digital Journalism* (Thousand Oaks, CA: Sage Publications, 2016).

CHAPTER 14

People Power

While the task of dispersing Big Tech's long shadow falls mostly to the industry itself, governments, and regulators, there are vital steps that you and I can take too. As private citizens and users, we must shoulder our share of responsibility for the chaos factory that surrounds us. After all, we were the ones who somehow agreed to barter away our private data and even the contents of our minds for the convenience of free search and maps, social media, video sharing, messaging services, streaming binges, subsidized taxis, home deliveries, and all the rest. We can always opt out. Change our behavior. Choose not to play along. Except most of us won't, and frankly can't, dispense with Big Tech altogether. However, there are certain things that we, as individuals, can still do to hold Big Tech's worst instincts at bay and play our part in bringing about a more empathetic, human-centric industry. It's all too easy to forget or ignore the fact that there are alternatives out there we can use instead (something I am guilty of myself) and collective action, coordinated or not, is a persuasive force. So here are some steps we can all take:

Give up a Bit of Convenience for a Little More Independence and Competition.

- Make DuckDuckGo our default search engine rather than Google.
- Swap our Gmail account for a secure privacy-preserving alternative like Proton-Mail, Tutanota, Runbox, or Posteo.
- Explore Fairbnb.coop, Innclusive, Homestay, or Vacasa as alternatives to Airbnb and HomeAway (owned by Expedia).
- Buy new books directly from an independent bookstore and vendors on bookshop.org (U.S. only at the time of writing unfortunately), Alibris, or BookOutlet; second-hand books from World of Books, Oxfam, or Thriftbooks; and ebooks from eBooks.com. And support our local library (some offer the borrowing of digital books and audiobooks).
- Call restaurants directly when we want to make a reservation or order takeout to save them the cost of reservation through a platform, or the up to 30% commission (plus sometimes other fees) food delivery apps usually charge.

- Pretty much every apparel brand now has a website that enables us to buy directly from them, while a myriad of additional e-commerce stores like Farfetch connect shoppers directly with individual boutique owners.
- Look at sites like Green America or Ethical Consumer that list ethical shopping alternatives.
- Where possible, subscribe directly from the service- or content-provider websites rather than in an app (where 15–30 percent of revenue of sold digital content goes to Apple or Google).[1,2]
- Vary use of Uber and Lyft with any of the myriad local ride-hailing apps on our doorsteps, such as Via, which wants to end single-occupancy journeys and pays salaries to its drivers.
- Use alternative messaging apps like Signal, Wire, or Wickr.
- Once social distancing rules are relaxed, shop at local brick-and-mortar stores when we can to help keep the local community alive.

Reduce Our E-Footprint and Drive Sustainability.
- Escape the tech upgrade cycle (also known as planned obsolescence) by maintaining and repairing hardware for as long as possible.
- Declutter mailboxes and empty junk email folders to reduce the energy consumed by the server farms required to store them.
- Consolidate online orders and limit same-day/next day deliveries to reduce cardboard waste and multiple transportations.
- Delete or deactivate old email accounts, social network accounts, and shopping accounts.
- If we can afford it, avoid shopping on Black Friday, when workers have repeatedly described warehouse conditions as inhumane.

Play Our Part in Paying People Fairly.
- Those of us who can afford it must routinely tip drivers, food delivery workers, and any gig worker whose services we book through an app so that they earn a livable minimum wage.
- Always check if the app gives 100 percent of the tip to the worker, and if not, leave the tip in cash, and then complain to the company about their tipping policy (and convince our friends to do the same) to get it changed.

---

[1]Ole Emil Lindberget, "When does Apple take a 30% cut of your app revenue and what can you do to avoid it?," Fuse, September 18, 2019, https://www.fuse.no/when-does-apple-take-a-30-cut-of-your-app-revenue-and-what-can-you-do-to-avoid-it/#:~:text=When%20does%20Apple%20take%20their, their%20progress%20through%20an%20app
[2]Brian Reigh, "Google to match Apple by lowering app subscription fee to 15 percent," Android Authority, October 20, 2017, https://www.androidauthority.com/google-match-apple-lapp-subscription-fee-15-percent-809047/

- If posting service requests on sites like TaskRabbit, Upwork, or Mechanical Turk, pay at least the minimum wage of the country we reside in.

Promote Ethical and Responsible Digital Citizenship With Children.

- Lobby schools to routinely teach the basics of digital literacy with children so that they learn how to use tech, protect their privacy, spot attempts to manipulate them, and follow the same ethical behavior on- and offline.
- Consider teaching a workshop at our kid(s)' school. There's plenty of supporting material available online.
- Advocate for schools to tightly regulate the use of technology during school hours.
- Prioritize the use of "safe" social networks specifically designed to protect children: CyberSmarties (Ireland only), What's What, giantHello, Skid-e Kids.

Actively Limit Data Collection.

- Install a browser add-on like EFF's Privacy Badger[3] to block invisible advertisers and other third-party trackers.
- Spend time looking at and adjusting, where necessary, privacy settings of the key websites and apps we use the most.
- Routinely adjust privacy/cookie settings when asked to do so by a website.
- Resist taking quizzes, however inviting, that require the sharing of personal information beyond the necessary basics.
- Support a nonprofit advocating for digital rights, in particular privacy: Electronic Frontier Foundation, Center for Democracy and Technology, Fight for the Future, Access, the Calyx Institute, Big Brother Watch, Privacy International, Liberty, and others.
- Protect our Amazon Echo privacy: regularly delete our recordings and transcripts, opt out of the feature allowing Amazon's employees to listen to our recordings to improve their voice assistant, and at the most extreme, learn to turn Alexa's mic off. Do the same, when possible, with other IoT devices.

Support Human-Centric Technology.

- Back organizations actively fighting for a more inclusive internet like Q (the first genderless voice) or Feminist Internet (fighting online abuse against women, lack of workforce diversity in the tech sector, and biased data collection reinforcing sexist privileges).

---

[3]https://privacybadger.org/

Fight Fake News and Unethical Digital Behaviors.

- Always flag or report hate speech/bullying/harassment on social media—to the platform itself, but also to regulators or, where truly egregious or sustained, to our member of Congress or Parliament.
- Say no to outrage: stop liking, retweeting, or reposting content that will add to the noise and anger. (Admittedly this is hard; I'm sometimes guilty of feeding the beast myself.) And systematically read the articles mentioned in these tweets and posts before doing so.
- Flag fake news. Report it, whenever we see it, and never, ever click on it. We shouldn't feed the trolls.
- Learn to say, "I don't know enough to have an opinion."

Pressure Big Tech into More Empathetic Behavior.

- Lobby businesses to stop advertising their company or wares next to inappropriate content. (For example, YouTube only changed tack after advertisers started to pull out over extremist content.)[4] And then support those that do by buying from them.
- Protest exploiters. When it comes to light that that tech giants and smaller unicorns are employing teenagers in Chinese factories or pushing courier drivers or riders to work lethally long hours, protest to the relevant regulator or member of Congress/Parliament, complain to the company, and highlight relevant articles on social media (if they're from credible news sources!).
- Ask questions. It often takes only a few shares to be able to ask questions at the annual shareholder meeting of all public companies.
- Follow those on Twitter and other platforms who advocate for more empathy in tech and amplify their message by liking, retweeting, and commenting.

Lobby for Better Legislation.

- Vote for representatives who actually care about these topics. This is at best usually a second-order topic when it comes to casting a vote.
- Launch petitions, where we feel strongly about some of the issues raised in this book and others, to be sent to our lawmakers.

---

[4]Olivia Solon, "Google's bad week: YouTube loses millions as advertising row reaches US," *The Guardian*, March 25, 2017, https://www.theguardian.com/technology/2017/mar/25/google-youtube-advertising-extremist-content-att-verizon

Epilogue: A Manifesto for Change

In the second half of this book I've set out my suggestions about what the tech industry's various stakeholders need to do to stem the crisis and neutralize the toxic impacts the largest companies have on the wider world. To leave the apocalyptic scenarios I described in Chapter 8 where they belong—in the realm of classic dystopian fiction—everyone must play their part, starting with legislators. While I am unapologetic about my opinion that revamped government regulation is both vital and long overdue (I wrote my first article calling for regulation in *Wired* in early 2015),[1] I'm also very much hoping that Big Tech firms will bring about most of the required changes themselves, thereby eliminating the need for externally imposed draconian controls. Having seen firsthand the impact of top-down regulatory overreach, I have no doubt that lighter-touch rules are better for all concerned.

As this book is first and foremost a call to action for people—whether industry leaders, board members, employees, government officials, journalists, or consumers/users—to drive change, I'm going to finish with a summary of the five most important actions (drawn from the many I've detailed in these pages) that Big Tech can take to beat the authorities to the punch. Alongside these, I have described the steps I believe Western governments are likely to take should tech leaders fail to change their behaviors and practices. My sincere hope is that as tech implements most of what is in the left-hand column, only very few of the measures on the right-hand side will need to see the light of day.

---

[1] Maëlle Gavet, "The data says Google and Facebook need regulating," *Wired UK,* March 5, 2015, https://www.wired.co.uk/article/data-google-facebook

Needed Changes	If Tech Self-Regulates	If Governments Feel Compelled to Act
Drive empathy into corporate culture and decision making.	▪ Include empathy in the company leadership principles and values. ▪ Review key processes, in particular people and product ones, to ensure that empathy is at their core. ▪ Be more forthcoming and transparent in providing information about what the company is doing and why. ▪ Dramatically improve diversity, especially at the top and in engineering. ▪ Create working groups that include people with non-engineering backgrounds to weigh in on key strategic decisions. ▪ Enable formal worker representation (regardless of status as employee or contractor).	▪ Make government contracts contingent on improved workplace diversity numbers. ▪ Impose diversity quotas for board members. ▪ Require worker representation.
Rein in the surveillance economy.	▪ Make it easier for users to have access to, to manage, and/or to delete all their data. ▪ Keep users more informed about data collection and targeting, and be more transparent about their data rights and implications of likes, follows, etc.	▪ Further develop GDPR/U.S. state privacy laws. ▪ Increase penalties for breaches and data misuse, including criminal charges. ▪ Impose algorithmic transparency and oversight, as well as right to explanation.

Needed Changes	If Tech Self-Regulates	If Governments Feel Compelled to Act
	▪ Make data mining and personalization opt-in. ▪ Make microtargeting available only to a very narrow subset of categories and advertisers. ▪ Implement alternative source of revenues to microtargeting/behavioral advertising.	▪ Ban microtargeting outright.
Become a better corporate citizen.	▪ Stop using tax havens and recognize revenue in the jurisdiction of the purchaser. ▪ Offer base benefits to all workers, regardless of their classification. ▪ Develop industry standards that include societal and environmental impacts. ▪ Work proactively with democratically elected governments. Refuse to work with autocratic regimes. ▪ Embrace B Corporation[2] standards.	▪ Reform tax codes to prevent the use of tax havens and loopholes and implement local digital taxes and minimum tax levels. ▪ Impose minimum wage, sick leave, unemployment benefits, and other employee benefits for all workers. ▪ Regulate technologies deemed strategic or having large societal and environmental impact.

---

[2]As per Wikipedia: to be granted and preserve the status of B corporation, companies must receive a minimum score on an online assessment for "social and environmental performance" and "satisfy the requirement that the company integrate B Lab commitments to stakeholders into company governing documents."

Needed Changes	If Tech Self-Regulates	If Governments Feel Compelled to Act
Defend facts, accuracy and civil discourse.	▪ Make moderation a business strategy rather than a cost of doing business. ▪ Crack down fully on false information and fake news. ▪ Differentiate freedom of speech from freedom of reach and adapt algorithms accordingly. ▪ Develop a zero-tolerance approach toward bullying, harassment, incitement to violence, and implement efficient reporting/action processes. ▪ More aggressively block fake accounts and bots.	▪ Reclassify all search engines and content platforms as information companies with similar obligations to media companies. ▪ Require detailed reporting on bullying, harassment, incitement to violence, and fake news.
Limit excessive tech power.	▪ Spin-off distinct subsidiaries (Instagram from Facebook, etc.). ▪ Cooperate with democratically elected governments and nonprofits to develop algorithmic transparency. ▪ Submit voluntarily to audit by credible nonprofits/NGOs focused on social and environmental issues, and publish results and action plans. ▪ Show up when requested to appear in front of government committees.	▪ Implement more stringent antitrust legislation and action and force divestiture. ▪ Treat tech companies as public utilities and regulate accordingly.

I understand that these steps will likely require a fundamental rethink of Big Tech business models. In the short term they may not be as big or as profitable, though they will still dwarf most companies. In the long run I believe their business will be healthier and more sustainable.

At the same time, with our societies now in the thick of the Fourth Industrial Revolution and with much turbulence still to come, large tech companies, with their unprecedented reach and power, have within their grasp the opportunity to make serious dents in the defining issues of our age, whether that's combating poverty and inequality, or tackling pandemics and climate change. The three earlier industrial revolutions, while painful and disruptive for many, brought about huge leaps forward for humanity, raising standards of living and life expectancy around the world. There is every reason to believe this tech-led revolution can achieve the same, if the issues highlighted in this book are successfully confronted. Indeed, the entrepreneurial stewards of this Fourth Industrial Revolution have an even greater opportunity—and responsibility—than their predecessors to create sustainable and inclusive economic growth because of their access to capital and the inherent scalability of the digital model.

It may be too late for the current crop of tech giants. As we've seen, arguably many of their teams have strayed too far from their original visions, have cut too many ethical corners, and have built an expectation of gravity-defying growth rates among their shareholder base that would make a wholesale change of direction all but incredibly difficult. But it's not too late for the many thousands of tech startups around the world, among them unicorns-in-waiting, and for other stakeholders—from boards and investors to casual users—who can demand from these companies more empathy.

If you've made it as far as this epilogue, I can recommend further reading. The World Economic Forum report, in collaboration with PwC, entitled "Unlocking Technology for the Global Goals,"[3] published in January 2020, identifies 10 vital Fourth Industrial Revolution technologies and how they can help meet the 17 Sustainable Development Goals[4] for a better world by 2030, agreed upon by United Nations member states in 2015. As the WEF report notes, with just a decade to go, the world has so far flunked many of these goals, which encompass eliminating poverty and hunger, building resilient infrastructure, and sustainable cities. Yet, in every one of these 17 objectives, tech can help move the needle. The majority of tech leaders and companies I know work in one way or another in one of these fields, even if only tangentially so. What if each tech worker, from top executive

---

[3]World Economic Forum, "Unlocking Technology for the Global Goals," January 2020, http://www3.weforum.org/docs/Unlocking_Technology_for_the_Global_Goals.pdf
[4]https://sustainabledevelopment.un.org/?menu=1300

to entry-level employee, alongside every tech company, were to measure their own progress against these benchmarks (at least those that are relevant to them)? That might mean that companies who "partner" with drivers or couriers or food delivery workers commit to higher pay toward helping "end poverty in all its forms" (#1 of the 17 UN goals) or "ensuring sustainable consumption" (#12), or social media giants pledging to help work toward "promoting peaceful and inclusive societies" (#16). Whether one (or more) of the 17 goals was part of a company's overall mission, or they served as guiding lights to inform decision-making and the inevitable trade-offs that business life involves, or companies empowered their employees to devote a portion of their time to any project related to one of these goals, I firmly believe that cumulatively it would bring us appreciably closer to achieving the UN's targets.

While I'm skeptical that we will ever live in a world where poverty is entirely eradicated, where everyone will have access to food, clean water, education, and healthcare wherever they live, and where nature is fully protected, I do think tech can truly make a difference if companies tested their actions against these goals.

As I write this final page, the COVID-19 pandemic is still raging, killing thousands of people every day around the world. Yet despite the pain it's inflicting on humanity, this virus is also an opportunity to hit reset and forge a new, more empathetic version of the tech industry. Indeed, we've seen glimpses of one already.

Apple's Tim Cook warned, "If you've built a chaos factory, you can't dodge responsibility for the chaos."[5] As an industry, we must own and repair our mistakes. And when we do, we can embrace a future in which the finest minds solve humanity's thorniest problems, and tech becomes a force for continuous progress in our world. We don't need less tech. We need more empathetic tech.

---

[5]Tim Cook, "Tim Cook: 'If you've built a chaos factory, you can't dodge responsibility for the chaos,'" *The Guardian,* June 19 2019, https://www.theguardian.com/commentisfree/2019/jun/19/tim-cook-if-youve-built-a-chaos-factory-you-cant-dodge-responsibility-for-the-chaos

Acknowledgments

It truly takes a village to create a book. A big MERCI to:

- James Silver: my writing partner, half Yoda, half Dr Watson. Without your long hours, infinite patience with my endless iterations, and ability to turn any idea and draft of mine into readable sentences, this book would simply not exist.
- Jonathan Krim: for your eagle eyes, ferocious red pen, and unaltered sense of humor at one in the morning. "Yet it has a bottom, beyond light and knowledge."
- Gabriella Lourie and Paul Sliker: for your incomparable frog-boiling technique and rolodex that led me to actually write this book without (almost) noticing.
- Leah Spiro: for believing in this book from the first time I met you and being as much my therapist as my agent during the whole process.
- Bernard Lukey: for being the first leader to show me the power of empathy in business. Forever imitated, never equaled.
- Janelle Monney: for guiding me on my journey toward more empathy through the roller coaster of life. People are not a problem to solve, but a reality to experience.
- Tom Killalea, Ailish Campbell, Christopher M. Schroeder, Peter L. Allen, Jon Keldan, Alfred Lin, Eytan Seidman, Michael Zaoui, Caroline Winter, Bernard Spitz, SS, JM, DC, MM, and BG: for reading many terrible drafts, answering endless questions, listening to all my doubts, and providing your generous (and very unfiltered!) feedback on the many areas for improvement you found.
- David Kabiller: for a memorable Spanish Inquisition–style dinner that made me run home, Louboutins notwithstanding, to rewrite quite a few chapters.
- Joshua Ramus: for making me see the world differently, from an unexpected painting and minimalist buildings to the cover of this book. Forever MIT!
- All the incredible women who have shown me the way, put me back on my feet when I needed it, and encouraged me never to be afraid to speak my mind. Sisterhood can move mountains.
- Countless employees, peers, and managers at BCG, OZON, Booking, Priceline, OpenTable, Compass, and a few entrepreneurial ventures of my own: for not giving up on me despite the constant process of trials and errors I put you through. I feel incredibly fortunate to have had the opportunity to work with and learn from you.

- The multiple people who agreed to be interviewed on record: Margrethe Vestager, Luciana Berger, Richard Stables, Ian Russell, Aza Raskin, Chris Meserole, Eric Feinberg, Hussein Kanji, Chris Gray, Deano Roberts, Professor Richard Walker, Damian Collins, MP, Martha Lane Fox (Baroness), Elaine Lu, Dr Tijion Esho, Gwyneth Borden, Russell Hancock, Jeffrey Buchanan, Anna Cash, Lupe Arreola, Flora Rebello Arduini, Samantha Bradshaw, Neil Weiss, Saul Klein, Beverly Blanchard, Thorben Wieditz, Sito Veracruz, James Higa, Arnaud Sahuget, Nicola Crosta.
- The Wiley team, in particular Jeanenne Ray: for betting on me as a first-time author and giving me the time and resources to write this book.
- And last but not least, my family and friends: for the words of support, hugs, EDM tracks, french fries, and drinks that have kept me alive and happy throughout the writing of this book, but also for the last 42 years.

About the Author

One of the tech industry's brightest stars, Maëlle Gavet has been named a Young Global Leader by the World Economic Forum, one of *Fortune*'s 40 Under 40, one of the Most Creative People in Business by *Fast Company* and was fifth among *Time* magazine's List of the Top 25 'Female Techpreneurs'. After six years as a Principal at the Boston Consulting Group, she went on to become CEO of OZON.ru, Russia's largest e-commerce site, and executive VP of operations of the Priceline Group, the largest online and travel agency in the world which includes brands like OpenTable, Kayak, and Booking.com.

Most recently Gavet was Chief Operating Officer at real estate platform Compass, valued at over $6bn. She has spoken regularly at the leading technology industry events and her writing has appeared in *Wired*, the *Harvard Business Review*, the *World Economic Forum*, *Fast Company* and *Fortune* magazine. *Trampled by Unicorns* is her first book.

For more information about Gavet and the Corporate Empathy test, visit www.maellegavet.com.

Index

1984 (Orwell), 91–2

A
Λ/B tooting, intogration, 65
Advanced Technology Review Council, 127
affective empathy, 106
Ahmed, Imran, 46
Airbnb
  culture bubble, 14
  voluntary tax arrangements, negative impact, 31
algorithmic surveillance, 94
algorithms
  audits, usage, 167–8
  standards setting, 166–71
Amazon
  activists, firing, 151
  antitrust investigation, 136
  employee activism (France), impact, 151–2
  federal tax rebate, claim, 34
  pricing attack, 88–9
  privacy, absence, 92–4
  productivity targets (reduction), firings (relationship), 39
  Rekognition facial recognition technology, shareholder pushback, 123
  secondary corporate headquarters contest, 30–1
  tax benefits (Luxembourg), 32–3

Amazon Europe Holding Technologies, revenue funneling, 32
ambient surveillance, 154
Amusing Ourselves to Death (Postman), 91
Andreessen, Marc, 77
anonymity, preservation, 119
anti-social networks, 43
Antitrust
  capability, reinvigoration, 133–9
  goals, alignment, 133–4
  investigation (Amazon), 136
  tool, 143–4
Apple
  investigations, 136–7
  philanthropic efforts, 29
  sales tax revenue, Cupertino share, 30
  work violations, 41–2
Arab Spring, 43
Arreola, Lupe, 27–8
artificial intelligence (AI), 139
  Big Tech claims, 62
  capabilities (Google), usage, 97
  dangers, warning, 167
  ethics board (Google), 101–2
  inadequacies, 56
  products, problems, 167
  standards setting, 166–71
  usage, 8, 10, 53
Ascension, Google (partnership), 97–8
Asimov, Isaac, 168
attention economy, 11
attention, monetization, 65–6

automation, impact, 40
Autonomous Revolution, The
(Davidow), 11
Avaaz investigations, impact, 47–9
Avakian, Stephanie, 83

B
Backrub, 14–15
Balsillie, Jim, 99
Bay Area
land use/housing policies, problems,
28
re-segregation, 26–7
behavioral controls, problems, 81–3
Benioff, Marc, 107, 128, 176
Berger, Luciana (bigotry campaign,
impact), 50–2
Berland, Laurence, 111
Bezos, Jeff
callousness/non-empathy, 87–8
decisions, impact, 147
pressure, application, 89
Big Data, role, 93–4
bigotry, campaign, 51
Big Tech
anticompetitive behavior, 130–2
authoritative content, increase
(claim), 45–6
backlash, 25
breakup, 129
building frenzy, 25
change, manifesto, 185–90
companies, lean payrolls, 40
data, disclosure (refusal), 12
feudalism, 37
fines, levying, 136–8
global tax gap, 31–3
government regulation, increase
(YouGov survey), 153–4
job destroyers, 40
leadership, diversity (absence), 18
lobbying expenditures, 61

median salary, 13
negative impact, 29–30
neutral conduit, perception, 161
news organizations, accountability
role, 178–80
overreach/data harvesting, concerns,
99–100
problems/errors, 3
profits, shuffling, 149
racial/gender diversity challenge, *17*
scrutiny, avoidance, 144
taxes, payment (low levels), 33
tax liabilities, reduction, 29–30
worker support, reduction, 39–40
Big Tech empathy
absence, 42
increase, pressure (increase), 184
Billard, Marianne, 157
Bird and Lime, first-mover advantage
(negative impact), 88–9
Black Lives Matter, 75
blitz scaling, 72
board of directors
corporate governance expectations,
122–5
empathy, increase, 124
Bolsonaro campaign, disinformation
(impact), 48
Booking.com, growth (problems), 68–9
Borden, Gwyneth, 23
Bosworth, Andrew, 57–8, 115, 158
Bradshaw, Samantha, 50
Brandeis, Louis, 133
Brave New World (Huxley), 91, 96
Bray, Tim, 151
Brazil (elections), misinformation
(impact), 48
Bregman, Rutger, 146
Brin, Sergey, 14, 15
broadband penetration, impact, 7–8
bro culture, 20–1
Buchanan, Jeffrey, 25

Bucks, Dan, 31–2
Bud Tribble project, 85
"Building Global Community"
   (Zuckerberg), 99
business
   differentiation, 127
   model, Big Tech nondisclosure, 154
   model, economics (relationship),
      119–20

C
calibration process, 117–18
California Consumer Privacy Act, 155
callousness, 87–8
Cambridge Analytica, scandal, 86–7,
   158
campus bubble, bursting, 115
Carnegie, Andrew, 175
Cash, Anna, 26
CCTV cameras, government usage, 95
Ceglowski, Maciej, 154
Center for Countering Digital Hate
   (CCDH), social media study, 46
chaos factory, 4
Charrie, Anthony, 146
Chaslot, Guillaume, 58–9
Chavern, David, 174
Chesky, Brian, 86
Chief Executive Officer
   empathy, impact, 108–9
   role, chairman role (separation), 126
children, ethical/responsible digital
   citizenship, 183
China
   censorship demands, LinkedIn
      agreement, 140
   company control, 140
   cyber troop activity, 50
   tech expansion, danger, 141
China Labor Watch (CLW), Foxconn
   report, 41

Christchurch (New Zealand) attack,
   Facebook Live
   footage, availability, 55–6
   usage, 54–5
Chrome (Google), emergence, 142
cities, Big Tech (negative impact), 29–30
civil discourse, preservation (fight),
   158–66
civil liberties, focus, 170
Clearview, AI facial recognition (law
   enforcement assistance), 170
climate change disinformation, posts
   (Facebook allowance), 159
Climate Informatics, AI (impact), 10
Coalition for a Safe Web, research, 56
cognitive empathy, 106
Collins, Damian, 52–3, 123
Communications Decency Act, Section
   230 (amendment), 162
communities, re-creation, 27
"Community Standards Enforcement
   Report" (Facebook), 102
companies
   breakup, 138–9
   control, dilution/loss, 71
   empathy-focused criteria, usage, 122
   financing criteria, 75–6
   growth, desperation, 72–3
   physical presence, tax basis
      (determination), 32
   psychopathic companies, creation, 81
competition, regulation focus, 146
computational propaganda, 49
content moderation
   dehumanization, 64
   problems, 64
   Zuckerberg discussion, 63–4
content moderators,
   micromanagement, 63
content reviewers, 63
Cook, Tim, 4, 190

corporate empathy, groups (impact),
    108–20
corporate governance, 121
corporate tax avoidance, negative
    impact, 34
"Cost of Next-day Delivery, The"
    (BuzzFeed investigation), 39
COVID-19, 2, 4, 8, 75, 101
    company perks, 14
    contact tracing, usage, 96
    Dorsey pandemic relief fund, 81
    misinformation, social networks
        (impact), *46*
    social distancing requirements,
        impact, 9
    spread, 38, 45
Crosta, Nicola, 9
CrowdTangle (social media monitoring
    tool), 48
cruelty, social media tolerance, 87–8
culture
    bubble, 13
    change, innovation (impact), 4
Curse of Bigness, The (Wu), 133
Customs and Border Protection, Google
    involvement, 112
cyber troop activity, 50

D
Daily Stormer, bigotry campaign, 51
Damodaran, Aswath, 71–2
data
    access/correction, focus, 156
    accuracy, focus, 170
    data-extractivism, 99–100
    enforcement, 157
    mining, microtargeting (impact), 163
    ownership, protection, 153–8
data collection, 154, 156
    active limitation, 183
data privacy
    Google track record, 98

guidelines/disclosure, strictness, 125
Davidow, William, 11
Davise, Brittany, 75
de Botton, Alain, 124
decision making, changes, 4
Demarta, Jean-Christophe, 164
democracy, social media attack, 47–50
democratic governments, security
    efforts (support), 120
democratic process, news media role
    (expectations), 178
digital behaviors, control, 184
digital economy, definition (vagueness),
    7–8
digital innovation, impact, 8
digital platforms, transparency
    obligation (France), 160
dispatch workers, work situation
    (problems), 41
Dodds, Laurence, 88
"do no harm" principle, 157
DoorDash, pricing problems, 72
Dorsey, Jack, 115
    Myanmar tweets, insensitivity, 79–80
    pandemic relief fund, 81
DoubleClick, Google acquisition, 138
"Double Irish, Dutch sandwich" tax
    loophole, 148
"Downtown West," 24–5
due diligence processes, 121–2
Duke, Paul, 112

E
economic absolutism, 134
economic progress, technology (driver),
    7–10
e-footprint, reduction, 182
embedding, VC offer, 68
empathetic company, appearance,
    107–8
empathy, 105
    absence, 42, 87–8

affective empathy, 106
business model/economics, impact, 119–20
cognitive empathy, 106
decision-making processes, 114–19
deficit, 3
groups, impact, 108–20
implication (Zuckerberg), 63
overuse, 106
promotion (Microsoft), 107
testing, 117
employees
empathy, impact, 109–12
right to fail, 118
employment protection, modernization, 151–3
engineers, knowledge (absence), 16–19
entrepreneurs, unicorn dreams, 76
ethics boards, absence, 12
European Union (EU) member, tax haven behavior (crackdown), 149–50
"Europe Firt for the Digital Age," 34
Europe, VC market, *69*
Everything Store, The (Stone), 89
exceptionalism, myth, 19–20
executives, empathy/humanity, 4
extreme content, policing (impact), 62–3
extremism, social media tolerance, 87–8

F
Facebook
Avaaz investigation, impact, 48–9
awareness, absence, 57–8
Christchurch atrocity, footage (availability), 55–6
climate change disinformation posts, allowance, 159
content moderation, problems, 64
content reviewers, 62
electoral manipulation, relationship, 48
fake news, relationship, 51f
guidelines, Italy breaches, 49
misinformation/disinformation reduction, failure, 47–8
negative impact, 44–6
platform (physical/social risks), leadership understanding, 58
privacy breaches, 153
rhetoric, 56
safety and security team, expansion, 62
targeting page, 164, *165*
"Ugly, The" memo, 57–8
voting suppression posts ban, 159
Facebook Journalism Project, 176
Facebook Live
one strike policy, usage, 55
usage (Christchurch murders), 54–5
Facebook Protect, 158
facial recognition
problems, 169–70
standards setting, 166–71
technology, Big Tech creation, 95
facts
preservation, fight, 158–66
social media, negative impact, 44–6
Fair Tax Mark (certification scheme), 33
fake news, 44
fighting, 184
First Amendment protection, 161
history (Facebook), *51*
FALCON Tipline software, immigration raid usage, 94
"Far Right Networks of Deception" (Avaaz), 47–8
Fear of missing out (FOMO), 73–4
Feinberg, Eric, 55–6
Feld, Harold, 143
Ferrary, Michel, 67
feudalism, 35, *38*

Firefox, emergence, 142

First Amendment, Supreme Court interpretations, 161

First Look Media, 176

Five Star Movement, social media infractions, 48–9

Forteza, Paula, 157

founder infallibility, myth, 81

Fowler, Susan, 112–13

Foxconn (Hengyang), wage problems (CLW report), 41

free speech, protection, 61–2

Friedlander, Hal, 97

Fry, Helen, 128

G

GAFA companies (Google, Apple, Facebook, Amazon), 132, 140

Galloway, Scott, 40

Gates, Bill, 147, 167

gay people, VC investment, 75

Genentech, culture bubble, 14

General Data Protection Regulation (GDPR), 145, 154–7, 164

genius-jerk theory, 19–20

gig economy
COVID-19, impact, 38
legislative changes, 152
problems, 36
work opportunities, 37

Gingras, Richard, 175

Gladwell, Malcolm, 43

global tax gap, 31–3

global tech companies, EU taxation (fairness), 149–50

goals, clarity (absence), 106

Goldman Sachs, policy change, 126

Google
AI capabilities, usage, 97
Ascension, partnership, 97–8
backing, 71
culture bubble, 14

data security policy violations, 111–12

dominance, e-commerce distortion, 131

fines, 136

personal health data, harvesting, 97

responsibility, knowledge, 28–9

search engine manipulation, fines, 131–2

self-interest, accusations, 175

Google Brain, usage, 58

Google News Initiative, 175

Gornall, Will, 68

government
erosion, corporate tax avoidance (impact), 34
interference, ineffectiveness, 91

Granovetter, Mark, 67

Gray, Chris, 64

grayscale mode (Apple), 102

Green Movement (Iran), 43

groupthink, presence, 74–5

guilt, absence, 86–7

H

Hacking Darwin (Metzl), 168

Hancock, Russell, 21, 24, 26–7

Harari, Yuval Noah, 96

Hare Psychopathy Checklist (Revised), 81, 89

hate
caste-based hate speech storm (TikTok), 52
crime, victims, 52
impact, 50–3
speech, 61–2

Hawking, Stephen, 167

health/life expectancy (improvement), technology (impact), 8

Hengyang Foxconn, CLW investigation, 41

Hershey, Milton, 14

Higa, James, 116

Holmes, Elizabeth, 19, 85
housing
  crisis, 28
  prices/rents, increase, 26–7
Hughes, Chris, 138
human-centric technology,
  support, 183
human depravity, 62–3
Human Resources (HR) empathy,
  impact, 112–14
Huxley, Aldous, 91–2, 100
  scenario, 96–9
Hypergrowth, focus, 70–2

I

Immigration and Customs
  Enforcement (ICE)
  Microsoft/Salesforce contracts,
    protests, 111
  Palantir, cooperation, 93–4
Impact46 (social impact accelerator), 9
independent journalism, media
  company objectives, 179–80
India, cyber troop activity, 50
individual welfare, promotion, 120
industry bodies, corporate governance
  expectations, 127–8
Infantilized culture, 15
information, buying (problem), 163
Information Commissioner's Office,
  data protection/information rights,
  155
information overload, 65
Infowars (Jones), banning, 58–60
innovation
  digital innovation, impact, 8
  impact, 4
  stakes, 130–1
Instagram
  Facebook acquisition, 135, 139
  Islamic State videos, appearance, 56

Institute of Taxation and Economic
  Policy (ITEP) study, 34
investment bankers, corporate
  governance expectations, 126–7
investors, corporate governance
  expectations, 121–2
Iran, cyber troop activity, 50
Islamic State videos, Instagram
  presence, 56

J

job destroyers, Big Tech role, 40
Jobs, Steve, 116
  humility/caring, absence, 19–20
  pathological lying, 85–6
job vulnerability, automation (impact),
  40
Jones, Alex, 102
  YouTube recommendation numbers,
    58–60, 163
journalism
  crisis, Facebook (impact), 176
  independent journalism, media
    company objectives, 178–9
Journalism Competition and
  Preservation Act, 179
juvenile delinquency, 88–9

K

Kaisser, Jonas, 59
Kalanick, Travis, 19, 113
  emotional responses, superficiality,
    83–4
Kamel, Fawzi, 83–4
Kanji, Hussein, 73
Khosrowshahi, Dara, 76
Klein, Saul, 61, 124
Kyi, Aung San Suu (genocide
  accusations), 80

L

labor protection, modernization, 151–3
Lammy, David, 52
Lane Fox, Martha (internet report), 52
Lindenberger, Ethan, 44–5
LinkedIn/China censorship agreement, 140
Living Goods, digital tools/information, 9
Livni, Ephrat, 80
local communities, tech teams (involvement), 116
local journalism, funding, 174–5
Lubetzky, Daniel, 105
Lu, Elaine, 41
Lyft, California lawsuit, 152

M

Magic Leap, 85–6
manual workers, work situation (worsening), 38–9
marginal tax rate, impact, 146–7
market
  definition, problem, 134–5
  dominance, 131–2
  repair, 137–8
Massive Open Online Courses (MOOCs), 9
mass surveillance techniques, usage, 95
McNamee, Roger, 100
media companies, Facebook/Google version, 177–8
media platform companies, reclassification, 177
medieval feudalism, unicorn feudalism (contrast), *38*
merger and acquisition (M&A)
  blocking, impact, 143
  validation process, 135–6
merger approval process, revision, 134–6
Metzl, Jamie, 168

Microsoft
  dominance, abuse, 142
  empathy, promotion, 107
  housing initiative, 29
  ICE contracts, protests, 111
  Windows 10 China Government Edition, 140
microtargeting, usage, 163–4
Mid-Market district, Big Tech (impact), 23–4
mid-range jobs, elimination, 25–6
Mikitani-san, 74
minorities, underrepresentation, 18–19
misinformation, problem, 102
monopolies
  breakup, purpose, 141
  perspective, 76–7
Multistate Tax Commission, 31
Musk, Elon, 19, 167
  behavioral controls, problems, 82–3
Myanmar Rohingya Muslims
  Dorsey tweets, insensitivity, 79–80
  Facebook culpability, 56, 64

N

Nadella, Satya, 107
National Society for the Prevention of Cruelty to Children (NSPCC), sexual grooming offenses report, 53–4
Nest, Google acquisition, 138
Netflix
  federal income tax payment absence, 34
  profit, channeling (accusation), 149
NetzDG law (Network Enforcement Act) (Germany), 160–1
Neumann, Adam, 19
  behavioral controls, problems, 92
news media, Big Tech (negative impact), 173
Newsom, Gavin, 27

news organizations, tech role,
178–80
news publishers, efforts (Google
profiting), 175
Newton, Casey, 62–3
#NewZealandMosqueAttack, 54–7
Nielsen, Rasmus Kleis, 180
nondisclosure agreements (NDAs),
impact, 113

0

O'Carroll, Tanya, 154
Office of Communications (OfCom),
online harms bill regulation, 61
Omidyar, Pierre, 176
on-demand/freelance-labor model, 37
Online Harms bill (UK), 53, 61
organization, values (injection), 4
Orwell, George, 91–2, 100
scenario, 92–6
Oxford Internet Institute, public
opinion manipulation report, 49
Ozon.ru (OZON), 1, 7, 16, 74, 115

P

Page, Larry, 15, 99
Pakistan, cyber troop activity, 50
pathological lying, 85–6
pedophiles, YouTube presence,
59–60
people
empathy, impact, 108–14
feedback, usage, 117–18
hiring, 117
independence, actions, 181–2
payment, fairness, 182–3
power, 181
separation conversations, 118–19
people of color, VC investment, 75
Peretti, Jonah, 179
personal data, Big Tech harvesting/use,
154

personal health data, Google
harvesting, 97
*Personality Types in Software
Engineering* (study), 16
Pfeifle, Mark, 43
physical social networks, destruction,
27
Picard, Robert, 173
Pichai, Sundar, 28–9, 144
planned obsolescence, 182
Pogba, Paul, 103
portable reputation program, creation,
152
Postman, Neil, 91–2
Power, Samantha, 159
privacy
absence, 91
data privacy, 98, 125
importance, 139
problems, 145
protection, 153–8
regulation focus, 146
product decisions, empathy (impact),
114–17
Project Dragonfly, 102
Project Maven (U.S. Defense
Department), Google
(involvement), 110–11
Project Nightingale, 97
Protection from Online Falsehoods and
Manipulation Act (Singapore),
negative impact, 160
proxy advisors, corporate governance
expectations, 126–7
psychopathic companies, creation, 81
psychopaths, personality traits, 3
public opinion, social media
manipulation, 49

Q

"Q&A with the CEO" audio recording, 63

quality assurance (QA), 116–17

Quest, Lisa, 146

Quidsi, Amazon pricing attack, 88–9

R

racial income inequality, *27*

Raskin, Aza, 65, 100, 162

Rebello Arduini, Flora, 48–9

regulation
  focus, 146
  role, 163

Rekognition facial recognition technology (Amazon), shareholder pushback, 123

remorse, absence, 86–7

remote working/office space (changes), COVID-19 (impact), 25

rent, caps, 27–8

research and development (R&D) expenditures, VC (impact), 68

responsibility, acceptance (failure), 86–7

Reynolds, Matt, 60

Ring, law enforcement video-sharing partnerships, 92–4

Rivers, Rebecca, 112

Roberts, Deano, 15–16

Rosen, Guy, 158

Russia, cyber troop activity, 50

S

safety, regulation focus, 146

Salesforce, ICE contracts (protests), 111

Salvini, Matteo (social media infractions), 48–9

Saudi Arabia, cyber troop activity, 50

Schifter, Doug, 36

science, social media (negative impact), 44–6

science, technology, engineering, and math (STEM)
  classes, women enrollment (problems), 17–18
  MindSpark focus, 9

search engines, change, 181

Section 230 (U.S. Communications Decency Act), impact, 60–1

self-interested beliefs, 20

self-worth, grandiose sense, 81–3

separation conversations, 118–19

sexual grooming offenses, NSPCC report, 53–4

shallow affect (superficial emotional responses), 83–4

Shanmugam, K., 160

shareholders, corporate governance expectations, 122–5

Sherman Act, 133

Shu, Catherine, 80

Sidewalk Labs (Alphabet), high-tech plans, 99

signaling, VC funding process, 68

Silicon Valley
  ethical contortions, 61–4
  mid-range jobs, elimination, 25–6
  racial income inequality, *27*

Silicon Valley Index data, 26

silo mentality, 42, 106

Singapore internet companies, government control, 160

singularity, 65

Slack, culture bubble, 15–16

social media
  apology, absence (Myanmar), 80
  hate crime, victims, 52
  hate, impact, 50–3
  manipulation, Zuckerberg dismissal, 47
  negative impact, 44–6
  problems, 43–4
  public opinion, manipulation, 49

toxicity, 52
social media platforms
  electoral interference, 50
  lawsuit protection, 60–1
social networks, negative impact, *46*
social progress, technology (driver),
  7–10
society (control), centralized power
  (impact), 96–7
soft skills, 1–2
software engineers, users (distance),
  16–17
Sonderby, Chris, 54–5
Spiers, Kathryn, 111
Spotify, culture bubble, 14
Stables, Richard, 130–1
stack ranking processes, 117–18
Stamos, Alex, 115
"State of Workplace Empathy"
  (Businessolver study), 108
states, Big Tech (negative impact),
  29–30
Steve Jobs Syndrome, 19–21
Stevens, Simon, 44
stock exchanges, corporate governance
  impact, 125–6
Stone, Brad, 89
Strebulaev, Ilya A., 68
Stuart, Spencer, 125
surveillance, 92
  algorithmic surveillance, 94
  ambient surveillance, 154
  mass surveillance techniques, usage,
    95
sustainability (driving), people
  (impact), 182

T

Tans, Gillian, 68
taxation
  avoidance/evasion, 32

avoidance exposure rule, blocking,
  149–50
fairness/equity, implementation,
  146–51
liabilities, minimization, 147
OECD solutions, 148–9
policy, EU repair, 150
rules (OECD redesign), 147–8
technology
  addiction, 65
  advances, side effects, 2
  company values, living, 106
  corporate governance, 121
  disruption, human impact, 35–9
  driver, impact, 7–10
  hidden effects, 10–12
  human-centric technology, support,
    183
  impact, opacity, 12
  innovation, impact, *10*
  negative impact, 11
  neutrality, belief, 20
  solutionism, myth, 20
  taxation, OECD solutions, 148–9
technology giants
  bubbles, vilification, 24
  juvenile delinquency, 88–9
  marketing, usage, 132–3
  power, responsibility (acceptance),
    3–4
Tech Workers' Coalition, 111
telemedicine services, increase, 9
Tenant Protection Act of 2019, 27
Tesla, fines, 82
Thiel, Peter, 76, 162
Thompson, Ben, 135, 143
Thompson, Nicholas, 139
Three Laws of Robotics (Asimov), 168
TikTok, caste-based hate speech storm,
  52
Time (Salesforce acquisition), 176
time off task (TOT), tracking, 39

"Trauma Floor, The" (Newton), 62–3
trolling, social media tolerance, 87–8
Trump presidential campaign, Russian disinformation (impact), 47
Tusome (literacy platform), benefits, 9
Twitter, abuse/death threats (increase), 52

U
Uber
  blitz scaling, 72
  California lawsuit, 152
  cultural problems, 112–13
  disruption/negative effects, 36
  drivers, suicides, 36
"Ugly, The" (Facebook memo), 57–8
unicorn feudalism, medieval feudalism (contrast), *38*
"Unlocking Technology for the Global Goals" (PwC), 189
urban displacement, domino effect, 27
U.S. Communications Decency Act, Section 230 (impact), 60–1
user data, absorption, 139
user privacy, problem (Schmidt dismissal), 87–8

V
vaccinations, decline, 45
values
  empathy/humanity, grounding, 4
  living, 106
vanity projects, 147
Venezuela, cyber troop activity, 50
venture capital (VC)
  embedding, 68
  Europe market, *69*
  funding process (signaling), 68
  funding sources, emergence, 76
  gender/racial diversity, absence, *74*
  impact, 67

  leadership, diversity (absence), 69–70
  management fees, 71
  Stanford School of Business study, 68
  valuation inflation, 73
venture funding, process (understanding), 70–1
Verge, The
  Alphabet investigation, 99
  content investigation, 62–3
Vestager, Margrethe, 34, 130–3, 136–7, 144, 150
vision, importance, 1–2
VMware, culture bubble, 14
voluntary collection arrangements, 31–2
voodoo doll model, 65–6
voting suppression posts, Facebook ban, 159

W
Waldman, Sophie, 112
Waldman, Steven, 174–5
Walker, Richard, 15, 17, 26
Warren, Elizabeth, 138
Warzel, Charlie, 55
Washington Post (Bezos acquisition), 176–7
Waze, Google acquisition, 138
WhatsApp, Facebook acquisition, 135, 138–9
Whistleblower (Fowler), 113
"Who Is the Fifth Horseman?" (Galloway), 40
Whole Foods, Amazon acquisition, 138–9
Wojcicki, Susan, 115
  non-apology, 86
women
  marginalization, 17–18
  VC investment, 75
women, harassment/bullying

AI solutions, Big Tech claim, 62
  description, 61–2
workers, Big Tech support (reduction),
    39–40
work insecurity/volatility, 38–9
workplace, changes, 9
Wozniak, Steve, 167
Wu, Tim, 133, 134, 140–1

X
Xi, Jinping, 94

Y
YouTube
  Google Brain, usage, 58
  homophobic harassment, Wojcicki
      non-apology, 86–7
  Jones access, 58–60, 163
  pedophiles, presence, 59–60
  recommendations, numbers, 58–60

Z
Zappos, Amazon acquisition, 138
Zero to One (Thiel), 76
Zhengzhou Foxconn (iPhone City),
    Apple violations, 41–2
Zoom, China (impact), 140
Zuboff, Shoshana, 100
Zucked (McNamee), 100
Zuckerberg, Mark, 99, 123, 135, 144
  decisions, impact, 147
  news perception, 174
  non-apology, 86–7
  pushback, problems, 139–42
  social media manipulation dismissal,
    47